The ▲ Abrams Guide to Period Styles for Interiors

BY **JUDITH GURA**

ILLUSTRATIONS BY **DAVID PERRELLI**   EDITED BY **RICHARD OLSEN**

HARRY N. ABRAMS, INC., PUBLISHERS

contents

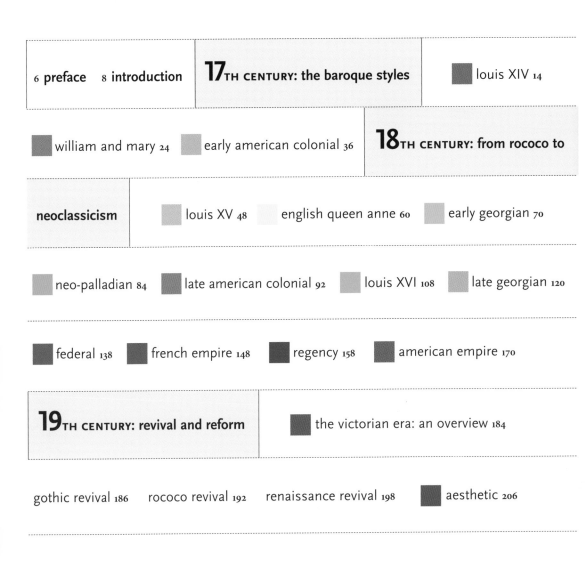

6 preface   8 introduction   **17**TH CENTURY: the baroque styles   louis XIV 14

william and mary 24   early american colonial 36   **18**TH CENTURY: from rococo to

neoclassicism   louis XV 48   english queen anne 60   early georgian 70

neo-palladian 84   late american colonial 92   louis XVI 108   late georgian 120

federal 138   french empire 148   regency 158   american empire 170

19TH CENTURY: revival and reform   the victorian era: an overview 184

gothic revival 186   rococo revival 192   renaissance revival 198   aesthetic 206

english arts and crafts 220   american arts and crafts 232   art nouveau 248

glasgow 262   **20**TH CENTURY: modernism and after   avant-garde: the wiener

werkstatte 274   international style 286   french art deco 298   midcentury modern 316

scandinavian 336   sixties 348   italian modern 358   post-modernism 370

minimalism 380   **21** ST CENTURY: an overview 388   **illustrations** 392

classical order 392   ornamental motifs 393   some distinguishing features of period furniture 395

glossary 398   **for further reading** 410   **index** 418   **credits** 424

To Martin

CONCEPT, PROJECT MANAGEMENT, AND EDITING: Richard Olsen
DESIGN: Brankica Kovrlija
PHOTOGRAPHIC RESEARCH: Leslie Dutcher
EDITORIAL ASSISTANCE: Isa Loundon
COPYEDITING: Sylvia Karchmar
PRODUCTION MANAGER: Maria Pia Gramaglia
GLOSSARY AND BIBLIOGRAPHIC RESEARCH: Sean Weiss

LIBRARY OF CONGRESS CATALOGING-IN-PUBLICATION DATA

Gura, Judith.
  The Abrams guide to period styles for interiors / by Judith Gura ;
illustrations by David Perrelli ; edited by Richard Olsen.-- 1st ed.
    p. cm.
  Includes bibliographical references and index.
  ISBN 0-8109-5914-3 (hardcover : alk. paper)
  1. Interior decoration--History. I. Title.

  NK1860.G87 2005
  747'.09--dc22

                           2005005852

Published in 2005 by Harry N. Abrams, Incorporated, New York

PRINTED AND BOUND IN CHINA
10 9 8 7 6 5 4 3 2 1

HARRY N. ABRAMS, INC.
100 Fifth Avenue
New York, NY 10011
www.abramsbooks.com

Abrams is a subsidiary of
LA MARTINIÈRE

acknowledgments

Most authors acknowledge a small coterie of friends and colleagues who have given aid and support in the development of their work. But for a broad-scope project like this one, with hundreds of images and thousands of details, I am indebted to a larger-than-usual number of people, without whose advice, cooperation, and patience this project could not have come to fruition.

For their enthusiastic help with my photo research: Chris Lacey at The National Trust; Stella Smith at Christie's Images; Rachel Lloyd at the Victoria & Albert Picture Library; Jennifer Belt at Art Resource; Susan Newton at Winterthur Museum; Ginger Yowell at the Society for the Preservation of New England Antiquities; Charles Lyle at Boscobel Mansion; Erica Stoller and Christine Cordazzo at ESTO; and Philippe Garner.

For digging into their files to supply images of various pieces of furniture: Julie Thoma Wright and Richard Wright at Wright; Anna Brouwer at Phillips; the staff of the Ariane Dandois Gallery; Barbara Lloyd at Associated Artists; Frank Levy at Bernard & S. Dean Levy; Martin Levy at S. Blairman; Beth Cathers at Cathers and Dembrowsky; Adriana Friedman and Monica Uribe at Delorenzo; Eric Baumgartner at Hirschl and Adler; Rachel Karr at Hyde Park Antiques; Jennifer Olshin at Ingrao; John Levittes at John Alexander; John and Michael Hill at Jeremy Ltd.; Benoist Drut at Maison Gerard; Lary Matlick at Macklowe; Crista Capello at Mallett; Robert Aibell at Moderne; Lucy Morton at Partridge; Richard Bryers at Paul Reeves; Evan Snyderman at R20th Century; Henry Leichter at Ritter Antik; and Martine Baverel at Vallois.

For helping me locate documentary textiles: Judy Straeten at Brunschwig; Jack Fields at Edward Fields; Terry Wendell at Prelle; Janice Langrall at F. Schumacher; Solveig Ek at Unika Vaev; Jane Mielo at Sanderson; and Ramona Denton at Bradbury & Bradbury.

For their invaluable contributions of time and talents: David Perrelli, an exceptional former student who thought that providing drawings for the book would be an interesting project; Sean Weiss, for enthusiastically taking on the bibliography and glossary, and doing a brilliant job on both; and Randi Mates, for getting photo research off the ground.

To the people at Harry N. Abrams: Leslie Dutcher, for pulling in and keeping track of all the images; Isa Loundon, for juggling all the elements with skill and good humor; Brankica Kovrlija, for putting it into an appealing design; and Maria Pia Gramaglia, for carefully presiding over the book's printing.

And finally, but perhaps foremost, the people without whom this book could never have gotten started: Inge Heckel, President of the New York School of Interior Design, who helped me find a publisher; Richard Olsen, my editor, whose idea of a style guide sparked the project, and whose skillful direction helped to bring it into focus; Eric Himmel, editor-in-chief at Abrams, who gave the project his full support; and Martin Gura, who at all stages served as sounding-board, tireless reader, chief critic, and constant support system.

preface

"WHAT STYLE IS THAT?" is probably the question most often asked by anyone looking at interiors and furnishings. Why does it matter? In part, because labels help us understand what we are seeing. Defining a style can place an object in historical context, so that we can appreciate its meaning for its own time and for ours. The primary purpose of this book is to make that task easier. ■ There are already a number of publications about period styles. So why deal with the same topics again? Because—with the possible exception of textbooks—most of these focus specifically on furniture or on the decoration of interiors. This book proposes to treat the two as part of a whole, to give an overview of each period and style in a clear, well-illustrated, and readable format. Summing up some thirty-odd styles and three-and-a-half centuries is a daunting challenge, but one worth the effort. ■ This is not a history of design— if it were, it would examine the styles of the Near and Far East, of India and Africa, of Mexico and Native Americans, as well as others that are limited in geography or sphere of influence. Instead, this book focuses on those moments, and places, in which a combination of design elements fused into a consistent aesthetic—what we refer to as a style. ■ Each of the styles I have chosen defines a particular time in history. Each could fill a book on its own; many already have. So the information here will be just a taste, but it is hoped a tantalizing one, of the inventiveness of designers and craftspeople, in the creation of exceptional interiors and the objects that go into them. ■ Each section includes the historical background and development of the style, descriptions of its typical interiors and furnishings, and the defining characteristics that distinguish it from those that preceded and followed. In addition to authentic period interiors, the illustrations include examples of each style in a variety of furniture forms. With few exceptions, I have chosen a range of typical objects, rather than the few museum pieces that appear in most texts. Also illustrated are period textiles and wall coverings, and color samples that suggest the chromatic accompaniments of the respective times. ■ A caveat to those in search of hard-and-fast rules: these descriptions are generalizations, not irrefutable facts. While they capture the essence of each style, they do not encompass its every interpretation. Nor can a single illustration of a style incorporate all of its elements. In real life, interiors and furnishings were—and are—as varied and individual as the people who create them and the people for whom they are created. ■ A final note: establishing firm start-and-finish dates for design periods is virtually impossible. With rare exceptions, a style evolves gradually and declines over time. Its designated parameters are either educated guesses, or approximations, about which few historians are in complete agreement. For purposes of consistency, I have used dates that accord with those in the *Getty Art & Architecture Thesaurus*. For styles and periods not specified by that source, I have used my own judgment.

introduction

THE EVOLUTION OF PERIOD STYLES ■ The design of interiors and furnishings predates by many centuries any attempts to define it. But the concept of aesthetic decoration—the conscious effort to plan those interiors—only began about four hundred years ago. Those years encompass the great period styles ■ Design, even at its most avant-garde, is seldom entirely new—styles evolve within a historical continuum, each reflecting the one preceding and incubating the one to follow. And each revival of style is a reinvention rather than a reproduction, inadvertently or arbitrarily tweaking the original to suit its new surroundings. This grafting of the new (or newish) onto the old is, to some degree, predictable. It may be brought on by political pressures and cultural change, by new production methods and materials, by expanding trade, by the foibles of fashion, and by the shifting preferences of those who design and those for whom designs are created. ■ Save for political upheavals, these changes take time to develop, as do the changes in style. But a new style is not necessarily an improvement over its predecessor—as any follower of history knows, change is no guarantee of progress. Nevertheless, the permutations of style through these centuries reveal a pattern, if not of specific progress, at least of gradual development toward a more complex and technologically advanced society, one in which design and its products are reaching an increasingly larger audience. ■ The term *design* originated during the Renaissance, drawn from the Italian word *disegno*, meaning "drawing." It was an era of capitalism, prosperity, and the beginning of patronage of the arts, leading to a new interest in domestic architecture and design. Renaissance style was actually the first occurrence of Neoclassicism—the return to design elements from ancient Greece and Rome. The classical orders were revived, objects like the tripod table and the curule chair were updated, and furniture makers began to win respect on a par with architects. ■ With the dawn of the seventeenth century, changing fashions and a taste for luxury brought the flamboyant Baroque, which improvised on the same classical forms in an exuberant, pompous, and materialistic style. Emerging in Italy, it was most influential in its French incarnation, spreading from there to England and other countries and dominating Europe for more than a century. ■ In that century and the one that followed, European designers created interiors and objects known to most of the present generation only through published images and museum exhibitions, though the few surviving furnishings are prized by those fortunate enough to afford them and copied by countless others. Over the ensuing years, successive reinterpretations of these defining styles merged national and international characteristics in unique and original translations that, mirroring the changes in society itself, began the slow and sometimes controversial transition toward modernity—of the contemporary era, rather than of any specific style. ■ The eighteenth century was dominated in its first half by the Rococo, which brought a new lightness and domesticity to interiors, and in its second by the most sophisticated and influential renderings of Neoclassicism among its many incarnations in the Western world. The styles of the eighteenth century, each capturing public fancy for a relatively brief but glorious reign, ranged from the modest Queen Anne to the more frivolous Louis XV, the equally refined classical inspiration of Louis XVI and Robert Adam interiors, and the furniture of Chippendale, Hepplewhite, and Sheraton in Georgian England, as well as individualistic American variants of the English-inspired styles. The styles of the eighteenth century are the most familiar, most easily recognized, and most frequently copied of any before the advent of Modernism. ■ The nineteenth century saw the growth of a new social order: an age of industrialization, urbanization, and conflict between a liberal new middle class and a conservative elite. In design, it was a time of both unprecedented options and cataclysmic change. On the one hand, the Industrial Revolution had made more goods available, in greater variety and at affordable prices, to a broader market than ever before. On the other, much had been lost in the rush to machine production, and there was a yearning to recapture the humanity of handcrafted styles, which, ironically, those same machines had made easy to replicate. ■ And so, for the first time, instead of using historical styles for inspiration, designers copied them literally. The result was an era in which revivals, rather than new concepts, predominated. Disseminated by improved transportation, exhibitions, and design guidebooks, the revival styles crossed national as well as historical boundaries, influencing architecture as well as design. This period marked the arrival of the new middle class, who signaled their status in society as had the aristocracy of earlier times—by filling their homes with the finest, and most fashionable, objects they could acquire. ■ The nineteenth century also brought revolutionary changes in technology that transformed the environments in which people lived and worked. In architecture and building, there were the development of cast iron, sheet glass, steel, and reinforced concrete; the engineering of bridges and railroads; the invention of the elevator; and the harnessing of electricity. In fabrics, wallpaper, and carpeting, the use of power looms, roller printing, and Jacquard weaving transformed production and made available to a mass market products previously affordable only to the few. ■ By the end of the nineteenth century, the design of a room was dictated more by individual preference than by its environment or even by prevailing fashion. There was, in fact, no prevailing fashion. With so many options, it was no longer possible for a single style to dominate a given period, as it had throughout history. That freedom of choice, more than any aesthetic, is the legacy of nineteenth-century design. ■ Design periods in the twentieth century are not nearly so easy to classify as are the preceding ones. Modernism, in its varied, and not always successful interpretations, sought to break new ground to meet the challenges of a changed, and still changing, world. Discarding the past in its search for the future, it moved in several directions, not all of them consistent in either philosophy or aesthetic. ∎ Moreover, although there were centers of style and arbiters of taste, none mandated fashion with the impact of either the monarchies or aristocracies of centuries past. Style leadership had passed from the elite to a broader and more democratic community. The rise of periodicals and design magazines had initiated still another sphere of influence—that of media professionals who were critics and dictators of design rather than its users or practitioners. ∎ In the twentieth century, the nature of fine furnishings was permanently changed: while no two Chippendale chairs are exactly alike—even if made from the same drawing—a pair of Marcel Breuer designs, for example, are identical products of a machine. The question of what constitutes an "original" when both original and copy are production-made is one that will generate debate for some time. ∎ Perhaps the most significant change of the Modern era has been the breakdown of relationship between interior and exterior. Far from being integral to the architectural structure, Modern interiors are often entirely independent of them. For the first time in history, people live in homes they did not build, in a style no longer current, and one which they perhaps do not admire. They may choose to furnish the interiors in the most Modern fashion, or may, just as appropriately, reprise a traditional aesthetic. Modern architecture itself may encourage these options: the relative neutrality of the spaces does not impose modernity on its occupants. Even the most admired styles of the twentieth century, like those of the nineteenth, have coexisted with several other, equally fashionable, possibilities. They have tended to polarize, either toward the architectural or the decorative, in an ongoing competition between restraint and extroversion. ∎ They have, however, agreed on certain standards: acceptance (if not always full embrace) of the machine and mass production, concern for functionalism as a defining element of design, and aversion to excess in ornament. This commonality lends coherence to the styles of the twentieth century and their coalescence under the general heading of Modernism. ∎ It should be mentioned that throughout the century just past, and into the present one, reprises of classical and eighteenth-century design have endured, continuing on a parallel track with variants of Modernism, and rejecting its perceived severity and its tendency toward understatement. Furnished with either period antiques or reproductions, these interiors break with traditional styles by choosing an unconventional vocabulary of color, a random mix of pattern, and an idiosyncratic mélange of accessories and ornament. In many cases, historic authenticity is second to visual effect, but it is through these interiors that the great styles of history are kept alive. ∎ **UNDERSTANDING STYLES OF ANY PERIOD** ∎ The style of an interior is defined by many elements—the size and shape of the enclosing space, the backgrounds created by ornament and color, the arrangement of the contents, and the contents themselves. All are described, in broad generalizations and specific examples, for the styles in this book. ■ Of these elements, the most important is the furniture, objects originally based on building forms and transmuted by technology and culture to a genre with its own vocabulary of shapes and ornament. Chairs, originally a sign of status, are the most distinctive and most accessible of furniture forms, and the objects most often chosen by designers to showcase their ingenuity and originality. They are almost always the most obvious signifiers of changes in style, and in new manufacturing techniques. ■ Case furniture, on the other hand, from simple chest to monumental armoire or bookcase, is more likely to reveal shifts in the social fabric of the home, in objects designed for particular rooms and specific purposes. ■ Color, in almost every period of history, has been used to define the mood of an interior. In choosing brights or muddy tones, in playing with saturated hues or soft pastels, the designer makes the choice between drama and subtlety, assertiveness or restraint, elegance or informality. ■ Finally, the element of pattern, or its absence, relates directly to the aesthetic or philosophical tenets of the style. ■ Looking at interiors and objects of the past several centuries presents a somewhat skewed picture. Unlike architecture, often erected with the expectation of surviving into posterity, interiors are meant for current use, rather than historic preservation. What survives has been, until relatively recent history, only the most costly and most carefully preserved, and does not reflect the way average people lived. It is, however, what determined the prevailing style to which the less privileged aspired. With that in mind, the picture they paint, if limited, is still authentic. ■ About generalizations: it is sometimes too easy, and often deceptive, but there are national characteristics that often are reflected in design. It is easy to make sweeping statements about French design, in which a preoccupation with intricate detail and exquisite workmanship is a heritage of the country's medieval guild system. And English design is often both a reflection of its less temperate climate and the sometime friction between political and religious factions. Of the major period styles, those originating in America are most quixotic. Every rule has dozens of exceptions, and for every fashion of the time, there are cases where the country's cornucopia of émigrés, materials, and skills, as well as a stubborn refusal to follow the standards of the continent across the ocean, make it the most difficult to pin down to specifics and often the most interesting to examine. ■ No single style is presented here as the best, or most desirable, although personal biases may escape between the lines and among the adjectives. Choosing a preferred style is not the point, though each of us has one or more that resonates with our own sense of beauty. The point is to appreciate that each era had its own standards and possibilities, and its most successful designs met those standards and exploited those possibilities. ■ All of these styles, therefore, are equally worthy of respect and admiration. This book, it is hoped, will help to encourage both.

17

CENTURY

the baroque styles

louis XIV

ABOUT THE PERIOD

The Baroque was born in Italy, but its ultimate expression was unquestionably French. The style was imported by Catherine de Medici, Italian bride of King Henri II, and nurtured by Cardinal Mazarin, prime minister under Louis XIII and the man who virtually ruled France until his death in 1661.

It was during the reign of Louis XIV (1643–1715) that Baroque came into its own, blossoming into the first of the great court styles placing France in the position of fashion leadership that it would hold for more than a century. In the golden years of the monarchy, Italian-trained architects and craftsmen traveled to the royal work-shops in Paris to create extraordinary, and extravagant, furniture and objects for Louis's palace at Versailles. The modest hunting lodge, originally built for Louis XIII, was transformed for his son by the architects Louis Le Vau (1612–1670), Jules-Hardouin Mansart (1646–1708), and Charles Le Brun (1619–1690), and landscape designer André Le Notre (1613–1670), into a spectacular six-thousand-acre estate that became the archetype for royal residences.

Originally a derogatory term, the name Baroque (from the Portuguese word *barroco* for an irregularly shaped pearl) mocked the overwrought aspects of the style—the extravagances of decoration that seemed the opposite of the refined Renaissance classicism from which it evolved. Excesses notwithstanding, Baroque was the first real expression of French decorative style. It established a tradition of royal patron-age of artists and designers that enriched French decorative arts and enhanced the prestige of the court. It is often called Louis XIV style.

The Baroque captivated much of Europe, where it was adopted for palaces and grand residences. It was particularly influential in Austria and Germany, where it intermingled with the Rococo that followed.

ABOUT THE STYLE

Magnificent is the word that best describes the Baroque interior. Its majestic scale and sumptuous ornament reflects the grandeur of French court life. It suggests, as well, the rigid formality that suffused every activity within its walls. A convergence of sculptural ornament, rich color, and costly materials, its sheer splendor is unmatched by any other style, in any other period of history. Though smaller in scale and freer in form than those of the Italian Baroque, these French interiors are designed to impress—and still do.

The Baroque room is high-ceilinged, rectilinear, and grandly symmetrical. Walls of boiserie, heavily carved wood paneling, are painted in light colors but given added weight with massive moldings, cornices, and classical elements like pilasters, entablatures, and arches. Decorations are applied to almost every surface, usually in high-relief carving, with fluid sculptural forms that create a feeling of dynamic movement. The upper part of the walls are adorned with painted murals or tapestries, and the ceiling is also decorated, perhaps with celestial scenes. Cherubs, floral ornaments, and acanthus leaves are frequent motifs, combined with architectural ones. Doorways and window frames are treated as architectural elements, and the enfilade, the alignment of doorways from one room to the other, enhances the visual flow of space.

The floors are of wood parquet or fine marble, sometimes laid with luxurious Savonnerie carpets in intricate, symmetrical patterns. The fireplace, with a heavily carved mantel, has become an important decorative element as well as a functional one.

Textiles are major elements of the decorative scheme. Windows, extending from floor to ceiling, are hung with heavy draperies befitting the grandeur of the space. There are sumptuous silks, velvets, or damasks in large-scale, formal patterns or intricate florals, executed in strong contrasting colors, and fringed or embroidered with gold and silver threads. The tapestries on the walls are produced by the flourishing industries at Gobelins, Beauvais, and Aubusson.

The color schemes in a Baroque interior are as rich as the materials themselves, tending toward the deepest hues, including golds, burgundies, and rich blues.

Monumental chandeliers of crystal, bronze, or gilded wood, and wall sconces or torchères provide illumination and additional ornament, although most rooms of the period are relatively dark. Also helping to brighten the space are large mirrors, inserted in the paneling—a mirror-making industry is developing in France, thanks to expatriate craftsmen from Venice, where the craft originated. Intricately carved, gilded frames surround the mirrors and the paintings.

Baroque furniture is overscaled to suit the proportions of the interiors. Too heavy to move, it is lined up against the walls of the room. Although retaining Renaissance forms, it has added extravagant decorations—carved cherubs and sea creatures, foliage, innumerable variations on columnar forms, and sculptural mounts of chased and gilded cast bronze—that often obscure the original silhouette. It is often made in suites with several matching pieces.

Chairs are imposing, and rectilinear, with thronelike high backs, ample seats, and ornate carved stretchers. Open arms and legs are usually heavily carved, as well. Tabourets, usually with X-base stretchers, are upholstered and fringe-trimmed. Storage pieces, large and elaborately decorated, might include cabinets on ornate legs, or the new commode, which has replaced the Renaissance cassone. Tables are massive, generally trestle-based, decorated with inlay or gilding. The console table is new in this period, as is the writing table or bureau. Four-poster beds, with testers, dominate the grand bedrooms.

Major pieces of furniture may be oak or walnut, but other woods, including ebony for the most elegant pieces, as well as chestnut, sycamore, and rare colored woods are used for ornamental purposes. Most pieces are intricately decorated with marquetry, intarsia, *pietra dura*, lacquer, and gilding or parcel gilding—every technique in the vast repertoire of guild-trained craftsmen has been employed to make each piece of furniture a virtual work of art.

French furniture is generally signed by the craftsman, and the names of the finest *menusiers* and *ébénistes* have become identified with particular styles or decorative techniques. The most distinctive of these is an intricate variation of marquetry in tortoiseshell and brass, combined with ebony and occasionally ivory. Perfected by André-Charles Boulle (1646–1708), the leading *ébéniste* of his time, it is so widely copied that the technique has become synonymous with his name.

PREVIOUS PAGE: A grand bedroom at Versailles Palace in France, its gilded furnishings and elaborate decoration exemplifying the lavishness of the French Baroque.

RIGHT: Rectangular center table by Andre-Charles Boulle, ca. 1680, of ebony, brass, and pewter marquetry, 45 x 29 inches. Its intricate ornament is enhanced by ormolu framing and cast ormolu mounts in the form of female masks and acanthus scrolled feet.

An unusual small bureau mazarin, ca. 1680, just 33 inches long and 16 inches deep, with virtuoso Boulle marquetry of tortoiseshell and brass, ebony, and pewter. The top unfolds to an expanded writing surface.

Highback armchair of parcel-gilt walnut, with needlepoint upholstery. Shapely serpentine arms have acanthus carving and scrolled supports. The multiple-turned legs are joined by a decorative pierced-and-carved panel. Late seventeenth century.

French Louis XIV fauteuil a la reine, an overscaled chair, ca. 1710, associated with royalty, with high back, square seat, and restrained carving on a gilded wood frame. Cabriole legs anticipate the Rococo.

Side table of gilded wood in bold architectural form, ca. 1700, 48 inches long, with marble top. The elaborate carving and pierced apron incorporate strapwork panels, flower garlands, foliate scrolls, and acanthus feet.

notes on the defining characteristics

MOOD opulent	**FURNITURE** massive, rectilinear, ornately decorated
SCALE grand	**TEXTILES** rich patterned fabrics, tapestries, carpets
COLORS rich and saturated	**KEY MOTIFS** columns, pilasters, pediments, cherubs
ORNAMENT abundant and elaborate	**LOOK FOR** Boulle marquetry, large mirrors

sample color palette and fabric swatch

This rich damask in gold and crimson was a complement to French Baroque interiors.

william and mary

ABOUT THE PERIOD

With the return of the British monarchy after the puritanical Reformation, interiors in England began to shed the somber look of Renaissance decor in favor of lighter and more appealing styles. The Restoration (1660–1689) saw a revived interest in luxury and royal patronage, acquired during Charles II's exile in France, and the Continental influence continued during the overlapping, and better-known, period that represents the Baroque in England.

William and Mary is an English translation of French Baroque, filtered through a Dutch sensibility. The reign of William of Orange and his wife Mary II, England's first constitutional monarchs (1689–1702), ended a long period of conflict between the crown and the nobility, bringing political stability, prosperity, and a burgeoning interest in design. The new rulers brought with them Daniel Marot (1661–1720), a French Huguenot, who became the period's most influential designer. Sir Christopher Wren (1632–1723), a follower of Inigo Jones (1573–1652), himself a disciple of the Palladian movement, was its most celebrated architect and was responsible for developing an English translation of the Baroque. This was a period of enthusiastic building that included lavish town and country residences, extravagantly furnished in the height of the new fashion. In the years that followed, Britain's affluent aristocracy of landholding nobility and wealthy merchants, rather than the court itself, would become the country's arbiters of style and good taste.

Like other interpretations of Baroque, William and Mary design was characterized by grand scale and massive forms, but unlike them, it avoided extravagant ornament in favor of more conservative expressions. Fueled by the trade of the East India Companies, Asian influences began to make themselves felt in accessories and ornament.

As the period drew to a close, architecture retained its majestic Baroque proportions, but English interiors became less weighty and more relaxed, foretelling the advent of the understated Queen Anne style.

ABOUT THE STYLE

The English Baroque interior is an intriguing study in contrasts, reflecting both the sobriety of British tradition and the lightening-up influence of French style. Though somewhat somber and forbidding, with dark backgrounds and weighty furnishings, it is relieved by a palette of rich colors and luxurious materials, the hallmarks of a style created for a privileged class.

Polished dark wood paneling, framed in heavy molding, covers the walls, often extending to the ceiling, and defines the space. The monochromatic tones are relieved by rich tapestries, decorative painting, or, for the less affluent, new flocked wallpapers. In the finest interiors, walls and even ceilings are adorned by cascades of fruit and foliage carved by the Dutch-born master Grinling Gibbons (1648–1721).

The traditional truss-beamed ceiling associated with English Renaissance interiors are supplanted by an elaborate plastered and painted one, with complex, curving forms that blend painting, sculpture, and architecture. The forms are less fluid than either Italian or French interpretations, giving a feeling of solidity rather than one of movement.

Floors are of dark oak, tile or stone, with black-and-white marble squares in great halls and other important spaces. Reflecting expanded trade with the East, they might be accented with Oriental rugs.

Windows are tall and narrow, often retaining the small leaded panes of earlier periods, and are hung with jewel-toned fabrics—damasks, tapestries, and velvets— over silk curtains that can be raised or lowered. In addition to their decorative function, heavy draperies help to retain warmth in the chilly English climate. Printed chintzes also appear on windows and sometimes bed curtains.

Color schemes, though rich, are in relatively somber tones, perhaps deep blues, crimsons, and green.

The fireplace, in all European countries throughout this century, remains a necessity and therefore a significant architectural feature. In the time of William and

Mary, it bears a heavy, carved stone overmantel signaling its importance as a source of warmth and light.

A brass chandelier provides light and accent, and accessories of brass or silver are embossed with floral ornament. Displays of blue-and-white ceramics—real Chinese porcelain or Delft look-alikes—reflect the porcelain mania that began in this period and would obsess collectors until well into the eighteenth century, when Europeans discovered for themselves the secret of making the coveted material.

William and Mary furniture is straight-lined, massive, and sturdy-looking. Chairs are slim and high-backed, fully upholstered or with seats and back panels of imported cane, framed in carved floral or scrolled motifs. The draft-blocking wing chair, its side extensions serving also as headrests, has been carried over from Restoration designs. Baluster, ball, or trumpet-turned legs and S-curve stretchers are preferred alternatives to the elaborate carving prevalent in French and Italian styles, and gold accents are rarely seen. Feet are finished in simple bun shapes or Spanish scrolls.

Case furniture is relatively heavy, with rectilinear chests and cabinets set on sturdy ball or bun feet for a solid, almost massive look. The weightiness is relieved by the extensive use of marquetry, rather than carving, as decorative ornament—delicate "seaweed" patterns and Dutch-influenced floral motifs are the most frequently seen. Inventing a new form, a chest of drawers has been mounted on a slightly wider chest, and the combination raised off the floor on six legs to make what would later be called the tallboy. Noteworthy also are the elaborate and lavishly draped state beds, more lavish than the French objects that inspired them, that are seen in English upper-class residences.

In the furniture of this period, oak is supplanted by walnut as the primary wood, sometimes in patterned burl, and occasionally beech or boxwood.

The Asian influence has led to the development of a technique called "japanning," in which shellac is applied over painted ornament to simulate the look of Japanese lacquer. Much furniture of this period, and even more during the Queen Anne to follow, was enhanced with this technique.

PREVIOUS PAGE: Among the impressive Baroque interiors of Beningbrough Hall, in Yorkshire, is the wood-paneled state bed-chamber, with a massive carved tester bed in the style of Daniel Marot, and a fine sea-weed-marquetry cabinet on turned legs. The Oriental rug and Chinese porcelains reflect the influence of Far Eastern trade.

RIGHT: A walnut and marquetry chest of drawers on bun feet ca. 1695, decorated on its top and sides with marquetry panels framing floral sprays in several different woods. Thirty-six inches wide.

A walnut cabinet-on-chest, 71 inches tall, on bun feet, ca. 1695. Decorated with seaweed marquetry using Roman acanthus and filigree motifs, it was probably inspired by French drawing books.

Cabinet-on-stand, ca. 1700, japanned in polychrome to imitate Coromandel lacquer, with incised Chinoiserie decorations. The giltwood stand has pierced apron and sides. Its elaborate carving shows the influence of French Baroque style. Sixty-eight inches high overall.

High-backed walnut and cane dining chair in the manner of Daniel Marot, ca. 1690. The unusual shaped back is carved with an intricate pierced crest, scrolls, and acanthus motifs. Legs are turned and carved, with serpentine stretchers.

The wing armchair was introduced in the mid-seventeenth century. In ebonized beech, this one has an upswept back, shaped sides, volute arms, and a loose cushion seat. Turned front legs are joined by turned stretchers.

notes on the defining characteristics

MOOD grand but conservative	**FURNITURE** rectilinear, massive, mostly walnut, ball turnings
SCALE monumental	**TEXTILES** heavy fabrics, tapestries
COLORS rich and somber	**KEY MOTIFS** fruit, foliage, scrollwork
ORNAMENT moderately heavy	**LOOK FOR** wood-paneled walls, "seaweed" and floral marquetry

sample color palette and fabric swatch

French damasks like this were popular choices in the Baroque English interior.

early american colonial

ABOUT THE PERIOD

The European settlers in the New World at the beginning of the seventeenth century (Jamestown, Virginia in 1607, and Plymouth, Massachusetts, in 1620), were seeking the promise of a prosperous life in a new land. Their first concerns were with the bare necessities of food, shelter, and the simple amenities that would help them survive under harsh circumstances; their next was to create surroundings recalling those of the homes they had left.

The styles grouped under the general heading of early American Colonial incorporate the period of the Pilgrims, including variants of Tudor, Elizabethan, and Jacobean design, and conclude with translations of William and Mary interiors and furnishings. These styles are found in the British-controlled colonies along the Atlantic coast, not the French colonies farther north, or the Spanish colonies farther south. Designs of furnishings were drawn almost entirely from English and also Dutch forms—but those of a generation past.

The earliest American Colonial homes were like peasant dwellings, single-story structures that gradually developed into wood-framed houses in English medieval style, covered with wood planks and clapboard siding, with brick chimneys. The classic Cape Cod cottage, a saltbox shape without foundation, also evolved in this period.

The limitations of the new environment were considerable; there was no established local trade, scarcely any skilled workers, and limited tools and materials. But Colonial carpenters adapted quickly, devising their own substitutes for pieces they could not replicate and for ornament that was beyond their grasp, in idiosyncratic objects that were quaint, charming, and often highly original.

As the settlements prospered, as mercantile trade expanded and imports increased, and as a growing market of potential clients encouraged European-trained craftsmen to establish their business in the New World, interiors in the American colonies began to catch up with those they had left behind.

ABOUT THE STYLE

The early American Colonial interior seems almost primitive when compared with the European models on which it is based, and the sensation of cramped space and makeshift furnishings can make one overlook its considerable merits. In a single-story structure with only one or two rooms, it is devised to serve many purposes, from kitchen and dining space, to guest parlor, to family room, to sleeping space. As the colonies develop, a second story and additional rooms will be added, but interiors for most of the seventeenth century remain simple, sometimes spartan, with little planned or coordinated decoration.

Despite its multiple functions, the space itself is small. Low ceilings with rough wood beams, walls of plain whitewashed lath and plaster, and wide-plank floors create a bare-bones background for furnishings that are more assembled than designed. The miscellaneous mix of objects includes both items brought from home across the Atlantic and those acquired or made locally.

Windows are small casement style, first with panes of oiled paper and later of leaded rectangular or diamond-shaped glass. Covering them are plain wood shutters, or simple sill-length curtains of cotton or linen. Homespun textiles—every Colonial housewife makes her own fabrics, for interiors as well as clothing—are supplemented by imported calico, India prints, and, only occasionally, English damask, brocade, and needlework. Floor coverings are simple handwoven or hooked rugs—imported carpets are too valuable to walk on and are used as table covers, if at all.

Like its counterparts in Renaissance Europe, the fireplace, here made of brick, is the most essential part of the room, providing the means for food preparation, as well as heat and essential light. Flickering tallow candles are the only other source of illumination in rooms with such small window openings that, even on sunny days, have little natural light.

Cheerful colors—bright primary reds, greens, yellows—are the most appealing and least costly way to relieve the gloom.

Candlesticks, later supplemented by Dutch-style chandeliers, might be pewter, (a tin-alloy substitute for silver) brass, or wrought iron. Pewter is used for tableware and mugs as well. Pottery is made locally, but clocks and mirrors, available only as imports, are rare until after the end of the century.

Furniture of the seventeenth century shows only rudimentary joinery skills, but its simplicity suits the Puritan ethic prevailing in the New England colonies. Such attempts at fashion as exist reflect late Renaissance design, with details that vary according to the national origins of the makers. The earliest furnishings are simple stools and benches, chests and tables, of local woods like pine, maple, oak, or cherry. Of basic plank construction, the chest is the most important piece of furniture— taller than European models, with a hinged top, it might be decorated with shallow "chip carving," or brightly painted with stylized motifs like tulips and sunflowers. In addition to its other attractions, furniture might be painted to conceal the fact that it was assembled from bits and pieces of different woods.

Chairs are of two types: the turned chair, assembled from spindles and requiring no special cabinetry skills, and the wainscot chair, with paneled back and shallow-carved ornament. Loose seat-cushions avoid the difficult task of upholstering. As colonial woodworkers hone their skills, ladder-back and banister-back forms are added to the repertoire, and the age of the joiner progresses to the age of the cabinet-maker. Objects like the three-panel-front Hadley, or Connecticut, chest, and the court cupboard are distinct Colonial inventions, as are combination table-chairs devised for their space-saving benefits.

William and Mary style appears at the beginning of the eighteenth century, in rooms that suggest the growing prosperity and sophistication of the American colonies. Spaces are larger, and more attention is given to decorating them attractively.

Taller and more graceful than earlier American Colonial furniture, American William and Mary pieces have ball-turned or trumpet-turned legs with ball or Spanish foot and stretchers. Chairs may be upholstered or have seats and backs of imported cane, decorative Baroque carving—though shallower than that in English pieces—and painted accents. The upholstered easy chair (from the English wing chair) appears, as well as a daybed with loose upholstered pad. Chests may be decorated with imitations of English japanning, to emulate Japanese lacquer. Gateleg tables, developed earlier in England, have become the indispensable space-saving solution in rooms that are still far smaller than their European counterparts. The tallboy chest, on six turned legs, soon will become the classic American highboy.

The Linebrook Parish room of Beauport, in Gloucester, Massachusetts, recreates the feeling of an early colonial interior through paneling taken from a seventeenth century house, diamond-pane windows, old beams, and an overscaled fireplace.

A William and Mary style walnut tea table with tray top and shaped apron. Its trumpet-turned legs reflect the influence of English baluster forms. Probably from New York, ca. 1710 to 1730.

An early version of the form that became the celebrated eighteenth-century american highboy—this one in black walnut—done with six William and Mary style turned legs and stretchers.

Made in Massachusetts, ca. 1716, this forty-two-inch-high pilgrim chest is named for the town credited with devising the original form. The Hadley, or Connecticut, chest marries a lidded top section with a two- or three-drawer lower one. Made of oak, with shallow "chip carving" and stylized naturalistic motifs, these chests generally bore the initials of the recipient.

ABOVE: The butterfly table, similar in function to the gate-leg table, converts from console to dining table by supporting the raised leaves on wing like brackets. This seventeenth century New England example is of painted and figured maple.

RIGHT: The kas, a Dutch form of the armoire with architectural lines, a prominent cornice, and geometric carving on the doors, was seen in early colonial interiors, reflecting the origins of many of the settlers. Generally oak, but this one is ebonized.

Ladder-back chairs, named for the design of vertical slats across the back, were generally made of any available local wood.

Simple turned chairs, of poplar or other local wood, were made by Boston-area cabinetmakers, ca. 1660 to 1690. This "Carver" chair has vertical spindles on the back (its counterpart, with spindles added to the sides, was the "Brewster" chair).

notes on the defining characteristics

MOOD unassuming	**FURNITURE** chests, benches, other simple shapes in local woods
SCALE modest	**TEXTILES** homespun
COLORS bright	**KEY MOTIFS** sunflowers and tulips
ORNAMENT uncomplicated turned-wood forms	**LOOK FOR** spindles, chip carving, painted furniture

sample color palette and fabric swatch

This resist-print colonial-era curtain fabric has clear colors and motifs from nature.

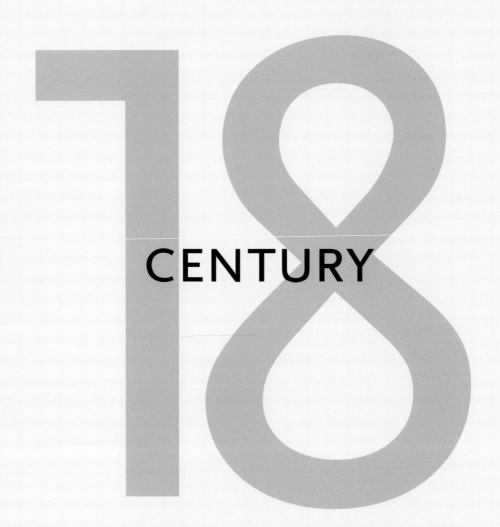

CENTURY

18

from rococo to neoclassicism

ABOUT THE PERIOD

As Baroque was the style of the court, so Rococo belonged to the nobility. Following the death of Louis XIV, Philippe II, duc d'Orleans, regent (1715–1723) for the young Louis XV moved the court from Versailles back to Paris, where the nobles enjoyed a less restrictive lifestyle in the *hôtels particuliers*, the elegant town houses that became the centers of life away from court. The pomp and formality of the Baroque gave way to the transitional Régence and then the Rococo, a style of romantic imagery inspired by fantasy, fable, and the exotic Orient.

Rococo mirrored a new intimacy and informality, in fashions set by social leaders like royal mistresses Mmes de Pompadour and du Barry. The name *Rococo*, bestowed after the fact as a pejorative, combines the French *rocaille* and *coquillage*, referring to the stones and shells that—along with stylized foliage, fish, scrolls, and asymmetrical curves—were its distinguishing motifs. Juste Aurèle Meissonnier (1693–1750) was the most prominent architect of the period, while Jean Berain I (ca. 1639–1711), his son Jean II (1678–1726), and Nicolas Pineau (1684–1754) were its most influential designers.

The Rococo style spread to other countries in central Europe, most notably Germany, where the Francophile princes, often employing French-trained designers, carried the style to its most enthusiastic expression. Italy remained mostly allied to classical forms, and Britain, save for the reserved interpretation of Queen Anne, rejected this charming but undisciplined style.

The improvisatory style of the Rococo was ultimately its undoing, encouraging its designers to frivolous and unrestrained expressions that were derided by critics as lacking in taste. It fell from favor, to be supplanted by the more restrained Neoclassical. Rococo is the most accessible of the French period styles; it would also prove to be the most influential, its influence visible in styles appearing centuries later. It is often called Louis XV style, after the king whose reign (1715–74) it dominated.

ABOUT THE STYLE

Smaller in scale than its pretentious Baroque predecessors, the Rococo interior is as luxurious but far more inviting, beguiling the eye with graceful curvilinear forms and soft colors. If linked to gender, Rococo is usually considered feminine. Its most uncontestable quality is that of charm.

Opening off a central salon, the typical room is well proportioned and might be in any of several interesting shapes, including ovals or octagons, depending on its intended function—as parlor or cardroom or intimate boudoir. The ivory or pale-painted walls are of boiserie, free of architectural or sculptural decoration: the tall rectangular panels are bordered in low-relief foliate carving, touched with gilding. Later in the period, colorful wallpapers, in scenic patterns or Chinoiserie motifs, might be set into the panels.

Overdoor and overmantel panels have the same rounded corners, with inventive carved and gilded ornament—the Rococo uses more gilding than any other French period. Decorative motifs, drawn from nature, are distinctively asymmetrical...bold S curves and C curves expressed in forms like shells, leafy tendrils, waves, and trailing ribbons. Ceilings, joined by cove moldings rather than cornices, had arabesque patterns of plasterwork, often enhanced by painted motifs or occasionally the illusion of cloud-dotted sky.

Floors are wood parquet or herringbone pattern, tile or terra-cotta, likely laid with elegant Savonnerie or Aubusson carpets in patterns designed with the characteristic floral and curvilinear motifs of the period.

At the full-height windows, cornice-topped draperies, generally in warm pastels, might be embroidered with patterns of flowers or foliage. Light is provided by airy crystal chandeliers, wall sconces, or girandoles. The chimneypiece, still a focal point, underscored a tall, elegantly framed mirror, celebrating the French mastery in producing larger sheets of glass. Mirrors might also be installed between the windows, over a console table.

An important component of the Rococo interior, the dominant colors are appealing mixes of ice-cream pastels, including soft blues, pale yellows, and seafoam hues.

Fanciful Rococo imagery also marks the decorative objects on tabletops and mantels, including gilded mantel clocks, gilt and bronze cherub candlesticks, Sevres porcelain vases, and imported Chinese ceramics. Ornament is central to Rococo decor, often to the point of subsuming form.

Rococo furniture is instantly identifiable by its graceful, rounded silhouettes and shapely cabriole legs, ending in small scroll feet. Invitingly curvy chairs and sofas exhibit a new variety of forms, all of them bearing names—*marquise, canapé a corbeille, veilleuse, duchesse*, and more. Elegant and light-scaled, with carved frames and shaped backs, they may be placed away from the walls of the room, and moved around as needed. Stretchers have disappeared, and arms are set back from the front of the seat to accommodate the billowing skirts worn by ladies of the period. Rich upholstery with overstuffed cushions reveals a new concern for comfort, as well as fashion, that reflects the domesticity of this style.

In its fully developed form, the commode is also curvilinear, with splendidly bombé sides, undulating fronts, and short, curved legs. A number of occasional pieces are available to serve particular needs—the music stand, the *bureau plat*, the *bureau à cylindre*, and the *sécretaire à abattant*. Though chairs are most often painted, case pieces employ a variety of decorative wood veneers—including mahogany, rosewood, cherry, pear, and ebony—and might be adorned with floral marquetry, inlaid porcelain plaques, paint, or Chinese lacquer. They also are accented with the gilt or ormolu mounts that distinguish most French period furniture. Leading craftsmen of this time include Charles Cressent (1685–1768), Martin Carlin (1730–1785), and Jean-Francois Oeben (ca. 1715–1763).

PREVIOUS PAGE: The delicate boiserie paneling, the curvilinear shapes of the furnishings, and the palette of lively colors are hallmarks of the period, as demonstrated in this Rococo salon at the Getty Museum in Los Angeles.

BELOW: Reflecting the picturesque style of its celebrated designer, Nicholas Pineau, this 78-inch-long giltwood console table, ca. 1725, is carved with intricate foliage, grotesque dragons, a central cartouche, and a large pierced shell.

A ca. 1740 bureau plat, 70 inches long, made of tulip-wood with ormolu mounts and sabots by Parisian ébeniste Pierre Migeon.

Graceful in silhouette but relatively simple in ornament, this amaranth and bois satine commode, ca. 1735, is decorated with fine marquetry and bold ormolu mounts. By Charles Cressent, one of the most skillful Rococo ébenistes.

This bombe-shape commode, ca. 1745, by Pierre Roussel is decorated with black, gold, and colored lacquer panels (probably cut from a Chinese screen) and set off by elaborate ormolu decoration of scrolling foliage and flowers.

ABOVE: a small ca. 1765 sofa, or canapé, with curving sides and a carved-wood frame (gilded) that is decorated with ribbon-tied bows.

LEFT: the frame of this giltwood fauteuil, ca. 1745, is richly carved with rocaille ornament; shells, scrolls, and stylized flowers. Made by Jean-Baptiste I. Tilliard, one of the finest chairmakers of the Louis XV period.

notes on the defining characteristics

MOOD relaxed elegance	**FURNITURE** curvilinear, veneered or painted
SCALE intimate	**TEXTILES** luxurious but light
COLORS warm pastels	**KEY MOTIFS** shells, waves, other naturalistic forms
ORNAMENT naturalistic, asymmetrical	**LOOK FOR** cabriole legs, overstuffed seating, lots of gilt

sample color palette and fabric swatch

The trailing pastel ribbons and flowers of this romantic print evoke the charm of the Rococo interior.

As the styles of the french court gained attention, they were popularized in less expensive and smaller-scaled adaptations for less ostentatious interiors. French Provincial, more informally known as French Country Style, mutes down the exuberance of Louis XV and XVI design into a less showy, more serene, and considerably less labor-intensive rendering of the Rococo, or occasionally Neoclassical style.

The French Provincial interior strips off the elaborate Rococo framework of boiserie and ornament, replacing it with walls paneled in light wood or fabric. The curvilinear silhouettes and asymmetry of the style adapt well to such understatement, which retains its outlines but avoids carving beyond simple panel shapes. In lighter and more accessible local woods, the furniture is both better suited to the ambience of a country residence, and more affordable as well. Finishes are less showy, avoiding the high-gloss, high-maintenance French polishes used in the court styles.

Window treatments are also simpler, often using the printed-linen toiles in bucolic pastoral scenes that have become associated with the style. French Provincial is an evolution of the most fashionable Gallic styles, but rendered with a lighter hand and a casual air.

This side chair has Neoclassical lines, but its spare carving and natural fruitwood are more suited to a country house than a city mansion.

A chestnut buffet in provincial style, without the ornament that would be expected on French furniture of the period.

This walnut armoire is another understated variation on a familiar form.

queen anne

ABOUT THE PERIOD

Under England's less autocratic monarchy, styles were not so defined by royal patronage as those in France, and were therefore less affected by transitions in the monarchy. English periods of the eighteenth century are not entirely contiguous with the reigns of their namesakes, and changes in design evolved gradually, with considerable overlapping from one period to the next. During much of the eighteenth century, in fact, several styles existed simultaneously at the height of fashion, often duplicating characteristics and always competing for dominance in the market.

As the century began, the Queen Anne style developed as the English version of Rococo, and was the first style of that country to emphasize curving forms. Though short-lived (as was Anne's reign, from 1702 to 1714), its influence was considerable. When the over-decorated Baroque fell from favor, English designers sought a simpler, refined look, but one that reflected their aversion to the "fancy" French aesthetic. They accomplished this by translating French Rococo with characteristic British restraint, modifying the shapely silhouettes into more subdued curves, with almost no decoration.

In its spare simplicity, the Queen Anne style was well suited to British taste. It also filled a need for lightweight, portable furniture that arose in the aftermath of the 1666 fire that had destroyed much of London, reflecting the need to rebuild and refurnish. It was only a matter of time, however, until the fashion-forward aristocracy began to look for more elaborate expressions with which to furnish their imposing town and country residences. What evolved, at the beginning of the Georgian period, was the grafting of carved ornament and decoration onto basic Queen Anne silhouettes.

ABOUT THE STYLE

The Queen Anne interior reflects its ladylike name—it is modest, understated, and evokes a sense of refinement. Though reprising the curves of French Rococo, it reduced them to their most pristine, free of the frilly asymmetrical decoration that marked the original. Rather than the frivolity of French Rococo, the English version projects a serious demeanor.

Queen Anne decor has moved away from the ornate plasterwork and pervasive ornament of English Baroque, and wood paneling, often cut back to dado height, gradually begins to give way to painted surfaces and plaster decorations, bringing a lighter and more inviting aspect to the rooms. Ornament is modest, though sometimes present.

Colors are softer and more inviting than the somber Baroque tones of the William and Mary period, with such tones as muted greens, ivories, and warm reds.

Windows are larger, as are the glass panes, and drapery treatments have taken on a lighter feel with fabrics in graceful floral or inventive designs with exotic motifs from the Far East. In addition to China and Japan, India is becoming a frequent source of inspiration, as crewels and chintzes begin their reign of popularity in English country houses.

Floors of polished wood parquet might be enhanced with Oriental carpets. Fireplaces, still important fixtures, keep the restrained lines of the period, and lighting fixtures are predominantly brass, rather than the showier crystal favored by the French.

Accessories, too, are simple—silver, though shapely and sculptural, bears little adornment. The influx of decorative objects from the China Trade has increased, with porcelain designed specifically for export in patterns and forms tailored to European taste. Most notably, the consumption of tea has transformed English daily life, impelling the creation of new objects linked to its use—these include not only tea services, strainers, and serving implements, but teapot-stands and a variety of serving tables.

Queen Anne furniture reprises the curves of French Rococo, though in a more moderate fashion. Form is central, rather than ornament—the most frequently used decoration being a simple version of the scallop shell, symmetrical and flattened in its English translation. It is retained into the Georgian period despite its associations with Rococo.

For chairs and tables in Queen Anne style, the single defining feature is a bold C-curved cabriole leg, with a more pronounced knee than in the French form, and customarily a pad foot. Chairs have lower backs than William and Mary designs, and are curved to fit the body. Their distinctive silhouette features a double-curved hoop back, urn-shape splat (derived from Chinese porcelain), and rounded front rail with drop-in seat. Often only the front legs are fully developed, the rear ones left plain, and stretchers begin to disappear. The wing chair, with comfortably-padded arms and back, reflects an increased interest in comfort, and will become a standard-bearer of British style. Except for its feet, the design will change very little in the decades to follow.

Queen Anne cabinet sides are straight: only the legs, and sometimes the tops, have the new silhouette. New composite furniture forms have been introduced; the bureau-secretary, cabinet-on-chest, and bureau-bookcase, all crowned with double-domes, or Rococo-curved, swan-neck pediments. Consoles, wardrobes, bureaus, and occasional tables fill other furnishing needs.

With almost no carving or intricate veneering, the wood—primarily walnut, but also elm and walnut burl—serves as its own ornament, though shapely brass escutcheon plates are added grace notes. The exceptions are the elaborately "japanned" pieces, with Chinoiserie decoration, that add dramatic statements to otherwise understated rooms.

PREVIOUS PAGE: the dining room of Canons Ashby, an Elizabethan country house in Northamptonshire, England, has the under-stated elegance of the typical Queen Anne interior, with fine oak paneling and a carved marble chimneypiece.

This upholstered walnut stool, ca. 1710, has shell-and-scroll carving on the knees of its cabriole legs. It is covered in petit-point needlework done with stylized flowers and scrolling foliage typical of the period.

Queen Anne chairs were charac-terized by their hoop-curved top rail and sides, urn-shape splat, cabriole legs, and pad foot, but within these parameters there was considerable variation. This one is a simple, probably early, example of the form.

This burr elm lowboy, ca. 1710, has the characteristically simple Queen Anne form, set on cabriole legs with pad feet. Subtle detailing appears at the corners and edges of the quarter-veneered top, and acanthus carving on the knees.

The walnut wing chair, ca. 1710, then also called the "easie chair," was designed for comfort rather than elegance, and varied little throughout the eighteenth century except for details such as the carving on the legs. This one has cabriole front legs and turned rear ones, with a turned stretcher.

The most elegant furniture of the period was in lacquerwork, like this striking brown-and-gold bureau cabinet (early eighteenth century), with arched broken pediment and gilt finials. The interior is fitted with drawers and pigeonholes, and the ornament throughout is exotic Chinoiserie.

notes on the defining characteristics

MOOD unpretentious	**FURNITURE** simple curving shapes, minimal carving
SCALE spacious	**TEXTILES** imports, Indian prints, and crewels
COLORS warm	**KEY MOTIFS** scallop shell
ORNAMENT restrained	**LOOK FOR** cabriole leg with pad foot, tea furniture

sample color palette and fabric swatch

Crewel prints were a popular import from India, part of the Eastern trade route.

early georgian

ABOUT THE PERIOD

The Georgian period in England was named for three successive rulers in the Hanoverian dynasty; George I (reign 1714–27), George II (reign 1727–60) and George III (reign 1760–1820). It spanned most of the eighteenth century—a prosperous time when several coexisting styles held sway, and society was an intriguing mix of elegance and dissolution. The reigns of George I and George II comprise what is designated as Early Georgian, the period when Rococo reigned supreme.

Early Georgian interiors and furnishings, reflecting the influence of French style, also revealed the growing sophistication of the English aristocracy, who were now setting fashion standards. With London a flourishing hub of creativity, England was at last in a position of cultural leadership to challenge France.

During these decades, the influence of a few prestigious architects and their affluent patrons initiated the "Golden Age" of English design, which brought the country's most exceptional design achievements. Architecture reigned foremost among the arts, and celebrated practitioners such as William Kent (1684–1748) and James Gibbs (1682–1754) built showplace townhouses and the palatial country homes that epitomized the height of fashion. A beautifully furnished residence became the means of displaying the good taste, and the social status, of its owners.

Other factors contributed to the sophistication of Georgian styles. Advances in furniture workmanship helped to produce objects of superb quality, an integrated furniture trade had developed to market these objects to consumers, and, perhaps most significant, widely disseminated pattern books made it possible for cabinetmakers in other parts of the country, or other parts of the world, to replicate the latest London styles.

After the middle of the century, cultivated Englishmen on the grand tour of the Continent would return with mementos of antiquity that fed a new interest in classicism, but until then, the Rococo influence informed the design of English interiors and furnishings, as it did on the European continent.

ABOUT THE STYLE

The Early Georgian interior moved away from the understatement of Queen Anne to take on the characteristics of a more assertive style. It distills the essence of English-ness, tempering aristocratic pomp with the restraint that separates most British styles from those of their French neighbors. It is deservedly admired and endlessly copied. While impressive and somewhat formal, it stops just short of stuffiness, walking a middle ground that mixes several elements of style.

Richer decoration has been added to what is essentially the same type of well-proportioned space that began the eighteenth century. The application of ornament conveys greater formality and bespeaks affluence and status.

Walls of off-white or stone grey have taken on moldings and decorative cornices, all painted white. Dark wood paneling is giving way to lighter treatments, with carved swags or garlands on the dado, and perhaps faux-bois painting to suggest lighter woods. There might also be tapestries, and either hand-painted Chinese or flocked wallpapers.

Colors are deeper than in the Queen Anne period—blues, greens, reds, golds, in muted or vibrant tones depending on the room.

Floors are oak plank or parquet, and might be stained or painted. In grand houses, marble is preferred. Oriental rugs are used in formal rooms, and perhaps canvas floor cloths in other areas.

Double-hung sash windows with rectangular panes, or three-section Palladian windows with arched semicircular cornices are the latest style. Soft festoons of fabric might balloon beneath a carved and gilded cornice, or draperies of heavy silk, coordinated with the upholstery fabrics, hang to the floor.

Toiles, chintzes, or printed Indian cottons are less formal alternatives to rich imported silks.

Fireplaces continue to be a focal point, with carved marble mantels and over-mantels projecting into the room.

Lighting is by means of candles or gas lights—tall candle-stands in the corners, wall-mounted sconces, or massive chandeliers, perhaps of polished brass or French crystal. Elaborate framed mirrors might be carved with scallop or shell motifs, classical scrolls, or Rococo filigree.

George I furniture looks much like that of the Queen Anne period, except for carving and ornament grafted onto the same basic forms. Early Georgian chairs retain the Queen Anne silhouette, but have become more elaborate. The cabriole leg remains, but a ball-and-claw, derived from an ancient Chinese image of a dragon holding a pearl, is the characteristic foot on Early Georgian furniture, supplanting the pad foot; a lion's paw is sometimes used as well. The proportions of seating pieces are broader, with wider backs and wider, flatter seats, the fronts of which have lost their rounded shape. The disappearance of stretchers requires the support of a broader knee, which is carved with graceful cabochons, volute ornament and, in George II chairs, more prominent motifs that might include lion masks or foliage. Carved ornament appears on the crest rail as well. George II chairs have high-relief carving and decorated seat rails, as well as carving on the splats.

Tall cabinets have finials added to Queen Anne–style double-dome tops, or are crested with broken or swan-neck pediments for a more architectural look. The chest-on-chest, on plinth base, replaces the tall chest on cabriole leg. In the Early Georgian period, a greater variety of furniture has come into use—tea tables are joined by several styles of drop-leaf and occasional pieces, and the card table reflects a popular new pastime, with a folding frame that allows it to serve also as side table. Beds, somewhat less elaborately draped than in Baroque times, have exposed, carved posts. In the George II era, bookcases and breakfronts begin to show strong classical influence, with cornices and broken pediments.

Toward mid-century, imported mahogany is replacing walnut as the material of choice, walnut having become scarce after a blight that destroyed much of the European crop. A harder wood, mahogany takes particularly well to carving, encouraging the interest in more ornamentation. Its decorative grain is also ideal for the expansive veneered surfaces of tables or cabinet fronts. Japanning and chinoiserie ornament continue in popularity, appearing on many tall case pieces.

LEFT: Rather than developing new forms, the early Georgian period drew on basic Queen Anne style. parlor chairs like this, ca. 1725, were embellished with shapelier sides and ball-and-claw feet.

The library armchair, with broad, low back, open sides, and upholstered armrests, was commodious and comfortable. This one, ca. 1740 by Giles Grendy, is upholstered in petit-point needlework and has elaborate scrollwork on its walnut arm-supports and legs, and hairy-paw feet.

ABOVE: This George I burr walnut side chair has shaped side rails, vase-shape splat with acanthus and scroll carving, and fine shell carving on the crest rail, ca. 1725.

ABOVE, RIGHT: The Far Eastern influence appeared in decorative objects like this mid-eighteenth century giltwood mirror, drawn from a pattern published by Chippendale. Its intricate frame carving combines Rococo elements with pagoda, ho-ho birds, and a Chinese musician.

This ca. 1755 George II chest on chest, a form that appeared throughout the century, is done in mahogany with brass inlays and has a simple, bracket-foot base. The flanking columns and molded cornice on the upper section indicate the new interest in classical ornament.

An exceptional George II mahogany knee-hole desk, with serpentine top and arched kneehole flanked by columns and draw-ers. The sides are fitted with drawers as well—four working, and four false.

notes on the defining characteristics

MOOD moderately formal	**FURNITURE** mahogany, with carved decoration on Queen Anne forms
SCALE imposing	**TEXTILES** Indian prints, chintzes, or imported silks and damasks
COLORS varied, muted, or bright	**KEY MOTIFS** shells, ribbons, acanthus, lion's heads and paws
ORNAMENT relatively restrained	**LOOK FOR** important chimneypieces, Chinese motifs, heavy carving, Rococo elements

sample color palette and fabric swatch

Textiles, like this one, often echo the chinoiserie ornament seen in Georgian interiors.

Much English furniture of the mid-eighteenth century is referred to as Chippendale, but the designation properly belongs only to pieces made in the London workshops of Thomas Chippendale (1718–1779). Chippendale was the leading furniture maker of his time, but his greatest achievement was producing the first major pattern books devoted to furniture. It is these catalogs that have made his name virtually synonymous with the period, and created the first style named for a maker, rather than a ruler.

There is, however, no single Chippendale style: *The Gentleman and Cabinet-Maker's Director*, published in 1754, 1755, and 1762, contained drawings for chairs, tables, commodes and other objects of furniture in all the fashionable styles of the time, including many that were not his own designs. They reflected several influences: French Rococo, Gothic, Chinese, and later Neoclassical variants, all grafted onto what were essentially the same basic forms. The *Director* was widely distributed in England as well as other countries, most notably America, where they became the basis for meticulous copies, adaptations, and improvisations on the originals.

The variety of influences notwithstanding, Chippendale-style furniture, particularly the chairs, can usually be identified by several distinctive characteristics: the yoke-shape crest rail, pierced splat, straight sides and (particularly if made at the Chippendale factory) skillfully carved ornament. Below the seats, however, there was considerable variation. Early Chippendale designs had Rococo elements such as floriate carving and cabriole legs, while later ones were more restrained, with Neoclassical motifs and square-section Marlborough legs with stretchers.

Chippendale case pieces are less easily characterized. On commodes, which adopted the French model, the Rococo is more restrained than that of Continental styles, with carving as ornament, rather than elaborate mounts. Bookcases and secretaries are often large and architectural in form, with mullioned glass doors and cornices, and broken or scrolled pediments. Later designs have classical pilasters.

This satinwood and marquetry commode, with shaped sides and ormolu mountings, was designed by Thomas Chippendale in the 1770s to reflect the "antique" style then coming into fashion. The form was derived from French commodes, but the ornament is clearly classical, including sunflowers and palm leaves on the frieze, ram's heads atop corner pilasters, Etruscan vases, and fretwork.

neo-palladian

neo-palladian ca.1730 to 1760

ABOUT THE PERIOD

Concurrent with the relatively understated Early Georgian, the Palladian, or Neo-Palladian, as it is known, is an assertive and monumental style, clearly based on classical architecture. Neo-Palladian style had no relation to prevailing English fashion, but was created by architects and designers for wealthy clients who favored grandeur over understatement, and could afford to commission whatever they chose.

The style was defined by the work of William Kent (1684–1748), who assisted his patron Lord Burlington in the design of Chiswick House in London, and who executed commissions for dozens of churches and public buildings as well as private residences. Disdaining the weightiness of the English Baroque, Neo-Palladian style drew instead on the more refined Italian classicism. Kent had studied Palladian architecture, as well as the seventeenth-century designs of Palladian-follower Inigo Jones, and then developed his own interpretations of the classical style. Though Kent's buildings were more elaborate than Palladio's rustic villas, the classical severity of the architecture was a striking contrast to the opulence within.

ABOUT THE STYLE

Neo-Palladian interiors are as grand in their way, though more austere, as almost anything in the French vocabulary of design. Their almost-monumental scale and symmetry reflect the English view of themselves, in the glorious days of the Empire, as inheritors of the Roman tradition. The typical Neo-Palladian room is a testament to the status of its owner.

In the high-ceilinged, symmetrical space, stucco walls are anchored by prominent baseboards, above which are three sections; dado below, field above, and entablatures or massive cornices at ceiling level. The field might be painted, or covered with patterned damask, tapestry, or occasionally wallpaper.

Ceilings, while not quite as elaborate as those in French interiors, are decorated with classical plasterwork that can be as three-dimensional as carving, and sometimes includes touches of Rococo. Doorways and windows have architectural detailing—

chunky moldings, scrolled brackets, friezes, and reliefs. Most are painted white, with occasional gilded accents.

Grand over-mantels with projecting cornices and imposing pediments highlight the fireplace, the focal point of the room, and stairs and balustrades are given similar treatment.

Window treatments are complex, with multiple layers of ornate and costly draperies, in rich, imported fabrics. Oriental rugs and magnificent objects contribute to the sumptuous effect.

Colors, in a varying palette, are more assertive than those of the usual classical interior, and reflect the preference of the individual client.

Kent was the first Englishman to design complete interiors, and the furnishings and backgrounds were carefully planned and coordinated. For these rooms, he and his followers designed furniture as imposing as sculpture or architecture. Forms are not new, but are magnified, corniced and pedimented, or enhanced with carved elements such as volute supports, fish scales, shells, or lion masks. Chairs might be painted, or accented with gilding. Case pieces and tables are grand in scale, and clearly based on architectural forms. Most of the furniture is mahogany, which takes well to detailed carving.

Matthias Lock (ca.1710–1765), working in this period, produced distinctive column-legged consoles with Rococo-like ornamentation, typically with carved swags and classical faces, painted white and generally gilded. Unlike other Georgian furnishings adapted from pattern books, most Neo-Palladian pieces are individual, idiosyncratic works of art.

OPPOSITE: The hall at Upton House in Warwickshire, England, conveys the stately grandeur of Neo-Palladian style, with its Kent-style chimneypiece, marble floor, and seventeenth-century Brussels tapestries.

RIGHT: The architectural character of Neo-Palladian furniture is shown in this 70-inch-tall mahogany cabinet, with shaped pediment, paneled doors, acanthus carving, and heavy paw feet. Probably by William Vile for Kensington Palace, it was made in the 1760s.

Eagle tables like this, done in gilded wood and marble, are generally described as being "after William Kent," reflecting the vigorous character of his designs, ca. 1740.

This 72-inch-wide, white-painted console, ca. 1740, and one of a pair, is a typical design of Matthias Lock, with its columnar legs with bracket supports, and the carved apron with frieze, swags, and classical mask.

notes on the defining characteristics

MOOD	**FURNITURE**
formal and austere	mahogany, massive and linear
SCALE	**TEXTILES**
monumental	rich silks and damasks
COLORS	**KEY MOTIFS**
intense	grotesques, swags, columns, pediments
ORNAMENT	**LOOK FOR**
grand scale	architectural forms, bold details

sample color palette and fabric swatch

A Georgian silk brocade inspired by Grinling Gibbons carvings has the stately air to complement Palladian interiors.

late american colonial

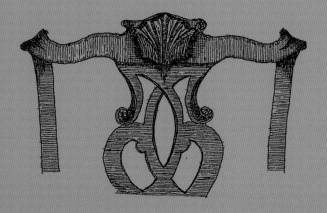

ABOUT THE PERIOD

Having survived the rigors of settling a new nation, Americans were gaining ground, both in the amenities of life, and in the stylishness and sophistication of their homes. With the emergence of a prosperous class of merchants and shipbuilders, there were more clients able to afford fine furnishings, and with the arrival of European-trained craftsmen, more local specialists to make them. Not only could the colonists import fine things from abroad, but they were increasingly able to copy or adapt them at home. However, the combined inconveniences of British taxes and restrictions, the great distances involved in trade, and the uncertainties of ocean transportation, led to delays in communication. Styles in the colonies lagged a decade or more behind those in England.

It is easy to describe American Colonial designs as scaled-down and simplified versions of European (mostly English) prototypes, but they are more interesting, and harder to classify than as mere attempts at reproduction. There are distinct differences between interiors and furniture in the two countries, reflecting both the changing taste and the growing independence of the young nation.

The Late Colonial period includes Queen Anne (which began after that monarch had died) and Chippendale styles. The two overlapped and intermingled, often with elements of both combining in the same interiors and objects. During this period, too, regional variations developed in the way the same designs were executed in different centers of the furniture trade.

Boston, the original center, relinquished some of its dominance to Philadelphia, where immigrant French craftsmen sparked a wave of creativity. Toward the end of the eighteenth century, New York, by then the most important port, also housed the country's leading furniture makers, and other centers developed in Newport, Baltimore, and Charleston. Although American furniture is generally unsigned, the names of exceptional craftsmen like Thomas Affleck (1740–1795), Benjamin Randolph (1721–1791), and William Savery (1721–1788) of Philadelphia, and John Goddard (1724–1785) and John Townsend (1733–1809) of Boston, have become recognized.

During this period, residential architecture made great strides, thanks in part to the availability of the first pattern books for buildings. Brick or wood houses, styled after those in England, now had larger windows, symmetrical plans and classical detailing. The changes were reflected in American interiors, as architectural details were added to the rooms and the furniture that filled them.

In 1776, the American colonies declared their independence from England, leading to even more radical changes that would affect design, as it affected every aspect of the colonists' lives.

ABOUT THE STYLE

As a general rule, although not as elaborately designed, the American interior of this era is often less predictable and a bit lighter in tone than its English Georgian counterpart. It has less architectural detailing, but uses similar elements, and while the furniture appears to be much the same, the idiosyncratic variations of American furnishings give diversity and individuality to the rooms they occupy.

As life in the colonies becomes more stable and prosperous, the decoration of interiors follows suit. Though ceilings remain low, spaces are more expansive, with paneled walls and floors of polished wood planks. Toward mid-century, classical detailing, simplified to suit Colonial taste and craftsmen's skills, appears—moldings, pilasters, and paneled doors.

Wallpapers, first imported hand-painted designs, and later locally produced ones, have become very popular, as they had in Europe. The Chinese motifs seen in England are favored in America as well, particularly with Chippendale-style furnishings.

Windows are double-hung, with larger panes, and accordingly more elaborate window treatments; floor-length draperies of imported textiles in more formal rooms; chintz (an Indian influence), calico or ruffled curtains in others. Textiles are important, with sturdy wools and horsehairs made in the colonies, but the demand for richer fabrics, also making this the single largest category of imports. Later in the period, Venetian blinds appear, offering a better means of light control.

Carpets, once only locally made hooked rugs, are now more varied, and include florals and geometrics. Imported floor coverings, primarily Oriental, are only in the best rooms.

Implements for serving and drinking tea are important symbols of a cultivated home as Americans adopted the customs of the upper-class British—at least until the revolution.

Colors have become brighter and more varied—medium blue or shades of green, accents of white and bright red are popular interior hues.

The fireplace is a focal point, though its treatment is relatively simple, with a carved mantel often bordered in Delft tiles. Later in the century, heavier moldings and architectural detailing become the norm.

Brass chandeliers and sconces are more decorative than wrought iron and less showy than crystal.

Oriental or other fine imported porcelains are displayed in glass-front cabinets or on mantels, along with decorative objects of brass or the new Sheffield plate that provides a middle-class alternative to silver. Clocks, imported or perhaps from local sources, are becoming popular, and gilt-framed mirrors, too, hang on the walls.

American furniture is now comparable to English in skillfulness of cabinetry and finish, more closely resembling the designs that inspired it, though lagging several years behind in style. But the resemblances are sometimes superficial. As American craftsmen come into their own, form has become more important than ornament— the furniture is generally lighter in scale, slimmer and more vertical than English pieces, which are horizontally oriented, weightier, and more deeply carved. These differences reflect not only the American dislike of pretension, but also the inappropriateness of heavy-looking furniture to rooms of modest size.

Beyond these general variations are more specific ones: the craftsmen in each furniture-producing community develop particularities of form and decoration, from the silhouettes of Queen Anne chairs, to the carving of shells or ball-and-claw feet, to the placement of escutcheons on highboys. Distinct differences in these and other details make it possible to identify the part of the country in which they were made, and often even the maker. Such highly individualistic departures from pattern-book models also make American furniture an intriguing study.

PREVIOUS PAGE, TOP: Quincy house, in Quincy, Massachusetts, was built by revolutionary leader Colonel John Quincy to serve as a country estate. The bedroom, with its understated but elegant furnishings, is an attractive reflection of Queen Anne style in colonial America.

PREVIOUS PAGE, BOTTOM: In its basic form, the American interpretation of Chippendale style varied very little from that of England, but the interiors reflected the smaller scale and aversion to ostentation of the colonies.

ABOVE: The highboy was perhaps the most important piece of eighteenth century American furniture. The wood and detailing varied with the region, and the maker—this 86-inch-tall one, constructed of cherry, with fan-like shell carving and a spiral finial, was made in Connecticut, between 1750 and 1780.

LEFT: Reflecting the regional variations in American furniture, the highboy form in Newport, Rhode Island, was flat-topped, with a slipper foot. This example from 1748 was made by Christopher Townsend, one of a family of celebrated Newport-based cabinetmakers.

The Philadelphia Queen Anne chair is a superb and original expression of the style. This mahogany example, one of the finest extant, incorporates the S-curve in every part of its frame, and has distinctive shell carving, slip-seat, and trifid feet. Made ca. 1740 to 1760.

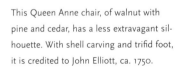

This Queen Anne chair, of walnut with pine and cedar, has a less extravagant silhouette. With shell carving and trifid foot, it is credited to John Elliott, ca. 1750.

Reflecting the sophistication of Philadelphia makers of this period, this lowboy, ca. 1745–55, has scrolls and shell carving at the knees, trifid feet, and a decorative shaped and carved apron. Mahogany with poplar and pine.

A fine example of a tall-case clock, this one, ca. 1755, has an arched pediment, corner columns, and hand-painted silvered-brass dial. The concave carved shell marks it as the work of the Townsend-Goddard cabinet-makers of Newport.

The slant-front desk was, in effect, the lower half of the English secretary-bookcase. This one, of mahogany with simple shell carving and bracket feet, was made in Newport, ca. 1760 to 1780.

The block-and-shell furniture of Newport, Rhode Island, is exemplified by this bureau table, with outer convex shells flanking a concave one. The central door is flush with the facade, in a variation on the more common knee-hole form. Made ca. 1790 by John Townsend, one of the finest Colonial cabinetmakers.

In the last—and most spectacular—
interpretation of the form (it disappeared after the Revolutionary War),
Chippendale highboys were marked by
virtuoso carving and ornament. This
one, made in Philadelphia ca. 1765,
combines bold Rococo scrolls and
shell motifs with scrolled pediment,
urn finials, and fluted columns that
foretell the coming Neoclassicism.

Chippendale chairs were translated in America directly from the pages of *The Director* but were freely interpreted by individual craftsmen. This one, done in mahogany with white pine and maple, was made in Massachusetts, ca. 1765.

The wing chair, brought from England and called the easy chair, was a luxury that required costly imported upholstery. This American Chippendale example, made in Philadelphia ca. 1765 to 1780, has deep foliate carving and ball-and-claw feet on cabriole legs.

In classic Chippendale form, this sofa, made
in Philadelphia ca. 1765, has a serpentine back,
volute arms, and Marlborough legs.

notes on the defining characteristics

MOOD understated and comfortable	**FURNITURE** mahogany, like English forms, lighter and more varied
SCALE well proportioned	**TEXTILES** Indian crewels, chintzes, imported silks and damasks
COLORS warm and varied	**KEY MOTIFS** scallop shell, ball-and-claw foot, interesting finials
ORNAMENT conservative	**LOOK FOR** highboy and lowboy, English styles done differently

sample color palette and fabric swatch

An imported English toile like this would have been a fashionable addition to a Queen Anne room.

The silhouettes of American Queen Anne furniture are based on the S-curved forms of English designs, but differ in several important areas: case pieces are slimmer, and the cabriole legs are curvier, with a pronounced knee, tapering ankle, and club or trifid foot. The ideal Queen Anne chair is made in Philadelphia, a fluidly sculptural design with elegant, shapely splat, balloon-seat and shell carving on knee and crest rail; and the upholstered easy chair, with either scroll or pillar arm, is another adopted English form.

A particular invention of American furniture is the highboy, a chest raised up on legs—for both convenience and a taller look—with a companion piece called a low-boy. The form continued until after the revolution, and became probably the most important item of furniture in most colonial homes. The classic Queen Anne highboy is a bonnet-top form made in Boston, on four legs, without stretchers, and with vesti-gial pendants suspended from the apron. In rooms with lower ceilings, the highboy top may be flat. Brasses and handles are simple, shapely, and mostly imported.

Other furnishings are both more sophisticated and more varied. Tilt-top, tea and card tables, drop-lid and slant-top desks (as literacy is more widespread), and chests of drawers are among the items of furniture produced in this style. Since the style began later in America, when walnut was becoming less fashionable, much Queen Anne furni-ture is of mahogany, though many American furniture makers continued to work in local woods like maple, pine, and cherry, especially outside the major port cities.

Queen Anne furniture remained the most enduringly popular style in the colonies until after the revolution, long after it had become forgotten in England. Beyond the appeal of its grace and simplicity, there is perhaps another reason. With simple lines and less carving, Queen Anne pieces are less costly to make than Chippendale ones, and that would have appealed to the conservative colonists. Americans, at that time, were more penny-wise than fashion-following.

As styles moved from an American interpretation of English Queen Anne to variations on Early Georgian, they also incorporated Rococo elements from France and the Far East. With the 1754 publication of Chippendale's *Director*, which was widely circulated in America, skilled craftsmen in the colonies could replicate the latest London fashions, though most American Chippendale is a free interpretation of Chippendale's originals.

The transition from Queen Anne to Chippendale furniture began with more linear forms, the addition of ball-and-claw feet, and a greater taste for ornament and carving. The new silhouettes, however, often retained elements of the old. Chairs might marry Queen Anne–style cabriole legs with a Chippendale body, though with flatter carving than that in English chairs. Seats are rectilinear, but generally less broad, and less flat, than English. Sofas are a larger, more comfortable alternative to settees, while the easy chair remains, with its squat cabriole legs, ball-and-claw feet, and no stretchers.

A new fashion appears—block-front furniture, in which desk, chest, or cabinet fronts are formed in three alternating concave and convex panels. Though not an American invention, the form has become associated with Newport, Rhode Island.

Chippendale highboys and lowboys show some of the most original stylistic touches of any American furniture. The tops have broken, curving, scrolled pediments, flanked with finials and centered with fanciful and finely-executed carving, usually combining shells with intricate foliage that turns apron and tympanum into virtuoso works of art. Highly figured, imported crotch mahogany veneers make the smooth surfaces as decorative as the carved ones. Brasses, too, are more decorative, reflecting the Rococo influence, though Americans, like the English, are restrained in their embrace of French frivolity.

Other furniture of the time includes tea tables with piecrust top and tripod column base with ball-and-claw foot, game tables, drop-front and slant-top desks, bookcases and secretaries. Toward the end of the period, acanthus carving, fretwork, fluted columns, and gadroon borders reflect the growing taste for Neoclassical forms.

ABOUT THE PERIOD

As its name suggests, Neoclassicism marked a return to the traditions of the past, and the search for a more refined and enduring style than the undisciplined and frivolous Rococo. In its rationality, it was influenced by the intellects of the Enlightenment, but its more immediate impetus was the excavation of ancient ruins at Pompeii and Herculaneum in Italy. Beginning in the mid-eighteenth century, these widely published findings became a rich source of inspiration for architects and designers, motivating a dramatic turnaround of style in France, and a simultaneous one in England.

Coming into its own after some years of transition, when the Rococo mingled with the incoming style, the early phase of French Neoclassicism combined the best features of Baroque and Rococo. It balanced the richness and symmetry of the one with the grace and delicacy of the other and, considering its merits, should have stayed fashionable for several decades.

To its misfortune, it coincided with the reign of Louis XVI (1774–1789), by whose name it is also known. As politics intruded on fashion, the association of design and patronage with the monarchy ensured its downfall. When the French Revolution of 1789 dethroned Louis and his much-maligned queen, Marie Antoinette, the style that marked the era was discarded with the royals and their court. The palaces and mansions were sacked or destroyed, and the trappings of wealth were disdained as unsuitable for the new proletariat. French design, however, would reassert itself under the rule of Napoleon.

Having avoided the excesses of its predecessor, the Neoclassicism of the mid-eighteenth century influenced design changes in many other countries, becoming the first of many revivals of styles tracing back to ancient Greece and Rome.

ABOUT THE STYLE

The Neoclassical interior is gracious and elegant, projecting an air of serenity achieved in large part from its emphasis on symmetry and order. It strikes a happy medium of mood, slightly more formal than the Rococo room but avoiding the pomposity of a Baroque one. It revives familiar classical ornament, but executes it with restraint.

The space is generous, but comfortably scaled, and may take any of several shapes, though all of them carefully balanced, projecting an air of calm sophistication. Boiserie on walls is outlined in slim, classical borders into neat, geometric sections, accented with classical motifs such as acanthus scrolls, rosettes, swags, or Greek-key motifs. The prevailing geometric forms of *le gout grec*, the early stage of the style, progress later to more decorative Etruscan and rich floral ornament. Wallpaper might be a fashionable addition—papers replicating the look of hand-painted silk are preferable to heavy tapestries, or scenic panels, newly introduced by Jean-Baptiste Reveillon, are attractive alternatives to frescoes or hand-painted murals. High ceilings are less elaborately decorated than in previous periods. They are centered with medallions, joining the walls in precise, geometric cornices rather than cove moldings.

To create the requisite symmetry, hidden doors or false openings might be created opposite real ones, and treated identically. Both doors and windows are framed in classical orders, and topped with cornices, pediments, or decorative panels. The chimneypiece, less intrusive and more gracefully proportioned than those of earlier periods, is given similar treatment.

Casement windows, to dado or floor, have arched or rectangular headings, and shutters to match the paneling on the walls. The glass panes are now larger, admitting more light to the interior. Drapery and portieres are coordinated with the rich fabrics used on upholstery, for a more unified look.

Floors, of parquet that may combine different woods, can also be faience, marble, or terra cotta, and carpets might be imported Oriental designs as well as Savonnerie or Aubussons, in geometric patterns.

The pastels of Rococo are retained, with white or pastel walls, but a palette of livelier colors in fabrics adds sparkle to the scheme.

Still a focal point, the Neoclassical chandelier has a refined silhouette, more vertical than that of the Rococo, with strands of crystals clustered around the central post creating a "waterfall" effect.

Mirrors remain important accessories, framed in the paneling, and contributing to the balanced proportions of the space. Other accessories, as might be expected, reflect the same type of classical ornament as the framework of the interior—porcelain shaped like Grecian urns, gilded clocks with columns and pediments, and candleholders with caryatids.

Having discarded the unrestrained forms of Rococo, Neoclassical furniture is slim and linear, with straight legs, gracefully fluted or reeded, and tapering to neat sabot feet. For chairs and sofas, curves are controlled rather than voluptuous, with oval, medallion, rectangular, or square backs, wide seats, and fluted legs jointed neatly to chair frames with rosette-carved blocks. The variety of forms introduced in the Rococo period continues, with silhouettes modified to suit the more restrained style. Exposed wood frames of beech, ash, or elm are often gilded or painted.

Though light enough to be movable, furniture is set in precise alignment with the walls of the room, creating an effect in pronounced contrast to the informality of the Rococo period. Other than chair backs, the only curves are simple geometric ones, shaping corners or rounding fronts of cabinets and tables.

Cabinetry continues to be attractively varied—the *bureau à cylindre,* the *bonheur du jour*, and specialized pieces for a variety of serving needs; larger commodes or tables topped with marble, in white or pastel colors; small tables, in square, oval, or demilune shape—often drawn from ancient classical forms.

Mahogany (*acajou*) is the new wood of choice, along with satinwood, ebony, tulipwood, and others with more varied and decorative grains. Linear cube marquetry, or more refined frieze veneer, are alternatives to floral marquetry to decorate commodes and cabinets, with graceful ormolu or gilt-bronze mounts shaped as swags or classical figures. Porcelain plaques, Japanese lacquer panels, and *pietra dura* are also seen as ornament. Wrought iron, inspired by Pompeii finds, is used for table legs. Trim is done in steel and brass.

A number of celebrated craftsmen worked during this period, but of them all, Jean-Henri Riesener (1734–1806), *ébéniste* to the king, is considered the most exceptional. Others include Adam Weisweiler (1744–1820), and the *menuisier* (carpenter) Georges Jacob (1739–1814), who founded the workshop that defined fine French chairmaking for several decades.

In the salon of Paris's Hotel de Bourbon-Conde by Alexandre Theodore Brogniart, Louis XVI furnishings are framed in classical architecture—pilasters, entablatures, and carved motifs such as lyres and acanthus scrolls.

Part of a suite of giltwood seating pieces, this ca. 1780 canapé by
Louis M. Pluvinet has a floral-carved crest and ribbon-and-husk
carved frame—all set on tapering fluted legs.

This writing table, ca. 1775, of tulip-
wood with marble top and ormolu
mounts, has a frieze drawer with
a hinged, leather-topped writing
surface. Straight lines and simple,
classical ornament mark it clearly
as Louis XVI style.

The fauteuil, an upholstered armchair whose form dates to the
Baroque period, has acquired a
shorter leg and shapelier arm.
The carved wood frame is generally gilded. Made by Andre-Pierre
Dupain, ca. 1775.

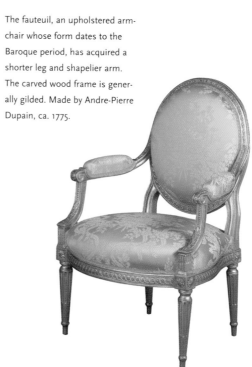

A breakfront commode, ca. 1780, of bois satine, amaranth, and rosewood, ornamented with intricate parquetry and ormolu mounts.

Reflecting the *goût grec* style introduced in France in the mid-eighteenth century, this ca. 1775 bureau plat has stylized Greek key parquetry inlay and classical-motif mounts.

This bureau à cylindre, made ca. 1780 in Paris by Ferdinand Bury, has geometric marquetry and restrained ormolu mounts.

Similar to a sideboard, though a bit smaller, this ca. 1780 console desserte by Charles Topino has two open shelves and is done in mahogany with ribboned trophy mounts of gilt-bronze.

notes on the defining characteristics

MOOD moderately formal	**FURNITURE** straight-lined, slim, and symmetrical
SCALE generous	**TEXTILES** silks, damasks, velvets
COLORS lively and varied	**KEY MOTIFS** classical pilasters, swags, rosettes, urns
ORNAMENT restrained and linear	**LOOK FOR** fluted or reeded legs, motifs from antiquity, cube marquetry

sample color palette and fabric swatch

A symmetrical design of floral motifs and classical figures, richly colored, characterizes this Louis XVI silk lampas.

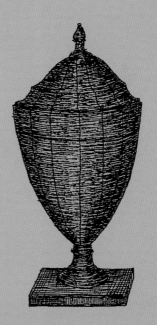

ABOUT THE PERIOD

During the reign of George III (1760–1820), English style entered a period of committed and continuous Neoclassicism, first overlapping and then gradually supplanting the Rococo. Inspired by the Pompeii and Herculaneum excavations that affected France, it marked a growing interest in antiquity and was contemporaneous with the change in French style. It was also an era that included the legendary designers of English interiors and furniture: Adam, Chippendale, Hepplewhite, and Sheraton.

Reaping the rewards of affluence, education, and travel, the English became committed collectors, amassing artworks as souvenirs of their tours of the Continent. They acquired etchings by Piranesi (1720–1778), or paintings by artists such as Canaletto (1697–1768) and Panini (1691–1766), depicting the beauties of classical architecture, and they commissioned architects and designers to translate the timeless aesthetic in building by remodeling and decorating their homes.

The most famous of these, Robert Adam, developed a design vocabulary that would dominate the Late Georgian period and is often called "Adam Style." Adam brought a sophisticated sensibility to the creation of interiors he described as "integrated," in that every element was planned as part of a coordinated whole. Designing or specifying all of the furnishings in the room, he created a pervasive and enduring style that represents the English interior at its most fully developed. In furniture, early Neoclassicism was linked to late Chippendale styles, and to furniture by George Hepplewhite and Thomas Sheraton, whose designs, particularly those of Sheraton, were embraced as well in American Federal interiors.

The fates conspired to bestow England with new resources for luxury products— Axminster (1755) for fine carpets, Worcester (1751) for England's first porcelain, Waterford (1783) for cut glass to rival French crystal, Matthew Boulton's factory for Sheffield silverplate (1762), and Josiah Wedgwood's pottery (1771), making jasperware that "channeled" the look of Roman cameo glass. Georgian England also produced the painters Joshua Reynolds (1723–1792) and Thomas Gainsborough (1727–1788).

As the century drew to a close, Neoclassicism continued to dominate English design, becoming more pronounced and explicit in the style that would be called Regency.

ABOUT THE STYLE

The finest Late Georgian interior can hold its own with the very best of French style—indeed, in its most formal incarnations, it shares many characteristics with its contemporary French Neoclassical room. There are, however, notable differences— though the same classical ornament is used in both, the execution and the furniture itself vary in approach. The Late Georgian room is elegant in its symmetry and refinement, balancing characteristic English restraint against the desire for ornamentation. In its sophistication, planning, superbly crafted furnishings, and worldly mélange of accessories, it represents the high point of English design.

The room itself is grand, without assuming extravagant proportions. It is probably rectangular, or sometimes round. Avoiding heavy paneling, cornices, or tapestry, the walls are painted in pleasant colors, with a dado of plaster rather than wood. Above it is perhaps an expanse of scenic wallpaper or patterned fabric.

Moldings and plasterwork are white and relatively understated, and ceilings are treated in similar fashion. Doors are paneled, or sometimes curved to conform to the shapes of circular rooms.

Tall windows with large rectangular panes might have newly fashionable roller blinds or are dressed in heavy drapery over sheer curtains, topped with a cornice or lambrequin. Bay windows have come into fashion during this period.

Textiles are increasingly varied and less weighty than in previous periods, as England has begun producing fine wood-block or copper-plate printed fabrics, as well as its celebrated printed chintzes. By the final decades of the century, all the textiles and upholstery in the room are coordinated, giving the interior a more unified appearance.

Floors of polished oak, stone, or marble in halls or foyers are covered with Axminster carpets, which are as desirable as imported ones.

In the standards set by Robert Adam interiors, colors are vibrant and appealing, with lively pastels lending warmth and variety.

Chandeliers and candelabra in crystal, brass, or bronze provide light as well as decorative interest.

More attention is being given to fine decorative accessories—mirrors, most often gilded and often with Chinoiserie motifs; clocks, busts of marble or bronze, *torchères* and candelabra, and mementos of foreign travel. Wedgwood jasperware is joined by vases of Sèvres porcelain, or Meissen figurines.

Early Chippendale designs carry the Rococo influence into Late Georgian furniture, with finely executed carving that reflects the various influences seen in his drawing books. As the period progresses, however, the Neoclassical influence takes hold, and furniture abandons asymmetrical ornament and foliate carving, returning to the symmetry and linearity of classical forms.

In the final decade of the century, Hepplewhite and Sheraton styles represent the Neoclassical ideal of Late Georgian furniture. Chairs are strikingly slimmer than those of the Early Georgian period. The cabriole leg and ball-and-claw foot have disappeared, to be replaced by slender, tapered legs, and slim vertical members. Some chairs recall French forms, though they are not always painted, and all have an air of delicacy.

In case furniture, heavy cornices and pediments are replaced by refined molding, and though cabinets are occasionally carved, the ornament is understated and generally limited to panels or framing. Glass-doored cabinets are defined in shaped wood mullions, and even the largest pieces have a more refined, lighter look than in the Early Georgian period.

Though mahogany is still widely used, satinwood and fruitwoods have become increasingly popular, often decorated with delicate inlays or contrasting banding. Characteristically, English designers continue to make use of wood as ornament, avoiding the gilt mounts that are a prominent feature of French period furniture.

PREVIOUS PAGE: Saltram House in Devon, England, boasts some of the finest interiors of the Late Georgian period. The dining room, designed by Robert Adam in 1768, is celebrated for its plasterwork ceiling and the Adam-designed Axminster carpet that echoes its classical motifs.

ABOVE: The sideboard, a new form credited to George Hepplewhite, melded a center table with side pedestals to create a practical item of dining room furniture. This George III mahogany piece has a serpentine front and skirt, with satinwood inlays and lion's-mask pulls.

A ca. 1765 silver table attributed to John Cobb, done with rectangular top and baluster-turned gallery, on square fluted and tapering legs with double-arched stretchers.

The decoration of this ca. 1760 George III breakfront bookcase with swan-neck, scroll pediment, and pierced carving, suggests designs by Thomas Chippendale.

The demilune commode, a French form, was adopted in England with painted or inlaid decoration in place of applied ornament. This one, ca. 1785, has fine detailing of urns, swags, foliate scrolls, and even simulated fluting on the legs.

A Late Georgian armchair, ca. 1760, in mahogany with serpentine top rails and straight sides, has carved detail on the arms and legs. Generally designated "French" by their English makers (to denote good taste), chairs like this bore little actual resemblance to those made in France.

Part of a grand suite of seating furniture directly influenced by the "French Chairs" of Thomas Chippendale, this extravagantly carved giltwood armchair, ca.1755, has high arched crests and cabriole legs with leaf-carved feet.

Made ca. 1760 by two of London's finest cabinetmakers, William Vile and John Cobb, the architectural form of this grand bookcase is typical of early George III furniture. Its decoration combines elements of Neo-Palladian classicism and Rococo-style carving.

notes on the defining characteristics

MOOD moderately formal	**FURNITURE** mostly mahogany, but varied woods, light-scaled, drawing-book forms
SCALE generous	**TEXTILES** silks and damasks, English chintzes
COLORS vivid and varied	**KEY MOTIFS** pagodas and parasols, then urns, rosettes, festoons
ORNAMENT Chinese, Gothic, then classical	**LOOK FOR** Chippendale, Hepplewhite, Sheraton furniture, Adam style

sample color palette and fabric swatch

This print of dancing figures has the lively colors and symmetrical refinement of the classically influenced era.

Robert Adam (1728–1792) was a Scottish-born architect and designer whose beautifully conceived "integrated interiors," designed during the Late Georgian period, represent the paradigm of early Neoclassical design in England. The son of a celebrated architect, his three brothers also architects, Adam traveled to Italy to study classical buildings and the work of Palladio, whose designs he concluded were too weighty. He sought, in his words, to bring "novelty and variety" to the spirit of antiquity, and his interiors combine the lightness and charm of Rococo with the precision and symmetry of Neoclassicism.

Most of Adam's architectural commissions were renovations rather than original construction, but his interiors were entirely his own, and they can be recognized by his meticulous attention to balancing all the elements in a room, and his finely executed vocabulary of ornament based on classical motifs.

An Adam interior feels spacious and airy, even when modest in size—the result of his delicate touch and superb sense of proportion. Walls, typically painted in white or warm pastels, are trimmed with white moldings and delicate low-relief plasterwork. The ceiling is an all-white composition of absolute symmetry, with plaster ornamentation that has its counterpart in the design on the floor. A hexagonal ceiling design, for example, is reflected in the hexagonal border of the carpet (which might now be made by England's own Axminster factory), or a similarly shaped motif executed on a marble floor.

Doorways and windows are balanced as well, each opening having its precise counterpart on the opposite side of the room. Where a door or window is not called for, a mirror of the same shape might substitute, or a tall recess for sculpture.

The mantel is an important element in the Adam interior, refined in scale and generally painted white, flanked by columns and decorated with ornament in scagliola that simulates marble, or is patterned like *pietra dura*, in familiar motifs like urns, rosettes, swags, ribbons, ram's heads, guilloches, and Greek keys. Though altogether distinctive, Adam interiors have a clear relationship to those of the French Louis XVI style. His selection of fabrics, though perhaps less elaborate, is equally elegant and refined.

Adam's color schemes favor warm-toned pastels, though he occasionally varies these with more saturated hues.

An elegant crystal chandelier and graceful wall sconces provide the primary illumination. Accessories include fine paintings and portraits, plaster casts of classical sculpture, and elegant silver objects by English or French craftsmen. Oval mirrors, in delicate gilded frames topped with classical urns and swags, are another distinctive Adam touch, and Wedgwood jasperware plaques or vases are particularly appropriate complements.

Adam oversaw every element of each project, making drawings for carpets to be woven to his specifications, specifying or selecting furnishings by the most skilled makers, or sometimes designing the furniture himself, in forms that seem more French than English. The interiors he designed remain among the finest examples of skillfully coordinated design.

Graceful gilded mirrors like this ca. 1800 design, with pierced carving of scrolls and folliage, and attached candleholders, were an important part of Adam's design vocabulary. 49 ¼ inches high, 32 ½ inches wide.

George Hepplewhite (1721–1786) and Thomas Sheraton (1751–1806) were furniture makers in London during the time of George III, but their names are known primarily because of the pattern books they published, which together form an encyclopedic vocabulary of English Neoclassical furniture. Like Thomas Chippendale, they each showed a range of current fashions, but since the prevailing fashion was dominated by a single aesthetic, their furniture has many similarities. Both Hepplewhite and Sheraton pieces are light-scaled, slim, and graceful, though Sheraton designs are somewhat more delicate, have more surface detail, and reflect a stronger influence from French styles.

George Hepplewhite died before the publication of his *Cabinetmaker and Upholsterer's Guide* in 1788, which was overseen by his wife. He is credited for the invention of the sideboard, which combined a cabinet and two flanking pedestals to form a single piece for the newly designated dining room. Hepplewhite style is particularly associated with several specific shapes of chair backs: shield, oval, heart, wheel, and camelback, and the use of the Prince of Wales feather motif. Hepplewhite furniture is usually mahogany or satinwood, with legs that are slim, most often square, and fluted or reeded. Carving is rare; classical figures or marquetry in contrasting light woods is the most frequent ornament. Hepplewhite designs appear in interiors by Robert Adam.

Thomas Sheraton published his *Cabinet-Maker and Upholsterer's Drawing Book* between 1791 and 1794. Sheraton designs tend to be more rectilinear and generally slimmer in silhouette than Hepplewhite, and, like Hepplewhite, his name is associated with specific chair forms: straight-lined, and light-scaled, with delicately carved splats that may be decorated with urns, swags, lyres, or other classical motifs. Cabinetry is varied and graceful, with smooth expanses of fine-grained veneers, generally in lighter woods like satinwood, often with delicate marquetry in string-banding, ovals or lozenges, or festoons. Sheraton case pieces may also have painted accents, and often use brass gallery trim and inlay. His books illustrated unusual accessory pieces, and he developed specialty items such as tambour desks, folding tables, or tables with vanishing drawers. The legs of Sheraton furniture, like those of Hepplewhite, are slender, tapering, and finished in spade feet or sabots.

Since furniture cannot be directly attributed to either of these cabinetmakers, pieces are designated as Hepplewhite or Sheraton on the basis of the book from which the designs were drawn rather than the shop in which they were made.

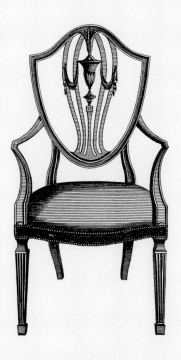

Hepplewhite drawing from the *Cabinetmaker and Upholsterer's Guide.*

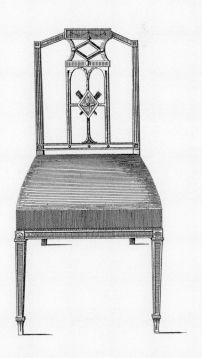

Sheraton drawing from the *Cabinet-Maker and Upholsterer's Drawing Book.*

LEFT: A shield-back arm-chair, ca. 1780, painted with garlands of terra cotta flowers on a black ground, reflecting the short-lived vogue for "Etruscan" decoration made popular by Robert Adam and seen in several of his interiors.

RIGHT: A ca. 1790 mahogany side chair in a familiar Sheraton form—low, straight back with vertical slats, and graceful tapering legs.

Sheraton case pieces, typified by this carlton house desk (ca. 1780), in figured satinwood with crossbanding and stringing in ebony and boxwood were generally lighter-scaled and more delicately ornamented than those of Hepplewhite.

late georgian hepplewhite and sheraton

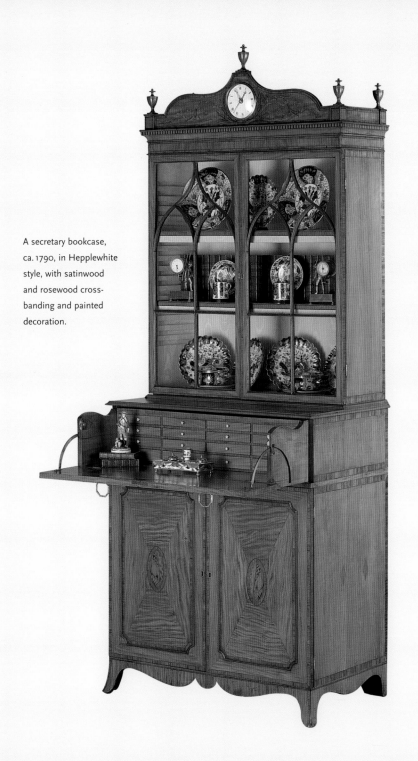

A secretary bookcase, ca. 1790, in Hepplewhite style, with satinwood and rosewood cross-banding and painted decoration.

federal

ABOUT THE PERIOD

The American Revolution of 1776 created a new nation, but its effect on design was not immediate. It would, however, prove considerable. When a new style emerged, a decade or so later, it was a movement toward refinement and elegance, reflecting several aspects of the young republic—the search for a strong national identity, the presence of a consumer elite, and empathy with the French, the revolutionary allies who staged their own revolt in 1789. The style was called Federal, after the name of George Washington's political party. It represented the early phase of Neoclassicism in America.

In the closing years of the eighteenth century, the classicism of Robert Adam became the height of fashion for a new and mostly native-born aristocracy of American merchants and ship owners, who filled their homes with Hepplewhite and Sheraton furniture. Reacting to the heavy ornamentation and Rococo forms of Chippendale design, Federal style focused, like its European precedents, on classical forms inspired initially by excavations at Pompeii and Herculaneum. As the style developed, it would draw more heavily on French designs, such as those of Percier and Fontaine.

New York was the center of trade and industry, and Federal furniture highlighted the skills of American craftsmen such as Samuel McIntire (1757–1811) in Salem, Massachusetts; John (1738–1818) and Thomas (1771–1848) Seymour in Boston; and Duncan Phyfe (1768–1854) in New York, though Phyfe became more closely associated with the Empire style that followed. Perhaps the most celebrated proponent of Neoclassical style, particularly in its French-influenced interpretations, was Thomas Jefferson (1743–1826). His gentleman-architect designs included the campus of the University of Virginia and, more famously, his own home at Monticello, a translation that owed much to Palladian architecture. Jeffersonian buildings have a smooth facade, a pitched roof, and gracefully detailed columns at the entrance, precursors of the more exaggerated Neoclassicism that would later captivate American architects.

Along with Queen Anne, Federal has been the most enduring and most influential, of all eighteenth century American styles.

ABOUT THE STYLE

More gracious and cosmopolitan than any previous American interior, Federal rooms exude the confidence that came with independence and a sense of national pride. They are more sophisticated, though also somewhat more formal, than Colonial interiors, with symmetrical plans and straight-lined furniture completely erasing any remnants of Rococo.

The Federal interior is geometrically shaped and relatively spacious. Smoothly plastered walls are painted white or perhaps in warm tones of blue, green, or mustard—subdued in public rooms, much brighter in private ones. There are white moldings, classically detailed, perhaps with plaster ornament like swags, garlands, and rosettes, sometimes accented in bright colors. The dining room or parlor might have wallpaper with patriotic motifs, or elegant scenics, imported from France.

Tall windows, often Palladian-style, take to fairly elaborate window treatments, perhaps with draped pelmets, swags, or tasseled pullback draperies over simple muslin or cotton curtains.

Floors are polished wood, graced with carpets. In wealthy homes, carpeting in geometric patterns might be laid in strips to cover the entire floor, then finished with a decorative border.

Fabrics, including fine French imports, are richer than any used previously in America, with patterns as well as solids embellished with appropriate classical motifs.

The classical revival has spurred the use of more color, muted pastels most often combined with white—straw-yellow, oyster, dove grey, green, and fawn. They reflect the lightness of Adam style.

Lighting has become more sophisticated, and fine chandeliers provide the requisite finishing touch for any important room—with crystal drops, or cut-glass shades. Primarily of brass, chandeliers and sconces still depend on candles, though the first oil lamp, the saucer-type "Betty," is introduced in 1790.

Decorations are more varied than in prior periods, and more distinctly American. The eagle, the national symbol adopted after independence was declared, is the ornament of choice for mirrors and other accessories, and a circle of stars, representing the thirteen colonies, is used as well. The Constitution mirror is a popular Sheraton style, with a painted panel depicting some patriotic event. Clocks are now widely made in America, and tall-case clocks—later called grandfather clocks—as well as the banjo form, have become symbols of status and national pride. So is silver by the smith and patriot Paul Revere (1735–1818). And portraits on the walls, suggesting the stability of family and home, might be by American painters like Gilbert Stuart (1755–1828) or Rembrandt Peale (1778–1860).

No longer multipurpose, the Federal interior reflects developments in room types and configurations. The parlor has emerged as the most important room, with its own type of furnishings, and the dining room is a newly designated space that also requires particular fittings.

Federal furniture is distinguished for its geometric forms, slim lines, and smooth expanses of mahogany or lighter-tone woods, often accented with contrasting banding and inlays. The "skin" of veneer has replaced carved decoration. A new range of objects has been designed for specific rooms—sideboards and large tables for the dining room, long sofas and matching chairs for the parlor, decorative tester beds, and a variety of occasional pieces such as sewing or card tables, sofa tables, side tables, the desk-bookcase (used as a china cabinet), and ladies' dressing tables.

The American highboy disappeared after the revolution, and has been replaced by the chest-on-chest and various storage pieces on platforms or bracket feet. Brought over from England, the ubiquitous and inexpensive Windsor chair has become the most popular and varied all-purpose piece in America. Though introduced earlier, it is most closely associated with the Federal period—in fan, comb, loop back, and other variations.

Despite the individuality of many objects, Federal furniture conforms more closely to pattern-book models than any preceding American styles. Benefiting from the finest imported veneers, and skilled, often European-trained, craftsmen to execute the designs, American Hepplewhite and Sheraton furniture could rival the finest English pieces.

PREVIOUS PAGE: The parlor of the Harrison Gray Otis House in Boston, Massachusetts, illustrates the elegance of Federal style, reflecting America's new interest in classical design. The plain-papered walls are bordered with an Etruscan motif. The house was designed by Boston's most celebrated architect, Charles Bulfinch, and built in 1796.

RIGHT: Inlaid with maple and flame birch, this mahogany secretary bookcase (Massachusetts, 1790 to 1810) is 88 inches high, with a shapely double-curved pediment and apron.

ABOVE, LEFT: The Windsor chair, and its many variations, was an inexpensive and versatile seating piece, made of any available wood and used in almost any room.

ABOVE, RIGHT: In a form derived from Hepplewhite drawings, this mahogany side chair has a shapely shield back with swag and feather carving. Made in New York ca. 1800.

LEFT: A Federal-style, eagle-topped girandole mirror made of carved and gilded pine, ca. 1815.

The sideboard was extremely popular in Federal dining rooms. This bow-front piece (New York, ca. 1800) has delicate string inlay and tapering legs.

This single-pedestal breakfast table in Sheraton style is a scaled-down version of a full dining table. Mahogany. New York, ca. 1810.

The multi-purpose pembroke table is a space-saving design, 28 inches high and 20 inches wide, and almost doubles that width when open. Mahogany with pine and cherry inlays. New York, ca. 1790.

notes on the defining characteristics

MOOD formal, with Adam influence	**FURNITURE** slim and rectilinear, with polished veneers and little carving
SCALE relatively grand for America	**TEXTILES** Indian crewels, chintzes, imported silks and damasks
COLORS varied and bright	**KEY MOTIFS** eagle, satinwood banding, and oval inlays
ORNAMENT strictly classical	**LOOK FOR** Hepplewhite and Sheraton furniture forms, Windsor chair

sample color palette and fabric swatch

Traditional toile in patriotic mode, this 1785 document depicts figures of George Washington and Benjamin Franklin.

ABOUT THE PERIOD

The impact of the revolution of 1789 resonated through every aspect of French life. The demise or departure of the monarchy and the nobles left designers and craftsmen without patrons for their luxury wares. In the search for new patronage, designers began to reflect the social climate, and the transitional Directoire style was named for the Directorate, the newly established legislature. Though retaining the concept of Neoclassicism, it distanced French styles from any association with the monarchy by adhering more closely to the forms and ornament of the ancient world.

The Directoire evolved into the majestic and overtly political Empire, named for the reign of Napoleon Bonaparte, the general who in 1804 declared himself emperor, dominating France and a good part of Europe until 1814. Napoleon sought to glorify his country and, more important, himself, in the tradition of ancient Rome, and design became the visual expression of his political aims. The classical world was idealized in art by the politically inspired painter Jacques David (1748–1825).

Napoleon was the last French ruler to pursue the tradition of patronage, and he commissioned furnishings for the palaces he had occupied, mandating a style that mixed his personal motifs with those from classical sources. After traveling with Napoleon's campaign in Egypt, his architects, Charles Percier (1764–1838) and Pierre Fontaine (1762–1853), published a book of designs for furniture and objects inspired by the exotic country, and the emperor's military triumph.

The emperor's followers in France, and in other countries under his influence, adopted the Empire style—possibly motivated as much by the desire to curry favor with its powerful progenitor, as by admiration of his taste. The exaggerated classicism of Empire spread across much of Europe, becoming fashionable in such widely separated countries as Italy, Austria, and Russia, each creating its own distinctive variations on the style. It also became a primary source of the popular Biedermeier, which evolved after the Empire itself had passed. Counterparts to the Empire style included the Regency in England and the American Empire, an extension of the Federal period.

With Napoleon's defeat, the Empire style fell out of fashion, though an interest in Neoclassicism continued to inform styles in France.

ABOUT THE STYLE

The Empire interior is a testament to imperial pomp and power, taking the basic elements of Neoclassicism, and magnifying their scale and ornament. Though amply furnished, it is in many ways less elaborate than that of the Louis XVI period, but its imposing furnishings and richer colorations are more dramatic, and it has an assertive, masculine air. A mélange of luxurious fabrics and polished surfaces, it conveys an air of palatial grandeur to rival that of the Baroque.

It is a grand space of strict geometric proportions, whose linearity is emphasized by prominent architectural details that replace the *boiserie* of eighteenth-century interiors. The walls are divided into sections by columns and pilasters, usually set on ornamental bases, often topped with gilt capitals and flanked by large paintings or mirrors that create striking backdrops for the furnishings.

The ceiling is flat or concave, or perhaps suggests barrel vaulting, and is decorated with classical moldings or other motifs drawn directly from those in Pompeii and adapted as precisely as possible.

A circular room, or even a square one, is probably enveloped in stripes, either with draped fabric or boldly patterned wallpaper, emulating the tents used in Napoleon's Egyptian campaign.

Doors and windows in the Empire interior are not overly elaborate, with restrained moldings and over-door panels, and large panes of glass. Windows are crowned with ornately sculptured valances, swagged over-draperies are pulled back to show secondary layers in contrasting color and fabric, each layer weighted with tassels and trim. The invention of the jacquard loom has made the weaving of multicolored textiles easier and less costly, and such elaborate window treatments, as well as upholstery and wall hangings, are the happy result. Scenic wallpapers are another option.

The brilliant colors of Empire style are a striking departure from the softer tones of most French periods. The patriotic Directoire tricolor palette of red, white, and blue has been supplemented with saturated shades like deep blue and green, golden yellow, rich red, and violet.

Floors, of marble or wood parquet, might be polished and left bare, or covered with a carpet patterned in precise, geometric motifs of the ancient world, or symbols associated with Napoleon, such as the bee, the wreath, or Empress Josephine's swan.

The chimneypiece is classical in form, with a marble mantel flanked by prominent columns or caryatids. Mirrors are large, and defined by similar motifs.

Most of the ornament is drawn directly from ancient wall paintings and Greek vases, though elements of Egyptian design punctuate the familiar vocabulary. Accessories in these rooms, from bronze chandeliers and sconces to classical statuary to Napoleonic plaques, reprise the same or similar motifs.

There are actually fewer individual items of furniture in the Empire interior, but these are grander, sometimes massive, in scale—rectangular armoires, pedestal-based tables, monumental beds, daybeds, and the now-classic Récamier chaise longue. Chairs retain the shape of the earlier Neoclassical, but with broader proportions and heavier frames. Legs are columnar, and armrests or arm supports may take the form of animal heads or mythical figures. In more complete translations from the antique, objects like the *klismos* chair, the Egyptian X-base folding stool, and the tripod table underscore the classical theme.

On the cabinetry, highly polished expanses of richly figured veneers have replaced decorative marquetry: the emphasis on unadorned wood, begun in the austerity of the Directoire, is retained in the extravagant Empire. Solid mahogany is the primary wood, with imported woods for accent, as well as elm, beech, ash, and others less exotic, often ebonized or gilded. Underscoring many of the case pieces, plinth bases emphasize the rectangular forms, though sometimes exaggerating their severity.

Gilt-bronze and ormolu ornament is applied in the shape of columns, swans, eagles, caryatids, and classical swags, as well as military or Napoleonic motifs.

The epitome of Empire-era luxury, the music room at Versailles, France, was used by Empress Marie-Louise, Napoleon's second wife. The furniture and accessories, and the strong color scheme, suggest the elegant pretentiousness of the period.

ABOVE, LEFT: The silhouettes and ornament of this early-nineteenth-century mahogany armchair reprises classical models: saber legs, carved lion's head, animal legs and feet, and rosette and palmette mounts. France.

ABOVE, RIGHT: Napoleon himself may have used this ca. 1810 secretary, an imposing design with finely figured veneers and bold ornament of classical and military motifs. By ébeniste Bernard Molitor and done in acajou with gilt-bronze mounts.

RIGHT: Used as a pedestal or occasional table, this three-legged mahogany gueridon has the classical-inspired form and ornament of Empire style. Mahogany with ormolu mounts.

Improvisations on Percier and Fontaine, this Russian armchair has ornately molded crest rails and arms formed as winged eagles. Painted and parcel-gilt, ca. 1815.

ABOVE, RIGHT: The Empire style was extravagantly translated in Russia into monumental pieces like this 94-inch-high secretary-bookcase of flame mahogany with gilt brass mounts. Its elaborate ornamentation is characteristic of the Russian interpretations of the style.

LEFT: The lit-en-bateau is a boat-shaped bed, similar to the sleigh bed. This one has a scroll-shaped head and foot and rests on distinctive pawed legs, recalling Egyptian chairs. By Jacob Freres, a celebrated family of menusiers, ca. 1803.

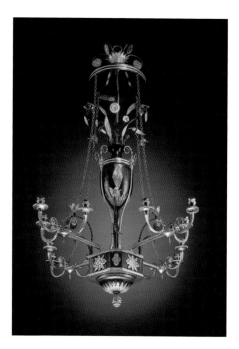

Contrasting somber patinated bronze and rich ormolu, this ca. 1795 directoire chandelier suggests the transition from courtly Louis XVI style to the more classical Empire.

Adopting the Empire style, this ca. 1795 German desk made of mahogany veneers with gilt bronze mounts has strong lines and restrained classical ornament. The urns reverse to form candleholders.

notes on the defining characteristics

MOOD pretentious	**FURNITURE** massive, architectural, polished veneers
SCALE grand	**TEXTILES** sumptuous
COLORS rich and saturated	**KEY MOTIFS** mythical figures and animals, military and Napoleonic symbols
ORNAMENT selective, but imposing	**LOOK FOR** tented rooms, Egyptian accents

sample color palette and fabric swatch

This Empire lampas fabric has bold, symmetrical motifs and strong color contrasts.

ABOUT THE PERIOD

The Regency denotes the late Neoclassical period in England, and was an evolution of the preceding style rather than a break with it. Regency design incorporated the refinement of Late Georgian classicism with a growing emphasis on historical accuracy, based on the forms and details of Greco-Roman models. The result was a more explicit, and often more exaggerated, interpretation of classical style. Regency is a counterpart to the Empire in France and the style of that name in America, and it shares many characteristics of interiors in those styles.

Though named for the period (1811–1820) from the death of George II until his son the Prince Regent ascended to the throne, the style can be seen several years earlier, and it continued through the reign of George IV to overlap with the revivals of the nineteenth century. During the Regency, the prominent architect Sir John Soane (1753–1837) designed strictly classical buildings, and interiors that moved away from the decorative Neoclassicism of Robert Adam. Apart from the ancient world, much of the inspiration for Regency design came from the colonial holdings of England, France, and Belgium, which had initiated a fascination with design motifs from foreign lands. Regency style became a quixotic blend of classical motifs and fantastic ornament from such esoteric sources.

Thomas Hope (1770–1831), the name most closely linked to Regency furniture, was a wealthy dilettante and dealer who created an environment for his collections in his own home, Flaxman House. His 1897 publication, *Household Furniture and Decoration*, encouraged an interest in Greek and Egyptian styles, though most furniture of the period was less extreme than Hope's designs.

The most exotic incarnation of Regency style was the fanciful redesign of Brighton Pavilion, whose extraordinary combination of Moorish, Indian, and Chinese design was created from 1815 to 1822 by John Nash (1752–1835), as a refuge for the Prince Regent from the formality of palace life in London. Its extravagantly overwrought interiors unleashed a passion for bamboo and reawakened an interest in exotica and all things Chinese. Once becoming king, George rarely enjoyed his country retreat, which remains an exemplar of the Regency at its most whimsical and certainly most decorative.

ABOUT THE STYLE

A combination of refinement, classicism, and charm, the typical Regency interior is refreshingly bold, for English style, with lively colors and more pronounced references to Greek and Egyptian sources than were seen in Late Georgian styles. It is more closely allied to Continental design than that of England, with lively color and refreshing touches of exotic ornament that coexist comfortably with classical motifs. A balanced and uncluttered arrangement of furniture and objects, it is more relaxed than its French Empire counterpart and less weighty than its American one.

The Regency room is a graceful, high-ceilinged space, punctuated with tall French doors and arched windows. The walls and ceiling, reflecting the classical aesthetic, might have white plaster rosettes, pilasters, and moldings, occasionally with subtle gilding. The walls themselves are painted in more vivid tones than the previous periods—turquoise, salmon pink, emerald green, saffron, or cherry, often enhanced with decorative painting in Chinoiserie or Pompeiian motifs. As an alternative, English or French wallpapers would be patterned in stylized fruits, flowers, or classical stripes. Doorways and windows may have restrained classical trim.

Window treatments might be filmy curtains, hung on prominent brass rods and overlaid with deep swags of heavy silk in stripes or dark solids, generously trimmed with golden cord and heavy tassels. Fabrics do not differ greatly from those of the Georgian era, though the colors are more intense and the designs, woven or printed, are more likely to be based on ancient motifs and classical architecture. Solids are used more often than patterns, heightening the effect of simplicity and focusing attention on line rather than ornament.

Room-size, all over-patterned carpet is increasingly popular, or patterned oilcloth as a less costly alternative, over parquet or black-and-white marble floors.

Color schemes, more vivid than the previous periods, might include such tones as turquoise, salmon pink, emerald green, or saffron gold.

Lighting comes from chandeliers, similar to those used in French Empire rooms—perhaps of metal rather than crystal, with brass accents in appropriate motifs from antiquity.

Classical urns and vases, in bold colors, may be of English bone china or ironstone. Plaster busts of famous Greeks and Romans, and shapely framed mirrors are other popular accessories.

Regency furniture is an update of classical symmetry, combining straight lines with modulated curves. It draws on heavier Greek forms rather than slender Pompeiian ones, but modifies the larger scale with relatively simple decoration. Hope's pieces, notable exceptions to this rule, are unrestrained in their exotic detail: relatively large-scaled, with animal heads and paws, columns and caryatids, or sphinxlike supports. Other Regency designs, considerably more understated, include extension dining tables with splay-legged tripod bases, imposing round center tables on pedestal bases, or sideboards with brass galleries.

Among the most typical Regency seating designs are bold Grecian-form sofas with scrolled head and footrest drawn from the French chaise longue, and occasionally lion's feet. There are highly decorative chairs in variants of the *klismos* shape, some with arms or legs carved with classical figures such as chimera or dolphins, and often gilded. Woods are generally dark, either highly polished mahogany or lighter rosewood and satinwood, accented by brass inlay, trellised galleries, or star-shape bolt heads and studs.

PREVIOUS PAGE: The dining room at Hinton Ampner in Hampshire, England, is a graceful interpretation of the light side of Regency design, its furnishings classical yet highly refined.

ABOVE: This shapely ca. 1820 daybed, done in rosewood with brass mounts and recalling both classical forms and those of French Empire, has a scrolled head and footrests and shapely scrolled legs with ball feet.

RIGHT: Open armchair in mahogany with ebony inlay, based on a model by Thomas Hope, who published a book of Grecian-inspired designs in 1807.

RIGHT: Brass accents often appear on Regency furniture, like this 5-foot calamander wood drop-leaf sofa table, ca. 1810, done with a border of brass and ebony. Lyre-shape trestle supports end in paw-footed saber legs.

BELOW: Serving table of mahogany with frieze of ebony inlay, with brass gallery trim centered on a classical lyre, ca. 1810.

The drum table, a classic Regency form, with a heavy pedestal base and deep apron (often fitted with drawers). This exceptional example, ca. 1810, done in rosewood and calamander, has intricate brass inlays on the top and sides, and ornately scrolled legs. Small leather-bound volumes fill the frieze.

The simple form of this mahogany pedestal desk, ca. 1820, is enhanced with spare ebonized stringing of Greek motifs. It sits on eight bracket-and-paw feet.

notes on the defining characteristics

MOOD relatively formal	**FURNITURE** weighty, with large expanses of polished wood, some gilding and ebonizing
SCALE restrained grandeur	**TEXTILES** luxurious
COLORS varied, saturated	**KEY MOTIFS** sphinx, caryatid, classical columns
ORNAMENT overtly classical	**LOOK FOR** *klismos*, Grecian chaise, exotic accents

sample color palette and fabric swatch

The restraint of this precise eighteenth-century silk lampas would flatter Regency furnishings.

Described both as an adaptation of French Empire and a simplification of the English Regency, Biedermeier is a style of furniture that developed as those periods had passed their peaks. Not so much a specific aesthetic as a general approach to design, it was intended as a simplification of Neoclassicism and a rejection of extravagant French style. Though generally less pretentious than those of the Empire style, Biedermeier pieces are often highly sophisticated.

Biedermeier is most easily recognized in case pieces with bold, geometric forms—fall-front desks with numerous compartments, armoires, display cabinets, and globe tables—framed by architectural elements like columns, pediments, cornices, and moldings that give the furniture a weighty, sometimes massive, look. In place of carving, highly-polished, figured veneers are the primary ornament such as rich mahogany, or ash, native fruitwoods and other lighter-tone woods, with veneers split to create bolder patterns. Ebonized columns are a frequent accent, as are applied gilt ornaments in the form of sphinxes, swans, and other stylized classical motifs.

Side chairs in Biedermeier style are strikingly varied in myriad and appealing designs with shapely, sculptural backs. Chaises, straight-back sofas, or settees have familiar classical silhouettes and polished wood frames.

The name Biedermeier, which like most style designations was bestowed after the fact, comes from a cartoon character satirizing the German bourgeoisie, the presumed consumers of this type of furniture, who aspired to the trappings of the aristocracy. However, it is something of a misnomer, in that the furniture itself is finely crafted and generally costly to make. Though associated primarily with Germany, Biedermeier was popular in much of Europe, including Austria, Hungary, and the Scandinavian countries. It was produced until almost the middle of the nineteenth century and has been revived several times since.

The sweeping form of this sofa, veneered with walnut on pine, is enhanced with a pair of Napoleonic eagles, appropriate for a piece owned by Napoleon's daughter. Attributed to Wilhelm Kimbel, Mainz, ca. 1835.

BELOW, LEFT: The sinuous silhouette of this side chair, made in Vienna ca. 1830, is enhanced with scrolls that frame the graceful center splat. Walnut veneers with ebonized trim.

RIGHT: Characteristic of the best of Biedermeier style, this 64-inch-tall secretary contrasts highly figured maple and bird's-eye maple veneers with bold ebonized column and brass mounts. By Wilhelm Kimbel, Mainz, ca. 1829.

american empire

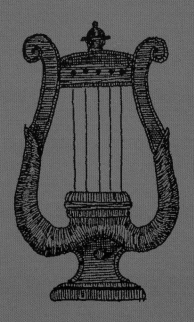

ABOUT THE PERIOD

America began to feel its strength as an independent nation, challenging the British again in the War of 1812, and starting its exploration of the uncharted Western territories. Empire seems an appropriate name for the style of this time. A counterpart to, and heavily drawing on, the Empire style in France, as well as the English Regency, American Empire overlaps the Federal style, of which is it often considered a part. More robust and overtly classical than its predecessor, American Empire was a once-removed continuation of the European romance with the ancient world. As always, however, America began with inspiration from Europe and went on to create a style uniquely its own. For the new republic, the Neoclassical had implicit political connotations, its symbolism suggesting a link to the democracy of ancient Greece.

Empire was also the first specifically French-influenced American style, the logical result of growing admiration for a country that had been an ally against England in the Revolutionary War, and many of the designs reflected the aesthetic of Percier and Fontaine's Napoleonic-era designs—most markedly the bold objects made by French immigrant Charles-Honoré Lannuier (1779–1819). Other important cabinetmakers in the major cities produced superb furniture in this period: the Seymours in Boston, Lannuier and Duncan Phyfe in New York, and John and Hugh Finlay in Baltimore working between 1799 and 1833 were only a few of an increasing number in this now-established trade. Phyfe, who became known during the Federal period, was the largest of these, employing dozens of craftsmen, and his name is often used to designate furniture of this era.

Though classicism remained a constant in American architecture, interiors in the nineteenth century grew more diverse. American Empire evolved into a style with projecting pillars, exaggerated scrolls, and an occasionally awkward weightiness. The Greek Revival style, by this time a paradigm for public architecture in America, was difficult to translate into interiors, which tended to repeat the same vocabulary of classical architectural details. It was, however, the first to be implemented in mass-produced furniture. Overlapping the Greek Revival were several successive intermingling styles that have been grouped into the designation Victorian. These were also inspired by the historical periods of the past and more successfully translated into distinctive interiors.

ABOUT THE STYLE

More striking than the Federal interior, though sometimes more pretentious as well, an American Empire room has strong overtones of French design, but is not as elaborate as its Continental counterparts. It is more spacious, reflecting the affluence of a well-established society, and its furniture and fittings are correspondingly larger in scale, enhanced with richer ornament, and showing a palette of darkish, contrasting hues.

Walls, with white baseboard, dado, and crown molding, might be painted a tone of mustard, blue, or brown, or will have the ornament of hand-painted French scenic papers, with a motif that evokes classicism or patriotic scenes. Classical motifs might be added in friezes beneath the molding, or above doors and windows.

Prosperity has made possible larger expanses of windows, with larger panes, and the style called for assertive treatments. The drapery treatment is a simplified adaptation of French Empire designs, in vivid colors, and fabrics such as satin, damask, or velvet.

Colors, as noted, are richer and more intense than those of the Federal period—royal blue and gold, dark greens and crimson, or other warm and saturated tones.

Parquet or marble floors would be covered with imported rugs, or the newly fashionable carpet—perhaps in a medallion pattern—laid from wall to wall.

Furniture has gradually grown larger in scale and more robust in appearance than earlier Neoclassical designs, with solid, geometric forms, darker woods, and broad expanses of polished veneer. Classical sideboards, chests, and wardrobes are low to the ground, sitting on broad paw feet or platform bases. Decorative carving is generally deemphasized in favor of a smooth surface in which the rich grain of fine veneers such as mahogany, the material of choice, serves as primary ornament. The demand for more elaborate furniture has brought more widespread use of brass inlays, ormolu and gilding, ebonized accents, faux-marble painted accents, or marble tops. Tables are important and varied: the pedestal-base dining tables, sofa tables, center tables on pedestals, pier tables, drop-leafs or card tables all generally followed English forms, but differed in their tendency to weightiness.

Decorative motifs are assertive and overtly classical: pillars or pilasters, lyre and acanthus motifs, sometimes lion masks. Nationalistic symbols such as eagles, or classical ones like dolphins or mythological winged creatures and caryatids, are also used, as are massive animal paws or colonettes of carved leaves in place of feet.

Chairs, often suggesting the form of the X-base *curule* or saber-legged Greek *klismos*, might be upholstered or open-backed, the latter often with a lyre motif, and tightly upholstered, wood-framed sofas or chaises in curvy classical form are popular expressions of the style. Suites of furniture have been introduced, consisting of several pieces with coordinated design, particularly in parlor seating. The low-to-ground sleigh bed, with same-height head and footboard, is a variant of French models.

PREVIOUS PAGE: American Empire interiors were markedly more influenced by classicism and French design than any preceding style. The rooms in Boscobel in Garrison, New York, show the elegant results, like this downstairs parlor.

ABOVE: American designers adopted the "Grecian" sofa form with enthusiasm and often extravagant ornament. This example is done in mahogany with paint-grained rosewood, bronzed and gold-stenciled, and has gilt-brass castors, rosettes, and moldings.

LEFT: Reprising the ancient Greek klismos form, this shapely mahogany side chair, ca. 1805, has carved legs and paw feet. By the most celebrated designer of the era, Duncan Phyfe, New York City.

This card table, ca. 1815, one of a pair, is typical of the most striking furniture designs by French expatriate Charles-Honoré Lannuier, with its winged figure, paw feet, and bold classical ornament. Carved and parcel-gilt rosewood. New York City.

The pier table, placed beneath a picture or mirror, was originally designed for the space between two windows. This one, ca. 1815, by Charles-Honoré Lannuier, is made of mahogany with kingwood, plaster, tole, ormolu mounts, and a marble top.

The understated design of this 69-inch-high mahogany secretary, ca. 1815, is enhanced with mirrored doors, ormolu, and gilt-brass mounts. Attributed to Duncan Phyfe, New York.

notes on the defining characteristics

MOOD formal, a bit pretentious	**FURNITURE** weighty forms, expanses of polished wood, some carving and gilding
SCALE grander than Federal	**TEXTILES** French-type silks and damasks
COLORS rich, varied	**KEY MOTIFS** Greek and Egyptian figures
ORNAMENT overtly classical, often exaggerated	**LOOK FOR** furniture in suites, variants of Empire and English Regency forms

sample color palette and fabric swatch

Recalling the textiles of the Napoleonic era, this rich lampas captures the stately aspirations of American Empire style.

19

CENTURY

revival and reform

victorian

gothic revival

rococo revival

renaissance revival

THE VICTORIAN ERA: AN OVERVIEW

The revival styles of the nineteenth century are often referred to as Victorian, after the British monarch who reigned from 1837 to 1901, when that country led the Western world in industrial and social growth. But there is no specific Victorian style: the period was a battle among several simultaneous styles, all reprising or reimagining designs from the past. Victorian eclecticism incorporated the Second Empire and the Restoration in France, and was seen in several European countries, but it is most closely associated with England and America. In America particularly, it saw the introduction of some half-dozen styles within one half-century, often in the same home, the same room—and occasionally the same piece of furniture.

The dominant influences were Greek, Gothic, Rococo, and Renaissance, each coalescing in a specific revival style—but the furniture forms remained essentially the same, varying only with the application of different ornament. There was little genuine innovation until late in the century, with the introduction of inventive mechanical chairs and multifunction furniture.

In most revival-style interiors, surface decoration supplanted originality of design: furniture was almost overpowered by carving; upholstery was grandly overstuffed, tufted, and trimmed; draperies were layered, fringed, and tasseled. Carpets and textiles were available in a variety of patterns appropriate to each revival style, and machine-printed wallpapers, by mid-century, were ubiquitous, offering a new and relatively inexpensive way to envelop an interior with pattern, with coordinated panels and borders to suit any setting and style.

As the decades passed, the lights of decorative oil or gas lamps faded in the enthusiasm for chandeliers, which waned in turn with the introduction of electric lighting in the 1880s. Colors shifted from soft to bright to dark, particularly in the final decade, when gloomy tones were considered the height of sophistication.

After the publication of books on color theory, varying color palettes were chosen for specific rooms—darker for masculine environments, paler for feminine ones, muted for private settings and lively for public ones.

The Centennial Exposition in Philadelphia, in 1867, awakening nostalgia for America's past, led to an interest in antiques, and Colonial Revival interiors. A strain of exoticism also appeared late in the century, though it was generally confined to the decor of a particular room or individual pieces of furniture and decorative objects. The fad for such conceits as Moorish smoking-rooms or Arab halls did not constitute a style, but was part of the mélange that made for this diverse and intriguing period in design.

The styles of the century conflated in the so-called Gilded Age, when the New York townhouses and Newport mansions of a new aristocracy evoked the Beaux-Arts and Baroque, exotica and eclecticism, in a fitting coda to the period that reprised the grandeur of centuries past.

Victorian interiors are often described in broad generalizations, most of them unflattering: a clutter of furniture and objects, a profusion of textiles, a plethora of pattern on every available surface—too much of not-good-enough things. But generalizations are misleading: albeit tending toward the overdone, these interiors are filled with life and personality. They are as creative in their way as any in history.

ABOUT THE PERIOD

During the eighteenth century, a wave of architectural preservation in England engendered an interest in medieval architecture, and its ultimate revival as a style for the industrial age. Gothic Revival, or Neo-Gothic, as it was called in England, was prefigured by Strawberry Hill (1758–1772), Horace Walpole's (1717–1797) fanciful reconstruction of his home in Twickenham, outside London, and its ultimate expression was Fonthill Abbey (1796), designed by James Wyatt (1746–1813) for the eccentric collector William Beckford.

For designers chafing under the strict symmetry of Greek Revival, the past of Arthurian legends, medieval poetry, and the novels of Sir Walter Scott seemed more picturesque and romantic. In addition to aesthetic appeal, there was the moral issue expressed by its most fervent proponent, Augustus W. N. Pugin (1812–1852), who saw the Gothic as a means of spiritual reform. The return to an ecclesiastical style could redeem industrialized society from the moral degeneration represented by pagan neoclassicism. Pugin's heavily gilded interiors for the Houses of Parliament in London (1836–68), and his exhibits in the Great Exhibition of 1851 are superb expressions of the Gothic Revival.

The most striking and pervasive of the nineteenth-century architectural revivals, Gothic Revival was appropriated by the English as a national aesthetic—the country had never really abandoned the Medieval style. It was translated for residential use in the villas and country cottages of Andrew Jackson Downing (1815–1852), and appeared in France during the Second Empire of Louis Napoleon and Empress Eugénie, most notably in the architecture of Eugène Viollet-le-Duc (1814–1879). In America, it was interpreted in the gable-roofed, flat-cut gingerbread-trimmed houses of Carpenter Gothic.

Later in the century, Modern Gothic followed the ideas of design reform as expressed by the Englishman Charles Locke Eastlake (1836–1906), whose influential *Hints on Household Taste* (1868) helped middle-class consumers deal with the plethora of available styles by teaching them principles of good taste. Published in England, it became even more popular in America, where Eastlake's name was appropriated for a style of furniture characterized by massive, rectilinear forms of solid wood, with medieval joinery and shallow-carved, flat decoration. Critical of machine-made furniture, reform designers pursued a more honest use of materials and restraint in ornamentation. Though sometimes poorly executed, their efforts marked the first tentative steps toward modernism.

ABOUT THE STYLE

The Gothic Revival interior has more charm than the sober Greek Revival, with which it competed. It is less rigid and somewhat less formal, though considerably busier and characteristically cluttered, in the manner of the prototypical Victorian home. It is also costly to execute, requiring intricate detailing and considerable hand-carving. At its best, it is winning; at its worst, weighty.

Architects like Alexander Jackson Davis (1803–1892) switched from Greek Revival to interpretations of Gothic. Interiors are high ceilinged, often ribbed, and walls are decorated with plasterwork tracery or dark wood paneling. Floors might be brick, tile, or marble in deep colors and geometric designs.

Windows and doorways are tall and slender, with pointed arches, sometimes with stained-glass panels punctuating the mullioned panes. Curtain treatments are simple, perhaps of embroidered wool or velvet with horizontal cross-banding.

Stylized patterns on wallpaper or textiles might include Gothic tracery or medieval panoramas, and carpets with medieval motifs are patterned in rich colors such as crimson and blue, or muddy tones of brown and olive, perhaps accented with gilding.

Elaborate mantels reprise the massive hearths of medieval halls. Flickering oil lamps cast a glow that add to the romantic, if a bit somber, ambience. Accessories might include collections of armor, stag antlers, or accents of stained glass.

Gothic Revival furniture is massive, often of oak, with detailing similar to that of the interior shell—tracery, rosettes, trefoils and quatrefoils, even heraldic motifs. The reprise of medieval themes includes some Elizabethan chairs, chests, and other "cottage" furniture, often with twist-turning on legs and chair backs.

OPPOSITE: Castle Ward in Northumberland, Northern Ireland, is a quirky mixture of styles. In the saloon, tall pointed-arch windows, fitted with fragments of seventeenth-century Flemish glass, dictate a Gothic Revival mood.

BELOW: This marble-topped mahogany center table, with hexagonal top and turreted apron, is among the most refined forms of American Gothic Revival furniture and relates to designs by architect Alexander Jackson Davis. Made in New York, ca. 1840–60.

ABOVE: Applying Gothic ornament to a familiar form, this mahogany bookcase (mid-nineteenth century) has pointed arches on the glass doors and the panels beneath.

This marble-topped rosewood dressing chest has Gothic arches on its doors and apron and an elaborately carved and pierced mirror. By noted cabinetmaker Charles A. Baudouine, New York, ca. 1840–50.

An iconic example of American Gothic Revival furniture, this hall chair, ca. 1850, with unusually high back of cathedral tracery and distinctive birdcage-carved front legs and supports. Of mahogany-finished oak with hinged plank seat and glove box, it is associated with New Orleans maker Henry Siebrecht.

Another hall chair, this one designed ca. 1840 by Augustus W. N. Pugin, the British architect whose ideas shaped the Gothic Revival. Of oak with painted crest.

ABOUT THE PERIOD

Throwing off the moral component of Gothic Revival, this style reprised the voluptuous forms of its seventeenth-century antecedent. An exaggeration rather than a
pure revival of Louis XV style, Rococo Revival drew on French pattern books and
was fashionable in England and Second Empire France. It crossed the Atlantic into
America, where it enjoyed a brief and flamboyant life, particularly in the South,
where it was known as "French Antique." Embracing florid scrollwork, marquetry,
gilding, and fanciful ornament, it is undeniably appealing—despite the excesses
committed in its name.

The Rococo Revival emerged when family life had become more informal, but
strict conventions still ruled the manner of entertaining and receiving guests. Rooms
were designed for specific purposes: the lady of the house received visitors in the
parlor, the library was a masculine preserve, and the dining room denoted social and
financial status, in the luxury of a room used only at mealtimes. With many styles
now available, there was no longer a reason to choose only one, and anarchy pre-
vailed over fashion. Interiors might vary from one room to the other, depending on
the desired mood.

As industrial production increased, many accessory objects were available through
mail-order catalogs, encouraging the impulse toward acquisitiveness and overdecora-
tion. Mass-produced lithographs, invented in late eighteenth century Germany, made
framed artwork available to a wide, if not always discriminating, audience. Woods
were more varied, and technical innovation led to the development of inventive new
types of furniture.

The Rococo Revival was too frivolous to enjoy a long life, and began to undo itself
with the kind of excesses that, a century prior, had encouraged the return of classicism.

ABOUT THE STYLE

The Rococo Revival interior is giddily charming and, despite its frills, very inviting.
Recalling the grace of eighteenth century French design, but considerably more

quirky and unpredictable, it combines exaggerated curves and richly carved ornament, sometimes applying the gilding that characterized the earlier style.

Walls and ceilings are dressed in a muted version of Louis XV boiserie and plasterwork, framing machine-printed, flocked, or embossed wallpaper, usually with coordinated borders. The patterns are most likely floral bouquets, swags, or ribbon-and-lace designs.

Windows have wood shutters, covered with heavy woven or printed draperies, elaborately trimmed with fringe or tassels and hung over lace curtains. Portieres, in similar fabrics, are hung at doorways. Upholstery fabrics, therefore, include a range of vivid velvets and tapestries, in addition to popular horsehair and leather.

Floors are wood parquet or patterned and colored tile, with rugs in large-scale botanical motifs, machine-made carpet laid fashionably wall to wall, or new patterned linoleum in a ruglike design.

Bold, polychromatic color schemes predominate, made possible with aniline and synthesized dyestuffs that can replicate the colors of natural dyes, as well as more intense shades such as mauve and magenta, widening the range of the available design palette.

Mantels, still used for function as well as decoration, are usually marble, carved with Rococo ornament. Chandeliers and lamps, using kerosene and, by the 1860s, gaslight, mix functional and fussy with painted-glass globes, brass trim, or crystal drops. Accessories include whimsical hat racks or whatnots with display shelves; arrangements of porcelains, figurines, or specimens from nature; and framed prints.

Suites of furniture are the height of fashion—matching or coordinated case and seating pieces are designed for parlor, dining room, and bedroom, each with complementary ornament and carving. Details translated from Rococo style include the cabriole leg, thicker than earlier versions, and carved with shell and floral motifs.

The development of metal-spring upholstery has brought new, comfort-conscious seating forms, including the oversized tufted ottoman, the balloon-back chair, and the single-ended sofa. All draw on traditional Rococo silhouettes, but are more exaggerated and often bulbous.

rococo revival

Woods are dark, rich, and highly polished, joined by other materials—iron and brass for ornate bed frames; real or faux bamboo and woven rattan for light-scaled seating and occasional pieces; and papier-mâché for accent furnishings, glossy-painted and sometimes inlaid with mother-of-pearl.

The most inventive developments in furniture, however, have come from new manufacturing techniques. Michael Thonet (1796–1871) has patented a method for steam-curving beech into joint-free, curvilinear chairs, and John Henry Belter (1804–1863) shapes furniture from layers of rosewood veneer, intricately carved in openwork floral patterns. Thonet's furniture prefigured Art Nouveau and Wiener Werkstatte modernist designs, and Belter's widely copied pieces are archetypes of the Rococo Revival.

PREVIOUS PAGE: Stanton Hall, in Natchez, Mississippi, is
a palatial home built in 1857 and furnished at considerable
expense. In the grand parlor space formed by two adjoin-
ing rooms, bronze chandeliers and rosewood furniture
suggest the frivolous excess of Rococo Revival.

ABOVE: This spectacularly shapely sofa of carved rosewood,
the crest pierced with carved scrolls, shells, and floral
motifs, is typical of designs by John Henry Belter, its
maker, who developed a process for laminating layers of
rosewood by machine, which was then hand-carved in
intricate, openwork designs. New York City, ca. 1850–60.

Cast iron furniture, then a new idea for outdoor
furniture, was the perfect medium in which to
execute rococo ornament. This garden bench
was made in Coalbrookdale, England, ca. 1870.

ABOUT THE PERIOD

Drowned in its own excesses, as had the original incarnation, the Rococo Revival was transmuted into an Italianate style known as Renaissance Revival. One of the cyclical reprises of classical ornament, this one made no attempt at authenticity, instead adopting elements of Renaissance architecture and French Neoclassicism in mass-produced furnishings that might incorporate *Neo-Grec* and Egyptian motifs and styles from other European sources. It was the most eclectic of all the revival styles. In Italy, Germany, and France, Renaissance Revival signaled a wistful nostalgia for regimes long past. In America, after the Civil War (1861–1865) it incorporated historical styles in a new show of diversity that gained strength after the centennial exhibition in Philadelphia, in 1876.

In architecture, a new style called Beaux-Arts had emerged under the liberal monarchy in France. Moving away from fixed classical forms, it fostered an aesthetic of classically influenced, but eclectically ornamented buildings of grand scale and great presence. Named for the *École des Beaux-Arts* in Paris, whose teachings it reflected, this expressive style spread to most of the Western world, lasting into the twentieth century to challenge the beginnings of the Modern movement. Renaissance Revival interiors, encompassing a cornucopia of influences, were its perfect complement.

As the Renaissance Revival waned, the Edwardian era, named for English king Edward VII (reign 1901–1910), brought the excesses of the Gilded Age, in which opulence was valued above any particular style, and the townhouses and mansions of a new American aristocracy sought to recapture the glamour of European royalty. It was a fitting climax to a century saturated with extravagant design.

ABOUT THE STYLE

The Renaissance Revival interior is distinctive for the imposing detail of its furniture, rather than the background that surrounds it. Walls, ceilings, and floor treatments are similar to those of the Rococo Revival, though the decorative motifs are more classical than naturalistic. Moldings and pilasters, Pompeiian-style painted panels or wallpaper, porcelain plaques and ormolu medallions evoke antiquity, adding pomp to accompany the clutter of furniture and objects.

Polished wood floors are covered with machine-made, patterned carpet or imported Oriental rugs, not necessarily with any relation to the style of the furniture.

At the tall windows, heavy tie-back curtains hang beneath elaborate lambrequins trimmed with loops, cords, or tassels. Textiles have more variety than in any previous period, thanks to new weaving machinery and roller-printing techniques, and the wallpaper might be hand-blocked French scenics, machine-made English patterns, or American interpretations of the most popular design motifs, including many inspired by Japanese design. Walls in three parts—dado, center panel, and frieze—are papered in classical patterns, or painted deep, muted tones, as backgrounds for a variety of framed artwork.

Toward the end of the century, the invention of the electric light revolutionizes interiors and lighting fixtures, making chandeliers less popular and increasing the use of individual lamps.

The abundance of color and pattern reflects the riches of a thoroughly industrialized society, with schemes in rich, tertiary hues such as olive, terra cotta, and old gold.

Renaissance Revival furniture includes familiar forms executed in a variety of woods, often elaborately ornamented. The distinctive three-section parlor cabinet, on a platform base, is flanked with columns or caryatids, and topped with pedestals for display. Sideboards, themselves imposing pieces, have shelves to show off china or collections. Many case pieces are accented with carved or incised decorations, ebonizing, gilding, or applied brass ornament—perhaps Egyptian or Greek motifs, or cartouches with urns or classical profiles, which can now be produced by machine. The vogue for *japonisme* is reflected in ornamental details. Furniture is customarily purchased in suites—a set of sofa and chairs is crested with matched plaques and carving, and a mirror mounted to the bedroom dresser coordinates with the decoration on the bed.

Many of the design changes are made possible by modern manufacturing techniques, which, unable to accommodate the curves of Rococo, adapted easily to producing ornament and trims for the Renaissance Revival.

A range of ingenious designs in patent furniture has added to the vocabulary of furnishings available even to homes of moderate means. By the 1870s in America, a furniture industry has developed in Grand Rapids, Michigan, to make products for a broad consumer market that emulates the style of specialty goods produced by firms like Herter Brothers for a more elite market.

PREVIOUS PAGE: The salon of the Victoria Mansion (the Morse-Libbey house) in Portland, Maine, is a fine example of a Renaissance Revival interior, with Renaissance ornament applied to almost every surface and a comfortably cluttered arrangement of furniture.

BELOW: The Wooten desk, a patented design made in Indianapolis, Indiana, ca. 1874, conceals multiple compartments and a hinged writing surface in its blocklike form. The carved crest and applied ornaments adopt Renaissance forms.

This parlor cabinet with pedestal top designed to hold sculpture or decorative objects is of rosewood with lighter wood inlays, hand-painted decoration, and gilding and carving. Herter Brothers, ca. 1870.

Renaissance Revival furniture tended
toward massiveness, but this carved
and parcel-gilt burled walnut dresser
is gracefully executed by the celebrated Herter Brothers, ca. 1875.

notes on the general characteristics

MOOD extroverted, exhibitionistic	**FURNITURE** generally imposing, basic forms with varying decoration
SCALE as grand as possible, even in confined spaces	**TEXTILES** myriad patterns, abundantly varied
COLORS increasingly varied, gradually darkening	**KEY MOTIFS** classical swags and columns, Gothic tracery, Rococo swirls, Renaissance swags, etc.
ORNAMENT more than in any other period	**LOOK FOR** dark rooms filled with furniture and layered with pattern

sample color palette and fabric swatch

Victorian textiles like this bold floral print were often set against deep-toned backgrounds, with a new color range made possible by synthetic dyes.

aesthetic

ABOUT THE PERIOD

The Aesthetic movement evolved during the era of design reform that followed the Industrial Revolution. Part of the search to recapture qualities lost in the shift from handmade to machine-made goods, it was parallel to and linked to Arts and Crafts and, like it, denoted an approach to style rather than any specific design vocabulary. It differed from Arts and Crafts, however, in rejecting moral values as a relevant issue in art or design: beauty was the sole consideration. The term Aesthetic, derived from the Greek word for perfection, referred to the appreciation of beauty in art, and "art for art's sake" was the movement's mantra. By appreciating beauty, one could transcend considerations of style.

Expressed in intricately patterned, meticulously detailed interiors and a lavish use of gold, tile, and intricate pattern, Aesthetic style exemplified the romantic excesses of the late Victorian era.

Originating in England, it was inspired in part by medieval art, but also drew on exotic Japanese, Ottoman, and Moorish influences—particularly those of Japan, which had only reopened its ports to Western trade in 1754, and whose designs were perceived as exquisitely refined and respectful of artisanry. The most vocal spokesman for Aestheticism was the author and playwright Oscar Wilde (1854–1900), and its most celebrated practitioners were the painter James A. M. Whistler (1834–1903) and the designers E. W. Godwin (1833–1886) and Christopher Dresser (1834–1904), who drew heavily on Japanese presentations seen in London (1862) and Paris (1867) exhibitions. *The House Beautiful,* published by Clarence Cook in 1887, defined the principles of the movement.

In America, fueled by Wilde's acclaimed national lecture tour in 1882, Aestheticism contributed to extravagant interiors, designed by firms like Associated Artists and Herter Brothers in the mansions and townhouses of Gilded Age industrialists. These made no claim to morality or restraint, wrapping grand spaces in rich materials, intricately detailed furniture, and a mélange of Eastern motifs. The Aesthetic movement was too extreme to be long-lived, but its influence was considerable, and many of its elements were absorbed into early Art Nouveau.

ABOUT THE STYLE

The Aesthetic interior is beguiling in its exoticism, and almost dizzying in its mix of color, pattern, and decoration. It resists classification, mixing elements from diverse sources in idiosyncratic renderings according to the designer's whim and client's preference, but it invariably provides a surfeit of visual stimulation. It is either the subject of instant attraction, or immediate dislike.

There are no specifics of shape or dimension particular to the Aesthetic interior. Though the abundance of detail often makes it appear modestly proportioned, its shape and scale vary according to the surrounding architectural shell. Rejecting the massive elements of the nineteenth century revival styles, the Aesthetic interior avoids Baroque carved and gilded frames, ornate mantels, or heavy draperies over doors. Instead, pattern is the primary means of organizing and decorating the space.

Wallpaper is the height of fashion for Aesthetic interiors, in coordinated patterns that enable designers to create intricate decorative effects. On walls divided into three sections—dado below, field or filling above, and frieze just below the ceiling—a different pattern and variation of color is applied to each area. The dado pattern is the most intense, the frieze the most elaborate, and the field the most understated, since it also serves as background for hanging paintings or prints. The frieze is often defined by a wood rail that serves also as a shelf for china display.

Colors, in wall coverings, textiles, and carpets, lean toward deep, subtle shades, such as dull greens, browns, and blues, with citrine as a frequent accent. Often there are shimmery accents.

Window treatments probably have patterned fabrics, often in motifs that suggest the Asian influence, which is a common theme of this period.

In accessories, Japanese and other Eastern sources provide many of the forms as well as the decorative inspiration for striking ceramics and metalwork—the Aesthetic era produced many objects of exceptional charm and originality. Chandeliers and lamps are as important, or more important, for their decorative value as for their efficiency as illumination.

The concept of "art furniture," rejecting the commercialism of most industrially made design, is an important contribution of the movement. Aesthetic furniture generally avoids the weightiness of most Victorian-era pieces, and its light-scaled forms reflect the influence of the Eastern aesthetic. Chairs, settees, and sofas are not marked by new forms so much as new decoration. The silhouettes of chests, exemplified by William Godwin's Anglo-Japanese designs, may suggest Japanese cabinetry. Others might be painted or incised with images of stylized birds and foliage.

Many items of furniture are painted or lacquered black or, later in the Aesthetic period, made of light-toned mahogany or satinwood. They are often carved with openwork motifs drawn from Oriental objects. Notwithstanding the movement's disdain of manufactured objects as Philistine, most Aesthetic-era furniture is actually production-made, as differentiated from those of the Arts and Crafts movement, whose followers believed that objects should be made by hand.

PREVIOUS PAGE: For the frontispiece of Clarence Cook's *The House Beautiful*, an 1878 decorating book, artist Walter Crane painted an archetype Aesthetic interior, with Asian-influenced furniture, stylized pattern, and accessories including Japanese fans and Chinese porcelain.

RIGHT: This grand ca. 1880 hall tree, combining mirror, bench, hooks for clothes, and a hinged seat for gloves, is made of ornately carved walnut, with lion's head and paw feet. Made in Philadelphia.

BELOW: This handsome Aesthetic style walnut bedstead, 78 ½ inches tall, is exuberantly carved with medallions and stylized panel of songbirds and foliage. Made by noted Philadelphia cabinetmaker Daniel Pabst (1826–1910) ca. 1875.

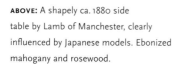

ABOVE: A shapely ca. 1880 side table by Lamb of Manchester, clearly influenced by Japanese models. Ebonized mahogany and rosewood.

ABOVE, RIGHT: A modest coal box, ebonized and gilded, has the type of stylized geometric ornament characteristic of the work of its designer, Christopher Dresser (1834–1904).

Exhibited at the Paris Exposition Universelle in 1878, this design by E. W. Godwin for William Watt, is characteristic of his celebrated Japanese-influenced Aesthetic furniture. Of walnut with split willow seat and back.

Framing an embroidered Oriental silk panel, this delicate ebonized firescreen, ca. 1880, has graceful carved detailing complementing its aesthetic form. American.

Pieces like this grandly proportioned sideboard, ca. 1880, were in striking contrast to more delicate, Asian-influenced, Aesthetic furniture designs. Of oak with carved and turned ornament, drawn from a design published by Bruce James Talbert, a leading English designer for commercial firms.

notes on the defining characteristics

MOOD fantasy	**FURNITURE** light-scaled, graceful, highly decorative
SCALE varied	**TEXTILES** intricately patterned
COLORS subdued, but richly varied	**KEY MOTIFS** Japonism
ORNAMENT delicate	**LOOK FOR** lots of pattern, lots of wallpaper, lots of gilded accent

sample color palette and swatch

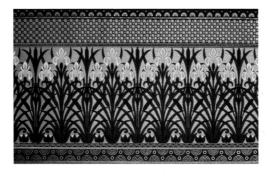

Designed by celebrated illustrator Walter Crane (1845–1915), "Iris Frieze" is a wallcovering design in the Aesthetic tradition.

In 1858, German immigrant Gustav Herter (1830–1892), who had worked for Louis Comfort Tiffany, opened a furniture and decorating business in New York that became Herter Brothers when his half-brother Christian (1839–1883) joined him in 1864. By the 1870s, the firm had become the most prestigious producer and purveyor of furnishings to a Gilded Age clientele. Herter Brothers designed complete and elaborate interiors, for which it produced the furniture in its own factory and sold textiles and accessories, much of which was manufactured to their own designs.

Refusing to design in the revival styles that were popular at the time, Herter sought more original expressions for their demanding and affluent customers. Although many of the firm's opulent interiors reflect the influence of the English Aesthetic movement, the unique interpretations were its own. Herter Brothers produced furniture in Renaissance Revival and other styles, according to changing fashion and the demands of their affluent customers, but have become most celebrated for their intricately detailed marquetry cabinets, with Neo-Japanese motifs executed in multitoned wood veneers.

Even in its more conventional designs, Herter furniture distinguished itself from its competitors by its exceptional quality and workmanship. It was superbly constructed from the finest materials and has hand-finished details.

Interiors for clients like William Vanderbilt, J. Pierpont Morgan, and Jay Gould were exquisitely crafted and impeccably coordinated, though rarely understated. Commissions executed by the firm included work for the White House. Christian retired in 1880 and Herter Brothers ceased operations in 1906, bringing to a close perhaps the last vestiges of America's most extravagant era in design.

The most celebrated piece for their most important client, this side chair of gilded maple with mother-of-pearl insets was made ca. 1881 by Herter Brothers for the New York mansion of William H. Vanderbilt.

An ebonized and marquetry library table, ca. 1875–85, from the New York mansion of financier Jay Gould, another prestigious Herter client. The finely detailed ornamentation is in Renaissance Revival style, one of several in which the brothers worked.

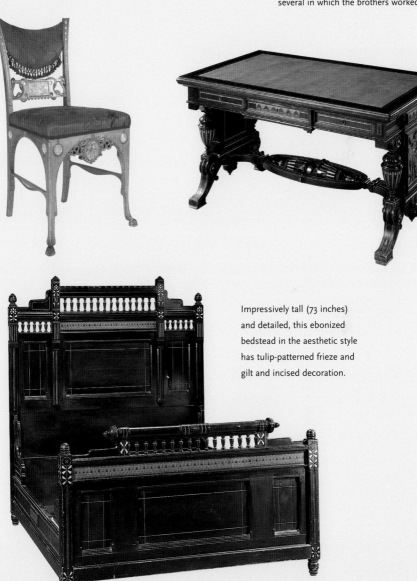

Impressively tall (73 inches) and detailed, this ebonized bedstead in the aesthetic style has tulip-patterned frieze and gilt and incised decoration.

The art and culture of the Far East is as old as, or older than, that of the Western world. It flourished for many centuries before the Europeans became aware of exotic lands like China and Japan. When Marco Polo visited Cathay in the thirteenth century, he led the way for other travelers to explore, and bring back treasures and legends from, the lands at the other side of the earth. By the sixteenth and seventeenth centuries, the East India companies carried silks, porcelain, tea, and carpets over land and ocean to decorate Western homes, and to influence design, particularly in the form of ornament drawn directly from, or inspired by, exotic Eastern motifs.

In the middle of the eighteenth century, when Japan opened its ports to the West after decades of excluding foreigners, the purity and simplicity of its design unleashed a new wave of enthusiasm, inspiring the Aesthetic movement and influencing the movement for design reform.

Interest in design from the East has not been limited to that of China and Japan, but has encompassed India as well, beginning in the era of British colonialism. Embroidered and printed textiles, lacquerwork, woodcraft, and metalwork in the West has freely borrowed, or adapted, decorative motifs and ornamental techniques developed in these countries.

Though most furniture of Far Eastern countries is specific to those interiors rather than those in the Western world, several elements—the ball-and-claw foot and urn-shape back of Queen Anne chairs, the yoke-shape back of Chippendale—can be traced specifically to Chinese sources.

ABOVE, LEFT: This folding horseshoe-back armchair dates to late sixteenth or early seventeenth-century China.

ABOVE, RIGHT: The shape of Chinese yoke-back armchairs like this jichimu example inspired Western furniture designers. They were made in the seventeenth century.

RIGHT: A classic Chinese piece with an unusual tapered form, this seventeenth-century cabinet is of huanguali wood with brass fittings.

OPPOSITE: A late seventeenth-century screen with the delicate and distinctive ornamental style of Japanese design, handpainted with cranes and pine trees by Kano Tsunenobu.

english arts and crafts

ABOUT THE PERIOD

In the 1860s, designer William Morris (1834–1896) became an enthusiastic convert to the reformist ideas of art critic John Ruskin, who had decried the taste of the Victorian public and the banality of mass-produced design. Arts and Crafts, a movement rather than a specific style, sought to create interiors and furnishings that would recapture the charm and personality that had been lost to industrialization. Morris favored a return to medieval craftsmanship, with honest finishes and nature-inspired ornament, and workmanship that showed the hand of the craftsman.

The movement was not named until almost three decades later, after the Arts and Crafts Exhibition Society (founded in 1888), but its roots were firmly planted in 1860 with the now-celebrated Red House by architect Philip Webb (1831–1915), with interiors by Morris. With Webb and other fellow Oxford graduates, the artists Edwin Burne-Jones (1833–1898) and Dante Gabriel Rossetti (1828–1882)—members of the self-titled "Pre-Raphaelites"—he formed Morris, Marshall, Faulkner & Company and later Morris & Company to produce well-designed goods for the general public. The group believed that art should be useful as well as beautiful, adding a moral element that was in pointed contrast to the ideas of the Aesthetic Movement, which paralleled it, although many designers of the period worked in both camps. Morris's Kelmscott Press, established in 1890, promoted the new philosophy in England and abroad. He was unrealistic in his total rejection of industrial production, insisting that objects be made entirely by hand, and most of the interiors and furnishings produced by his workshops were affordable only by a small, affluent clientele. His ideas, however, led to the formation of a variety of guilds and workshops, some of which made use of machine production.

Arts and Crafts overlapped with Art Nouveau, gradually merging into the latter and linking through it to Glasgow Style and that of the Wiener Werkstatte. Despite its failure to reach a large audience, the Arts and Crafts movement stimulated an interest in handcraft that had been lost since the French Revolution, and its back-to-basics design ideas mark an important landmark on the path to the Modern era of the twentieth century.

ABOUT THE STYLE

The Arts and Crafts interior is studiously unpretentious and carefully avoids the suggestion of having been designed for aesthetics alone. Evoking a medieval manor or a country cottage, it is charming in its simplicity, though that simplicity is often deceptive. Considerable time, effort, and often expense, have gone into the design of a room intended to look artlessly unplanned, and to follow the tenets of the movement. As William Morris famously cautioned, "Have nothing in your house that you do not know to be useful or believe to be beautiful."

Often, the simple rectangular shell of the interior is given the conceit of ceiling beams or timbering to reprise the look of a medieval hall. Walls are usually partially wood-paneled; above that, they may be painted white, or wallpapered with patterns in medieval themes or stylized florals.

Sash windows might be shuttered or given simple curtain treatments, with pretty prints that complement those on the walls. Cottons or linen are likelier choices than pretentious silks or heavy wools.

Floors are generally wood, over which are deep-tone, flat-woven carpets that anchor the furniture arrangement and ground the mix of patterns. The inglenook, a recess with cushioned benches framing a fireplace opening, is a popular architectural feature.

Most Arts and Crafts interiors include some element suggesting Gothic style—a genre that has remained enduringly popular in England. Other ornament is drawn from nature, though the heart motif appears frequently in textile patterns or as a cutout element on furniture.

English Arts and Crafts textiles are intricate and colorful, depicting highly stylized florals, birds, and other motifs from nature, rendered on backgrounds of white or subtly muted earth tones. Wallpapers, perhaps the most successful of Morris's designs, are meticulously printed with copper plates in delicate tints, and may provide the starting point for the coordinated scheme of the interior, whose objective is to create a total environment—either highly decorative or country-cottage plain.

Even the most ordinary objects are important in achieving the desired effect. Arts and Crafts accessories emphasize the handcrafted look in ceramics, metalwork of iron or brass, and embroideries. Painted tiles and mosaics may decorate the walls or frame the fireplace. Decorative stained glass, another idea inspired by medieval design and an important product of Morris's workshops, are extremely popular, appearing as small roundels or elaborate scenic panels.

In contrast to styles of the Victorian revival, which it overlaps, or those of the Aesthetic movement, the arrangement of furniture and objects in the Arts and Crafts interior is spare and uncluttered. Furniture forms are simple rectilinear shapes, most typically in oak, though other woods, including mahogany, are used as well, with detailing that emphasizes the handmade qualities of the furniture. Wood joints are deliberately exposed and finishes replicate the rough-textured, hand-hewn look of medieval objects. Even commercially produced Arts and Crafts furniture, from later in the period, tries to suggest the same handcrafted look.

Seating, in the form of straight-back chairs and open-back benches, is usually cushioned rather than fully upholstered, with cutouts, turnings, or through-tenons the only ornament. One innovation of this period, the adjustable-back Morris Chair, introduced the concept of reclining seats.

Carving is rare, though decorative cabinets and chests might be elaborately hand-painted with medieval figures and allegorical scenes.

PREVIOUS PAGE: Wightwick Manor in Wolverhampton, England, was built for a wealthy industrialist in 1887, but its Morris & Company interiors reflect Arts and Crafts principles. This is a section of the Grand Parlor with its massive mantelpiece, William Morris wallpaper, handpainted tiles, and inglenook seating.

ABOVE: An oak settee, ca. 1905, with three-sided spindle back made by Liberty & Company, a firm that pioneered bringing good design to manufactured furnishings. Oak with loose upholstered cushions.

The "Sussex" armchair, designed by Philip Webb and based on a rural prototype, was the most popular piece made by the Morris firm, produced from 1865 until well into the 1930s. Ebonized beech, with rush seat.

This oak armchair was designed ca. 1900 by architect Charles F. A. Voysey (1857–1941), a follower of Morris, who also designed fabrics, wallpaper, and furniture, often using a heart motif.

Not all Arts and Crafts furniture is simple, a point exemplified by this intricately inlaid sideboard designed by Reginald Blomfied (1856–1942) and made ca. 1893 by Augustus Mason. Mahogany inlaid with maple, rosewood, and gilded brass hardware.

This ca. 1865 sideboard is an early example of furniture designed by Philip Webb for Morris & Company. Walnut with the simplest adornment of brass hardware.

notes on the defining characteristics

MOOD unpretentious	**FURNITURE** simple lines, rough finishes, hand detailing
SCALE mostly modest	**TEXTILES** neat, allover prints
COLORS muddy but rich	**KEY MOTIFS** stylized birds and flowers, hearts
ORNAMENT naturalistic	**LOOK FOR** medieval forms, handcrafted look

sample color palette and swatch

This floral wallpaper by William Morris is typical of the stylized designs of Arts and Crafts textiles. Muted colorations reflect the use of vegetable, rather than chemical, dyes.

Emulating the medieval guild system, a number of British organizations were formed in the wake of the design reform movement to carry out its principles by encouraging the practice of all types of handicrafts. Their objective was to reawaken interest in the rural lifestyle and to elevate the status of crafts to that of the fine arts. The most important of these groups were the Century Guild (1883–1892), established by Arthur Mackmurdo and Herbert Horne, the Guild of Handicraft (1888–1907) established by C. R. Ashbee, and Kenton & Company (1890–1892), whose founders included William Lethaby and Ernest Gimson.

Though these groups met with limited financial success, their efforts led to changes in design education that would strengthen the ties between the fields of art and crafts, and bring greater recognition of the value of handicrafts. In America, Associated Artists (1879–1883), founded by Louis Comfort Tiffany, Candace Wheeler, and Lockwood DeForest, was the American counterpart of William Morris's firm, designing entire interiors as well as individual products. Later groups that followed a more rural Arts and Crafts model included crafts colonies like that of the Roycroft Workshops (1895–1915), and the Byrdcliffe Colony (1902–1915).

A landmark design, the "Century Guild" chair was designed by A. H. Mackmurdo and made ca. 1883. The undulating curves of its openwork back are considered the earliest precursor of Art Nouveau. Honduras mahogany with colored accents.

A revolving bookcase designed by
C. R. Ashbee and made ca. 1905 by
the Guild of Handicraft. Oak inlaid
with pewter and ebony.

Sophisticated simplicity—this linen
press in poplar wood, with a panel
of carved tulips, was made ca. 1904
at the Byrdcliffe Colony, in Woodstock, New York.

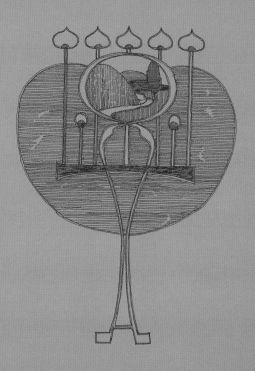

ABOUT THE PERIOD

Though inspired by its English namesake, the Arts and Crafts movement in America, commonly known as the Craftsman movement, did not begin until very late in the century. Though the styles are defined separately, there was extensive intermingling and overlap between them: the American practitioners shared the ideals of their English Arts and Crafts predecessors, but differed in the execution of their designs. Focusing more closely on materials than on decoration, they were also far more practical than William Morris and his colleagues, utilizing the efficiency of industrial production to assemble furniture by machine and finish it by hand. This combination of operations made their designs more affordable and therefore accessible to a wider audience.

By far the most prominent figure in American Arts and Crafts was Gustav Stickley (1858–1942), one of four German immigrant brothers producing furniture in upstate New York. He opened his own firm in 1898, introducing his first collection of "Craftsman" furniture in 1900. Stickley also published designs for houses and interiors in his magazine *The Craftsman,* and his catalogs included drawings that showed customers how to make the furniture themselves. Despite its initial success, Stickley's firm went bankrupt in 1916, but his influence was considerable in awakening interest in Arts and Crafts ideals.

Frank Lloyd Wright's Chicago-area Prairie Style houses reflected an aesthetic similar to that of the Arts and Crafts practitioners, although his translation was very different and evolved into a more modern aesthetic. The residences designed by the brothers Charles Sumner Greene (1868–1957) and Henry Mather Greene (1870–1954) in Pasadena, California, are the most refined and successful American expressions of Arts and Crafts style.

A subset of American Arts and Crafts, known as Mission Style, drew on the design of Spanish missions in Mexico and the American Southwest. In its willingness to move beyond the traditional forms of English style, it suggested America's growing confidence as an independent nation. The Arts and Crafts movement in America, like that in England, also spawned the creation of crafts communities, potteries, and other handicraft endeavors around the country.

Despite its large audience, Arts and Crafts in America did not survive the upheaval of World War I, and the new interest in modernism that arose after it ended. The style was rediscovered and enthusiastically revived in the 1970s, when the sturdy good looks of its furniture, the charm of its ceramics and metalware, and the worthiness of its ideals brought it back into favor.

ABOUT THE STYLE

An American Arts and Crafts interior is conscientiously rustic, simulating the rough-hewn surfaces of a preindustrial age, but wisely making the most of its cost-cutting possibilities. It has overtones of Colonial style in its strict simplicity and hints of English moderation in its lack of fussiness or frills. It combines almost-modern design with the warmth of the handicraft tradition.

White plaster walls and low ceilings are fitted with broad, exposed wood beams to create a cottagelike atmosphere. Modest-size windows, squarish in form, are punched into the walls without architectural ornament or framing. They often have leaded-glass panes. Shutters or, more likely, simple woven or printed curtains, are hung to the sills.

Ornament is relatively simple and carefully applied by hand. Decorative stenciling is used as friezelike trim on walls, or to decorate otherwise-unadorned furniture and curtains. Wright and the Greene brothers made sophisticated use of stained-glass accents, evoking the Japanese sensibility that influenced both.

Plain wood floors, in planks rather than parquet, are fitted with hand-knotted Orientals or homemade rag rugs.

The colors in the room reflect the soothing hues of the landscape: muted greens, browns, deep golds. Plants, too, are important, as another reminder of nature's bounty.

The setting is relatively spare, but comfortably accessorized. Lamps and fixtures in wrought iron, brass, or copper cast a warming glow, as do simple fireplaces, often faced with handmade tiles that may have been painted by the lady of the house.

Furniture of the type produced by Stickley and others is relatively large in scale and, despite its unassuming simplicity, can be imposing. Its sturdy, rectilinear lines are executed in rough-textured, dark oak. This fumed oak, darkened by exposing the wood to fumes of ammonia, simulates the natural weathering that comes from age and oxidation. The furniture is finished (deliberately) with visible joints, and accented with brass hardware and occasional stenciled motifs. Despite details that look handcrafted, it is made mostly by machine.

Typical seating pieces include wide, low-seated chairs with broad slats, square legs, and loose-cushion upholstery, covered in dark leather. There are only a few forms, and these are repeated in variations of size and proportion, but always with the same basic silhouettes. Case pieces are similarly limited to craftsmanlike, rectilinear forms that include square and rectangular tables, with sturdy legs or trestle bases, chests, buffet-servers, and bookcases with mullioned glass fronts. The few occasional pieces include desks, stools, and small tables. On some of these, wrought-iron accents suggest medieval inspiration.

Among the most distinctive and successful products of the American Arts and Crafts movement are the ceramics produced by amateur and professional potteries, which sprang up in the wake of the new interest in handicraft. They offered an unusual, and previously unavailable, opportunity for women to earn money through their artistic endeavors. The best-known of these are Rookwood, Grueby, and Newcomb, but there are many others that provided avocations for upper-class women and much-needed employment for many others.

PREVIOUS PAGE: The dining room of the Gamble House in Pasadena, California, is American Arts and Crafts style at its most sophisticated. Architects Charles Sumner Greene and Henry Mather Greene were influenced by English Arts and Crafts, but their interiors also reflect an affinity for Japanese design.

BELOW: This mahogany writing desk with gallery top has mother-of-pearl inlays and ebony detailing. Designed by Greene & Greene for the Blacker House in Pasadena, ca. 1907.

The sturdy, unadorned furniture made by Gustav Stickley, like this bookcase and chair of quarter-sawn oak, are the best-known expressions of American Arts and Crafts.

George Washington Maher (1864–1926), another important Arts and Crafts designer, made this oak side chair with unusual curved-splat back for the L. L. King House in Homer, Minnesota, ca. 1902.

Stickley's interpretation of the Morris Chair, with flat arms and slatted sides, was made ca. 1902 in his Eastwood, New York, factory.

Of hammered copper with mica panels, the "warty" table lamp is typical of designs by Dirk Van Erp (1850–1933), who opened his San Francisco workshop in 1910.

The Arts and Crafts movement in America produced distinctive ceramics as well as furniture. This stoneware vase, ca. 1900, was made by Grueby Art Pottery of Boston, Massachusetts.

A ca. 1903 music cabinet with tapering form, of oak with pewter, copper, and inlays of dyed woods, designed by Harvey Ellis (1852–1904) for Gustav Stickley & Company.

notes on the defining characteristics

MOOD	**FURNITURE**
conscious simplicity	simple forms of unfinished oak
SCALE	**TEXTILES**
modest	handwoven look
COLORS	**KEY MOTIFS**
limited palette, muted tones	some Japanese, some Gothic
ORNAMENT	**LOOK FOR**
restrained, some Japanese	rough finish, brass fittings, distinctive ceramics

sample color palette and swatch

The nondirectional leafy "Glenwood" pattern has the unpretentious character of Arts and Crafts style.

Probably the most creative American architect of the twentieth century, Frank Lloyd Wright (1867–1956) began his career in the last decade of the nineteenth century, and enjoyed a long and colorful career that lasted almost seven decades and spanned a number of design aesthetics, from Arts and Crafts to International Style and biomorphic modernism. Of the more than a thousand projects he designed, less than half were built, but those that were have influenced the course of modern architecture and design.

Although in the last decade of the nineteenth century Wright designed a few houses in the then-fashionable Queen Anne style, he quickly broke with the establishment. Most of his early work was a radical departure from cluttered Victorian design, compatible with Arts and Crafts ideals, yet reflecting his own distinctive aesthetic.

The so-called Prairie houses, in suburbs outside Chicago, exemplified Wright's organic approach to architecture. He believed that a building should evolve naturally from its surroundings and the land on which it was built, and these houses did precisely that. Their rectilinear forms hugged the ground, emphasizing horizontals rather than verticals, with projecting rooflines and broad strips of windows that blurred the boundaries between interior and exterior space. In later designs, he moved even further, sometimes even reshaping the landscape itself in order to fit his concept of integrating site with structure.

To Wright, a single-minded and autocratic man, the relationship between the elements of a design was more important than any specific form: every part must relate to the organic whole. He was adamant in controlling every facet of his projects—including the smallest accessories and often even his client's clothing.

Although it cannot necessarily be said that there is a single Frank Lloyd Wright style in interiors, most of the homes he designed share several characteristics. The typical Wright interior has a relatively low, beamed ceiling, and rooms that flow seamlessly from one area to another. Horizontal bands of windows, sheltered by overhanging roofs, are punctuated by stained-glass inserts. A palette of understated colors, drawn from nature and the surrounding landscape, is given variation by contrasts of tone and texture—unfinished wood grain, stone, rough plaster, and brickwork. Stained glass, in exquisitely precise geometric designs for windows or lighting fixtures, might be the only strong color in these spaces.

Wright's furniture was designed specifically for the interiors in which it is placed, though it is not always graceful and often not particularly comfortable. It is distinguished by sharply angular forms, often emphasizing horizontal lines, and with cantilevered elements that echo the architecture. Made of stained or fumed oak, it has surfaces that are relatively rough and unadorned. Intersecting horizontal and vertical planes, like those in his architecture, are largely free of ornament; what ornament he added was either geometric or highly stylized.

Many Wright interiors include built-in seating or storage that provide the most efficient use of space and underscore the absence of clutter or extraneous ornament. These carefully composed spaces reflect the influence on Wright of Oriental art, particularly the Japanese wood block prints he collected. The Usonian houses of his later career are the translation of his concepts into affordable, middle-class housing.

Though he refused to acknowledge the influence of either history or other architects, Wright's designs evolved in the course of his career. Many elements of his mature work, particularly the horizontal planes, the flowing spaces, and the continuity between interior and exterior, are compatible with the aesthetic of the International Style.

ABOVE: Wright furniture was substantial, sometimes almost massive, as this ca. 1900 library table demonstrates. Quarter-sawn oak.

RIGHT: Wright also used geometric forms in his windows and lighting fixtures. This lamp, 1902, made of leaded glass and bronze, was done for the Susan Lawrence Dana House, in Springfield, Illinois.

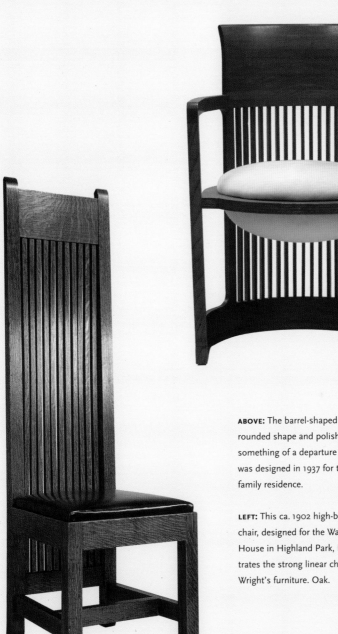

ABOVE: The barrel-shaped armchair, its rounded shape and polished oak finish something of a departure for Wright, was designed in 1937 for the Johnson family residence.

LEFT: This ca. 1902 high-back dining chair, designed for the Ward Willets House in Highland Park, Illinois, illustrates the strong linear character of Wright's furniture. Oak.

art nouveau

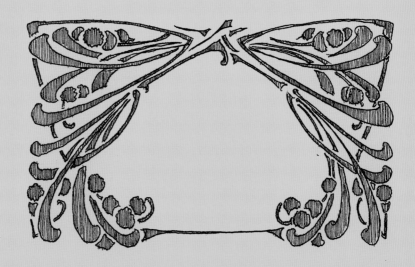

ABOUT THE PERIOD

Art Nouveau is considered the first "modern" style. As its name suggests, it sought to throw off the restraints of tradition by inventing a design vocabulary for the industrial age. Born as the nineteenth century was ending, it flourished for a brief but glorious time in the early part of the twentieth.

Despite its rejection of historicism, it drew on such diverse sources as French Rococo, Gothic, the Far East, Symbolist art, and even Celtic manuscripts, making it more a blend of several related styles than a single one. Overlapping Arts and Crafts, it took another direction—instead of calm evocations of nature, it used forms that vibrated with life; instead of rejecting modern materials and techniques, it embraced them.

Art Nouveau emerged in Belgium, in the architecture and interiors of Victor Horta (1861–1947) and Henri van de Velde (1863–1957), and France, where its best known practitioners included designers Louis Majorelle (1859–1926), Emile Gallé (1846–1904) and Hector Guimard (1867–1942). It was named for the Paris gallery *La Maison de l'Art Nouveau*, opened in 1895 by Siegfried Bing, that became the major showcase for objects in the new style.

Embraced up by a fashion-minded audience, *l'Art Nouveau* spread to many countries, assuming other names and national characteristics. It was *Jugendstil* in Germany, *Stile Liberty* or *Stile Floreale* in Italy, and *Tiffany Style* in America. It incorporated the eccentricities of Antoni Gaudi (1882–1926) in Barcelona and Carlo Bugatti (1856–1940) in Milan. The primary example of Art Nouveau design in America was in the opalescent and favrile glass objects created by Louis Comfort Tiffany (1848–1933). At its apogee, the style was celebrated in the Paris *Exposition Universelle de 1900*.

Art Nouveau furniture began with established forms and sculpted them into variations that reflected the organic, asymmetrical, curvilinear characteristics that define the style. French-made pieces, in particular, combined masterful carving with elaborate marquetry, requiring a high level of craftsmanship and making most of the pieces too costly for any beyond the cosmopolitan coterie who were, in any case, its greatest admirers. Furniture in other countries was generally less ornate, with a wide variety of interpretations that reflected a desire to develop individual national styles.

Art Nouveau was an important movement in architecture, and left a heritage of curvilinear facades in Brussels and Paris, as well as in such diverse locations as Prague, Helsinki, Moscow, and Barcelona. It encompassed many other areas of the arts, particularly influencing jewelry and graphic design: illustrations by Alphonse Mucha (1860–1939) and Aubrey Beardsley (1872–1898) were among its most successful interpretations.

In their search for originality, Art Nouveau designers committed excesses of taste, and the style was as mocked for its frivolity as it was applauded for its flair. The outbreak of World War I dealt the final death blow to the remnants of an era.

ABOUT THE STYLE

Walking into an Art Nouveau interior is like entering a fantasy—it elicits a smile, and a sense of escape from reality, enticing the eye with exuberant celebrations of the whiplash curve that painter William Hogarth (1697–1764) called the "line of beauty."

The style is created by more than merely furnishings; in effect, the entire room is designed as part of an ensemble that early German modernists called *gesamtkunstwerk,* a total work of art. The vertical and horizontal planes of walls and ceilings seem to dissolve into asymmetrical curves and undulating surfaces, transforming the shell of the room into a sculptural surround. Carved paneling might frame wallpapers patterned with stylized flowers, foliage, or Japanese motifs on pale grounds. Elaborate iron staircases resemble tendrils and vines, and the fireplace is framed in decorative tiles.

Window treatments are relatively uncomplicated, with shaped pelmets hung over draperies patterned with stylized floral motifs. Upholstery fabrics use the same stylized motifs, embroidered on linen, silk, or wool—many by celebrated Art Nouveau designers.

Colors in the Art Nouveau interior seem luminescent; intense pastels like lilac and mauve, salmon, and indigo enhance the effect of a room enveloped in pattern;

notwithstanding their search for modernism, Art Nouveau designers inherited the enthusiasm for ornament of the late-nineteenth-century Victorians.

The types of ornament associated with Art Nouveau include both nature-inspired and feminine motifs: nymphs with flowing hair, peacocks, dragonflies, irises and morning glories, waves, seaweed, and other botanical forms. These motifs are translated onto wallpapers, textiles, and woven rugs or carpets, laid over wood or tiled floors.

Lighting elements using gas, kerosene or, now, electricity, are organic forms, frequently of brass, or brilliant-colored Tiffany lamps and fixtures. On the walls, paintings, prints, perhaps Japanese wood blocks; on tabletops and mantels, many small objects of ceramic, silver, and pewter. Glass artware would include objects by the Gallé or Daum firms.

Despite its references to classical French forms, Art Nouveau furniture is another genre altogether. Unmistakable in its exaggerated curves and flowing ornament, it is as elaborately detailed, in its way, as the eighteenth-century styles. Yet the overall effect is one of lightness and delicacy, in part due to the finely executed ornament, but also from the use of a variety of decoratively grained, light-toned woods.

Virtually every object is designed as much for its visual appeal as for its function, with function sometimes seeming secondary. Chairs and settees are strikingly varied, with sensual, carved wood frames that upstage even the most elegant upholstery.

Cabinets, in a variety of shapes and sizes, are sculpted with intriguing suggestions of asymmetry, so that their familiar forms seem entirely new inventions. Some may have intricate marquetry ornament on door fronts; others have open glass shelves, sometimes arranged asymmetrically, for the display of the decorative ceramics and glass that are among Art Nouveau's finest expressions. Gilt mounts may be used, as on traditional French furniture, though with naturalistic, asymmetrical ornament. Round or rounded-square occasional tables, nesting tray-tables, and strikingly sinuous desks carry the distinctive lines and decorative detailing of the style. Despite the individuality of Art Nouveau design, many of the objects were not individually commissioned, but were produced in multiples.

PREVIOUS PAGE: Seen from the curvilinear metal staircase, a view of designer Victor Horta's own house in Brussels, an iconic statement of Art Nouveau style, built in 1898.

ABOVE: Sweeping curves in a rocking chaise longue, ca. 1880, by Gebruder Thonet, Vienna, the firm that pioneered bentwood furniture. Solid beech and cane.

Hector Guimard, a leading French exponent of Art Nouveau, is known for his entrances for the Paris Metro. He designed this shapely, carved pearwood side chair in 1912.

Belgian architect Henri Van de Velde designed this ca. 1897 oak armchair whose form reflects Art Nouveau, yet anticipates modernism.

LEFT: Art Nouveau produced unconventional designers such as Carlo Bugatti, whose individualistic furniture—using parchment, mixed metals, and exotic inlays—showed Oriental and Moorish influences. This arm-chair dates to ca. 1900–1910.

OPPOSITE, LEFT: Emile Gallé (1846–1904), celebrated for his glass, also made furniture. The motifs on this graceful pearwood cabi-net with openwork carving and marquetry, ca. 1900, resemble those used in Gallé glass, and suggest Japanese designs.

OPPOSITE, RIGHT: Louis Majorelle, a leader of the school of Nancy, designed this narrow cabinet, ca. 1900. Wrought iron and wood marquetry.

Majorelle's "chicoree" vitrine, ca. 1900.
Carved oak and marquetry, fitted with
shelves for display.

art nouveau

notes on the defining characteristics

MOOD exuberant	**FURNITURE** extravagantly curved, highly decorative
SCALE generous	**TEXTILES** rich and richly patterned
COLORS jewel tones	**KEY MOTIFS** nymphs with flowing hair, waves, peacock feathers
ORNAMENT naturalistic, resolutely asymmetrical	**LOOK FOR** "whiplash" curves, Tiffany lamps

sample color palette and fabric swatch

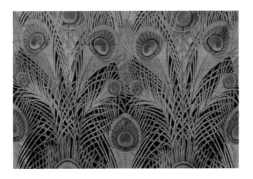

"Plumes de paon,"
an exotic weave of
peacock feathers, inter-
prets an often-used
Art Nouveau motif.

A multitalented artist, designer, and inventor, Louis Comfort Tiffany (1848–1933) was the only important American exponent of Art Nouveau style, and probably the first designer from America to become internationally celebrated. Trained as a painter, he spent most of his career working in glass, designing windows and then lamps, vases and decorative objects, whose unique qualities were derived from two important processes he invented.

His work in designing interiors, however, spans the transition between the Aesthetic movement and Art Nouveau style. Pursuing his desire to plan and coordinate entire rooms, he formed the firm Louis Comfort Tiffany, Associated Artists in 1879 in partnership with textile designer Candace Wheeler and then furniture maker Lockwood de Forest. In its short existence, the partnership designed homes and interiors for Gilded Age clients in Aesthetic style, though some of Tiffany's own work in stained glass began to reflect the aesthetic of the move toward Modern.

When Tiffany began, in 1883, to pursue his interest in glass, Wheeler took over the company, which closed in 1907. Tiffany continued to design interiors, but his most enduring contributions were his unparalleled achievements in glass technology, and the objects he created in his preferred medium.

In 1881 he patented a method for producing colored window glass that was opalescent rather than opaque, producing shimmering tonalities of color. It created remarkable effects of light and shadow in the leaded-glass windows he designed, though it was rejected as too fanciful by admirers of the monotone surfaces of traditional stained glass. Tiffany used the same material in the leaded-glass lamps and lighting fixtures that his firm produced in great quantities until 1919, offering customers the option of pairing their choice of shade with any of several designs of cast-bronze bases to customize what were essentially production goods. Other, more elaborate designs, were produced to order in limited numbers.

Tiffany's other major discovery, which he called *favrile*, was an iridescent glass whose luminous qualities gained immediate acclaim, and which was used in brilliantly colored glass vases and other decorative objects.

Tiffany exhibited his designs for windows and blown glass at international venues like the gallery L'Art nouveau, the 1900 *Exposition Universelle* in Paris, and the 1902 *Prima Exposizione d'Arte Decorativa Moderna* in Turin, Italy (where the Glasgow group and the Vienna Secessionists also showed). Tiffany also designed enamelwork and jewelry.

Lamps and fixtures of leaded glass with bronze bases, notable for their rich colorations and varied patterns, made Tiffany lighting among the most desirable accessories for the early twentieth-century interiors. Here, a ca. 1900 "Wisteria."

Tiffany designed leaded glass windows for clients of his decorating firm. This example, ca. 1900, features a peacock, a frequent motif of Art Nouveau design.

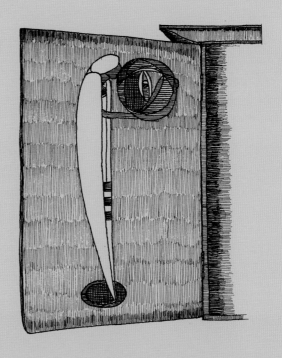

ABOUT THE PERIOD

Named for the birthplace of Scottish designer Charles Rennie Mackintosh (1868–1928), with whose name it is most closely associated, this style is both entirely unique and extremely difficult to categorize. While it straddles the fence between Arts and Crafts and Art Nouveau, it is linked as well to the modernism of the Vienna Secession. Mackintosh, his future wife, Margaret MacDonald (1864–1933), her sister Frances MacDonald (1865–1902), and Frances's husband, Herbert MacNair, were fellow art students who developed the elements of the design aesthetic. "The Four," as they were called, worked together on several projects, but it was the partnership of Mackintosh and Margaret MacDonald that actually defined the style, with furniture forms and construction that recall Arts and Crafts objects, and curvilinear ornament that vividly prefigures Art Nouveau.

Despite its connections to both strains of design reform, Glasgow Style is also a precursor of Modern. The celebrated "Rose Room" designed by the Mackintosh group in the 1902 *Prima Exposizione d'Arte Decorativa Moderna* in Turin, Italy, was enthusiastically received by the Vienna Secessionists, who saw in Mackintosh a fellow modernist rebelling against the design establishment. His use of linearity and intersecting planes, his progressive spatial planning, and his imaginative contrasts of solids and voids were clearly explorations of an avant-garde aesthetic.

In his architectural commissions, Mackintosh drew on elements of Scottish vernacular, combining them with more modern notes: asymmetry, cast-iron ornament, and plate-glass windows. Though he received critical acclaim in Europe, his work drew little interest in England, and his architecture and interiors projects were limited to the Glasgow area. His most noted designs include the Glasgow School of Art (1897), Hill House (1902), and several tearooms, particularly the Willow Tea Rooms (1904).

The combination of severity of form and sensuality of decoration, the yin and yang of male and female elements that are apparent in the collaboration of Margaret and Charles Rennie Mackintosh, make the Glasgow Style an example of design that, while drawing on influences of the past, is translated into something uniquely original. Despite a relatively brief and only intermittently successful career, Mackintosh is considered an important forerunner of Modernism.

ABOUT THE STYLE

An interior in Glasgow Style is in a class by itself. Entirely original, it is identified by the strong geometry of its attenuated furniture forms and the bold contrasts of light and dark. The Mackintosh interior is striking for its minimalism and simplicity, in an era of clutter-and-pattern-filled rooms. It projects the elegance of understatement, in a composition of simple elements with sophisticated touches of ornament.

The room might be somewhat feminine in feeling, with all-white backgrounds and white or black painted furniture. In a bedroom, for example, white walls and carpeted floors form a backdrop for slender chairs and cabinets, arranged with spare precision into linear compositions, and relieved by occasional accents of color. In other spaces, perhaps a dining room, a more masculine ambience might be evoked by the use of dark woods, posts, and beams.

Mackintosh rooms take no specific shape, but are articulated around the furniture arrangement, with built-in cabinetry, Arts and Crafts–style inglenooks, or small alcoves. These irregularities are reflected in the exterior of the building, which might be punctuated by randomly placed windows, curving bays, and turrets recalling Scottish Baronial architecture. Walls are most likely enhanced by gessoed or silvered panels painted by Margaret, with romantic fantasy figures, sinuous floral forms, or motifs including a stylized rose.

Window treatments are light and airy, and apart from the contrast of furniture against background, there is relatively little additional decoration and a minimal use of accessories. Making skillful use of light and shadow, Glasgow Style interiors are deliberately simple, yet have a spare elegance that accounts for their appeal.

The characteristic color scheme, as noted, is white with black, sparked with accents of lively pastels.

Mackintosh designed fabrics as well as furniture, in precise and unpretentious patterns that complement the simplicity of his interiors.

Furniture by Mackintosh is more distinctive for its design than for its workmanship. Though the cabinetry is relatively unsophisticated, and the construction undistinguished, the shapes are dramatic and the ornament delicate and highly refined. It is consistently rectilinear, with visible joints, plain straight legs, and rough-textured finishes. The forms of his cabinetry are rarely unusual, though the decoration is—geometric cutouts that create bold contrasts of solids and voids; inlays of mother-of-pearl or silver; doors with contrasting stained-glass inserts or painted motifs on exterior and interior faces, so that they present varying aspects when open or closed.

Mackintosh chairs are in another category: with their angular forms, assertive height, and distinctive openwork, they have become iconic images of early Modernism. The ornament includes hearts, crescents, or a gridlike piercing that suggests the designs of Wiener Werkstatte silver.

The furniture is generally of simple oak, often painted white or black, ebonized, or sometimes silvered for decorative effect.

PREVIOUS PAGE: Two rooms were combined to form an open, L-shape space in the Mackintosh House in Glasgow. Mackintosh furnished it with his own designs, in an all-white environment with restrained accents of sharp color.

LEFT: Made for the Willow Tearooms, this wraparound seat was for the manager's desk. The rounded form contrasts with the pierced geometric pattern on the back.

RIGHT: One of the most distinctive Mackintosh designs, this ca. 1897 chair was made for his first major commission, Argyle Street Tearooms in Glasgow. The unusual high back gave a feeling of privacy to diners. Oak and rush.

LEFT: Its exaggerated ladder-back, with slim horizontals and checkerboard cresting, was designed ca. 1902 for Hill House, one of Mackintosh's most important residential commissions.

notes on the defining characteristics

MOOD	**FURNITURE**
exuberant	angular rectilinear forms, distinctive silhouettes
SCALE	**TEXTILES**
modest	understated patterns and textures
COLORS	**KEY MOTIFS**
white and black, jewel-pastel accents	stylized rose, square cutouts on furniture
ORNAMENT	**LOOK FOR**
suggests Art Nouveau	white rooms with black or white furniture, flowing painted panels

sample color palette and fabric swatch

Although Mackintosh used leather and solid weaves more than patterned textiles, the stylized plant forms of this Art Nouveau design are compatible with his style.

CENTURY

modernism and after

avant-garde: the wiener werkstatte

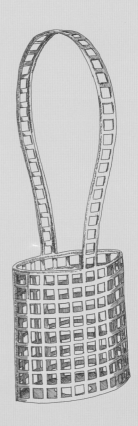

ABOUT THE PERIOD

Although the reformers of the nineteenth century took the first steps away from tradi-tion, their designs were not able to break entirely with the past. The early years of the new century, however, saw the first real stirrings of change. The secessionist move-ments of the early twentieth century—though the 1897-founded *Wiener Sezession* (Vienna Seccession) is the best-known of these, there were several similar groups—sought to separate themselves from the art-and-design establishment, to seek a new modern aesthetic, to erase the distinction between the fine and applied arts, and to improve public taste. In these objectives, they were influenced by the English reform movement. In their designs, however, are visible the first signs of Modern.

A key concept for these and other avant-garde designers was the understanding that industrialization had radically changed the very process of design, and their efforts were directed to take advantage of the possibilities offered by that change.

One of the tenets of the new aesthetic was expressed in a widely published 1908 essay by architect and theorist Adolph Loos (1870–1933). Entitled "Ornament and Crime," it justified the rejection of ornament as "unnatural" and inappropriate for modern society. Dicta such as "form follows function," and "less is more" would become battle cries of the Modern movement—though it was never formally organized, nor a single move-ment, but a series of independent and often loosely organized groups.

One of the most influential of these was the Deutsche Werkbund, founded in Germany in 1907, which brought together all those involved in design—artists and designers, artisans, and manufacturers—in the search for a solution to the new chal-lenges. Some of the most innovative designs of the time were introduced at Werk-bund-sponsored exhibitions in the period before the outbreak of World War I and Germany's subsequent ostracism by much of the Western world.

Influential early modernist groups included De Stijl, in Holland, which insisted on impersonal abstract design, seen in the designs of Gerrit Reitveld (1888–1964), whose angular forms and primary colors recall the paintings of Piet Mondrian (1872–1944). Other early Modern movements included Russian Constructivism, which strongly influenced modern graphic design, and Italian Futurism, which celebrated the aesthetic of the machine and speed, and produced Antonio Sant'Elia's (1888–1916) vision of the glass-towered modern city. But only one of the groups developed what can be considered a fully realized style, and that was the Wiener Werkstatte, founded in 1903 by designers Josef Hoffmann (1870–1956), Kolomon Moser (1868–1918), and their patron Fritz Warndorfer. The Werkstatte, whose key members were also members of the Vienna Secession, was a series of workshops for applied arts, reacting against Art Nouveau, and modeled somewhat on C. R. Ashbee's Guild of Handcraft (1888–1907) of the Arts and Crafts era. The Wiener Werkstatte (Vienna Workshops) took a functional approach to design, employing linear forms and its own vocabulary of ornament—almost entirely geometric, although the designs later became more exuberant and decorative. The products of the Werkstatte, which briefly established a showroom in New York City, were, like so many early attempts at design reform, very costly and therefore available to only a small market of affluent clients. Its designs, however, represent a milestone in the early part of the Modern movement.

ABOUT THE STYLE

For Werkstatte designers, all elements of a project are part of a coherent plan—the *gesamtkunstwerk*—and are designed to coalesce into an integrated whole. Although Secessionist design includes elements of Art Nouveau, its curvilinear forms are soundly rejected by Hoffmann and his colleagues. Werkstatte interiors are notable for their striking rectilinearity and their elegant simplicity.

The space itself is defined by the interplay of horizontals and verticals: white walls might be slashed with bold vertical lines to form a surround of slim, rectangular panels, each accented with stylized floral or geometric motifs. A stringlike design runs horizontally, to visually link the windows as a unit. Despite the severity of the individual elements, Hoffmann's interiors for important clients are luxurious, enriched with sumptuous materials such as marble and rosewood, parquet flooring, mosaics, and suede or velvet upholstery.

avant-garde: the wiener werkstatte

The Werkstatte designers did not eschew pattern, but rather stripped it down to the barest essentials: the pure geometry of checkerboards, squares, and sometimes circles. A favorite grid pattern is applied to floors, windows, and vivid textiles, appearing most intriguingly on pierced silver accessories that are among the most identifiable of the group's designs.

Probably the most characteristic Werkstatte color scheme is bold black-and-white, and an interior might include accents of red, brilliant yellow, deep blue, or other high-intensity hues.

In one of their more successful ventures, small-scale geometric motifs are also arranged symmetrically in the fabrics and carpets designed by Hoffmann and Moser and produced by the workshops. The interior might also show Hoffmann-designed geometric wallpaper.

Among the most innovative, and most recognizable, objects from the Wiener Werkstatte are the distinctive metalwork designs: silver, less costly and more durable than gold, is used for elegant lighting fixtures, clocks, bowls, boxes, and vases decorated with hammering or perforated grid patterns—a motif that was also used by Charles Rennie Mackintosh. The workshops also produced striking works of color-accented glass.

Furniture by Hoffmann and his colleagues follows a similar reductivist aesthetic, with angular construction, sometimes decorated with inlays of contrasting materials—Moser, in particular, devised sophisticated effects with a minimalist vocabulary, using rare woods and sometimes mother-of-pearl or semiprecious stones. The most famous of all Wiener Werkstatte furniture, however, are the charming and distinctive bentwood objects designed, mostly for J. & J. Kohn, using a process developed by the German-born Michael Thonet (1796–1871) a half-century prior. The factory-made chairs, settees, and tables, many with pierced geometric ornament and several of which have become iconic symbols of modernism, are the only Werkstatte designs that achieved the objective of making modern furniture accessible to a broad market.

PREVIOUS PAGE: Weiner Werkstätte of America salesroom at 581 Fifth Avenue, New York, 1922.

ABOVE: The "Sitzmachine," ca. 1902 by Josef Hoffmann, combines straight lines and bentwood curves, and has an adjustable back. Stained beechwood with plywood seat and back.

This bentwood, glass, and aluminum cabinet was designed by Kolomon Moser, one of the founders of the Wiener Werkstatte, and made by J. & J. Kohn, ca. 1904.

Shaped of bent beechwood, the frame of this settee, ca. 1908, by Josef Hoffmann for Thonet has a circular motif, rather than the more common diamond shape.

notes on the defining characteristics

MOOD severe	**FURNITURE** simple linear forms, dark wood, no carving
SCALE varies	**TEXTILES** flat-woven in bold symmetrical patterns
COLORS bright, bold	**KEY MOTIFS** checkerboard
ORNAMENT strictly geometric	**LOOK FOR** bold black-and-white, grid pattern, striking color accents

sample color palette and fabric swatch

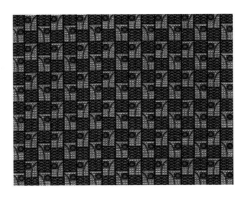

"Paradis," with its precise geometric motifs, is a Joseph Hoffmann woven textile in Wiener Werkstatte style.

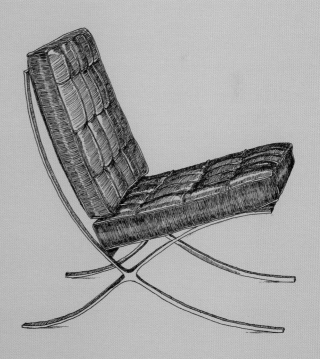

ABOUT THE PERIOD

In 1932, Philip Johnson and Henry Russell Hitchcock curated *Architecture: An International Exhibition,* at the Museum of Modern Art in New York. The style it documented, named after the accompanying book, is considered the purest expression of twentieth-century modernism. Evolved from the concepts of Bauhaus masters Walter Gropius (1883–1969), Ludwig Mies van der Rohe (1886–1969), and Marcel Breuer (1902–1981), and their contemporary Le Corbusier (Charles-Edouard Jeanneret, 1887–1965), International Style architecture celebrated geometric form and modern materials. Its buildings were severe, flat-roofed structures of steel and concrete with broad swaths of windows and without ornament, a revolt against traditional architectural styles, and it launched a new look with interiors that were open, light-filled, and furnished with objects that followed the tenets of functionalist design.

The International Style was embraced as a statement of modernity for the rectilinear, curtain-walled corporate headquarters that dotted the American landscape in the boom years after World War II. It was ideally suited to the demands of postwar construction: both economical and efficient, it provided maximum floor space and facilitated the use of machine-made modular elements.

Emphasizing structure and functionality rather than warmth and creature comforts, the style failed to gain the acceptance in residential design that it did for office structures such as the celebrated Seagram Building in New York, the paradigm of twentieth-century corporate culture. It was more successfully applied to high-rise apartments than to single-family residences, except perhaps for the innovative California homes designed by Rudolf Schindler (1887–1953) and Richard Neutra (1892–1970), precursors of the casual, split-level homes of Midcentury Modernism.

Like the architecture that surrounded them, the design of International Style interiors was sometimes limited by the constraints of the Modernist vocabulary, and, though often surprisingly sumptuous, were generally regarded as too severe. Despite its high profile, the International Style was considered passé by the 1970s; its principles were too demanding to sustain in the face of an interest in historicism, and the pendulum-swing of fashion.

ABOUT THE STYLE

The International Style interior is inviting, expansive, and suffused with light. Walking into the space becomes not one but a series of experiences, with the conventional layout of separate rooms replaced by an open plan of interlocking volumes, articulated by screens or wall sections. Individual areas are defined by islands of furniture in precisely arranged compositions that avoid the walls. Following Mies van der Rohe's often-quoted dictum "Less is more," the interior is furnished with a carefully edited selection of objects, chosen from a vocabulary of industrial-age designs and materials. The single drawback of International Style rooms can be the predictability of their furnishings.

Smooth white walls, stripped of moldings or other architectural detailing, enhance the seamless flow of unbroken space, and the ceilings are flat and often not overly high, emphasizing horizontal rather than vertical space. Glass is an essential element in International Style architecture, and it dominates the interiors as well: the concept of exterior as an extension of interior is expressed in floor-to-ceiling walls of glass that erase any feeling of separation or enclosure, bringing the surrounding landscape into the composition. Curtains, if used, are as unobtrusive as possible, or clean-lined blinds may provide an alternative covering for necessary light control.

Colors are primarily neutrals like grey, beige, or black, with careful and limited accents in clear, assertive hues.

The textiles of choice are either tightly woven natural fibers or smooth leather in natural colors—primarily black or brown. Occasionally, a more luxurious textile may be used for dramatic effect, but patterns are avoided. Richness is more likely to be seen on the walls, with materials such as marble, rosewood, and ebony, while steel and chrome provide light-catching luster.

Lighting for the most part is concealed to avoid interrupting the linearity of the space, though an occasional clean-lined fixture may be seen. Accessories and accent pieces are almost altogether eliminated, though the walls provide an ideal background to set off large-scale abstract paintings or modern sculpture.

The most prominent objects of furniture in International Style interiors are likely to be designed by one of the celebrated Bauhaus masters—iconic pieces that follow the strict parameters of the Modernist aesthetic. Even the most costly of these, in sharp contrast to earlier styles, have been industrially produced.

The most dramatic of these are the chairs, benches, or chaises by Mies, Breuer, or Le Corbusier, with bold silhouettes shaped of tubular or flat bent steel, and upholstery in leather, cane, or wicker. Cabinets are low and rigidly linear, of polished wood with steel hardware and legs. Storage is often built in, to minimize clutter. Tables are steel-based, topped with glass or perhaps marble.

The pure International Style interior rarely mixes its furnishings with those of other periods, though occasionally an item of antique furniture might be inserted as a contrasting work of art.

PREVIOUS PAGE: Mies van der Rohe's glass-wrapped Farnsworth House in Plano, Illinois, is a pure expression of International Style, erasing the visual boundaries between indoors and out. Built ca.1950, it showcases Mies's now-classic Modern furniture.

RIGHT: The distinctive silhouette of Mies van der Rohe's "MR" chair, ca.1927. Chrome-plated tubular steel with fabric seat and black-painted wood armrests.

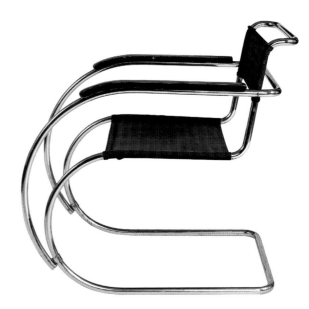

Many designs by members of the Bauhaus have become icons of International Style. Among them, Breuer's "Wassily" chair (ca.1925)—named for the painter Wassily Kandinsky, a Bauhaus master. Metal-plated tubular steel.

The cantilever chair, introduced in 1925, was a radical innovation to replace conventional legs. The "Cesca" armchair, probably the most widely copied version, was designed in 1928 by Marcel Breuer for Thonet. Chrome-plated tubular steel with stained beechwood arms and woven cane seat.

An International Style classic—the chaise longue designed in 1928 by Le Corbusier, Pierre Jeanneret, and Charlotte Perriand. Chrome-plated tubular steel with leather upholstery on painted steel and rubber base.

Companion to the X-base chair designed
for the German Pavilion at the Barcelona
World's Fair in 1929, the "Barcelona table"
by Mies van der Rohe is a sleek expanse of
polished steel and plate glass.

This bookcase, pictured in one of many
varying configurations, was designed in 1953
by Charlotte Perriand for a Paris university.
Made by Les Ateliers Jean Prouvé. Pine and
painted aluminum.

notes on the defining characteristics

MOOD pristine	**FURNITURE** sleek forms, industrial materials
SCALE generous horizontal expanse	**TEXTILES** leather, flat-weaves, solids
COLORS mostly neutrals	**KEY MOTIFS** avoidance of pattern
ORNAMENT avoided	**LOOK FOR** open-plan interiors, expanses of glass, iconic Bauhaus furniture

sample color palette and fabric swatch

The Bauhaus revolutionized textile design, introducing new approaches to woven fabrics by masters like Gunta Stolzl (1897–1983), one of whose patterns is shown here.

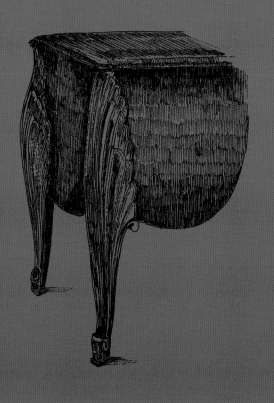

ABOUT THE PERIOD

Often referred to as the last of the great period styles, Art Deco began to develop in Paris in the first decade of the twentieth century, as a reaction to the excesses of Art Nouveau. With antecedents in Glasgow Style and the Wiener Werkstatte, *Le Style Moderne*, as it was originally called, found immediate inspiration in the avant-garde—cubist forms, Fauve colors, and the dazzling sets and costumes designed by Leon Bakst for the Ballets Russes—but also drew from sources as diverse as ancient Egypt, Africa, and the Jazz Age.

The designation Art Deco was bestowed long after the fact, on the occasion of its revival in America in the late 1960s. It was named for the 1925 Paris exhibition that provided its most prominent showcase. *L'Exposition Internationale des Arts Décoratifs et Industriels Modernes* sought to reassert France's fashion leadership in the face of German innovations in modern design, but the exhibition actually celebrated a style that, in its embrace of luxury and rich materials, was already behind the times.

Despite its wish to express modernity and its stated rejection of ornament, *Le Style Moderne* was closely linked to the guild-based tradition of French eighteenth-century design. Embraced by style-setting couturiers like Jacques Doucet, Pierre Poiret, and Jeanne Lanvin and interpreted by Paris *ensembliers* like Émile-Jacques Ruhlmann (1879–1933), and the design studios of the great department stores, French Art Deco design was impeccably executed, costly, and elitist. Its extravagant interiors and labor-intensive objects were the antithesis of democratic design for the industrial age.

Some designers sought another direction. The Union des Artistes Modernes was formed in 1930, and avant-gardists like Rene Herbst (1891–1982), Irish-born Eileen Gray (1879–1976), and Robert Mallet-Stevens (1886–1945) would help to bring new vitality to French design in the years to follow.

Le Style Moderne was brought to a halt by the Wall Street crash of 1929, after which such extravagance was no longer either tasteful or affordable. Tied to a heritage of artisanry, and requiring time-consuming handicraft techniques, it proved too costly to survive the trials of the Depression. It would be translated in other European adaptations, and altogether transformed in its equally striking but more egalitarian American counterpart. And it would be preserved for future generations in the fantasy interiors of great ocean liners, grand public spaces, and glamorous Hollywood films.

ABOUT THE STYLE

The French Art Deco interior is a study in soigné sophistication, possessed of generous proportions and wrapped in rich and exotic materials. Even in period photographs and faded drawings, the splendor of these interiors is striking. They are discernibly modern, but the most luxurious modernity imaginable, and clearly designed for only the most elegant and affluent occupants.

Grand geometric volumes of space are defined by stylized architectural elements, distilled from the classical vocabulary. Columns, moldings, recessed coves, and, often, elaborately tiered ceilings create a dramatic background. Despite the style's professed avoidance of Art Nouveau excesses, almost every surface of the space is decorated—but in a manner so subtle that the overall effect, despite its richness, generally stops short of ostentation.

The walls are most likely upholstered or covered with velvety, flocked, wall-coverings and rich damask and velvets are used on furniture and for window treatments. At the tall windows, draperies either hang straight or in fluid pullbacks.

Floors of dark polished wood are covered with carpets in intense colors and over-scaled stylized patterns, contributing to the luxury of the surroundings.

The patterns on textiles, walls, and floorcoverings are stylized motifs from nature and classical sources, or sweeping curves that suggest abstract painting. The same stylization lends a refined symmetry to three-dimensional decorative effects like reliefs, murals, and mosaics that are often applied to walls.

Color schemes may be chosen for theatrical effect—with unexpected combinations of intense, almost-clashing hues—or will use more conventional mixes in deep tones such as brown, purple, or black.

Focal-point lighting fixtures create their own drama, with cascading, multilevel crystal chandeliers, wall sconces, torcheres, or table lamps, often of frosted or etched glass as well as intricately worked metal. Metals such as bronze and wrought iron, most notably in the work of Edgar Brandt (1880–1960), are used for screens, fireplace ornament, and accent furniture. Finishing touches might include enamel-on-copper bowls or vases by Jean Dunand (1877–1942), bronze-and-ivory figurines by Dimitri Chiparus (1888–1950), silver by Jean Puiforcat (1897–1945), and frosted-glass objets by René Lalique (1860–1945).

Exquisitely crafted furniture of masters like Ruhlmann, Louis Sue (1875–1968) and Andre Mare (1887–1932), and Andre Groult (1881–1967) has conservative silhouettes in the tradition of Louis XV, Louis XVI, and Empire designs. Chairs, chaises, and loveseats are either variations of Rococo and Neoclassical models, stripped of extraneous ornament, or angular geometric forms, framed in polished wood.

Case furniture, too, is often rectilinear, with cabinets and armoires massed on platform bases, desks on shaped and saboted legs, tables on pillars or trestle supports. Many of the pieces draw on classical models. The French designers considered such straight-lined shapes more modern than curved ones, and they generally preferred extravagant finishes, rather than applied ornament or marquetry, for ornament. Cases might be sheathed in exotic woods such as amboyna, macassar ebony, amaranth, and zebra, layers of mirror-finish lacquer, or rare skins like shagreen, snakeskin, and Moroccan leather. Unable to resist the intricacy of detail that characterized traditional French design, they often added delicate inlays of ivory, or accents of parchment or gilt bronze. Other surfaces may be covered in silver leaf or parchment. Elegant detailing avoided a massive look, even on the larger pieces.

The Art Deco period also produced a variety of unusual desks and vanity tables, coffee tables, consoles, and unusual occasional pieces inspired by African sculpture.

PREVIOUS PAGE: The stylish salon of couturier and collector Jacques Doucet (1853–1929) is one of the most familiar interior images of *Le Style Moderne*, a bold statement combining African objects, cubist art, Lalique glass doors, and modern French furniture.

ABOVE: The lines of Louis XV furniture, updated and with spare carved ornament, executed ca. 1927 by Louis Sue (1875–1968) and Andre Mare (1887–1932). Polished rosewood.

RIGHT: Clearly influenced by African sculpture, this ca.1924 carved wood chair was designed by Jean Dunand (1877–1942) and Jean Lambert-Rucki (1888–1967).

This armchair, framed in Macassar ebony, was designed ca. 1923 by Pierre Chareau (1883–1950). The simplicity of line and avoidance of ornament are characteristic of his style.

The French ocean liner "Normandie," launched in 1935, was a showcase of French Art Deco design. From a salon, this glass panel, silvered, gilded, and reverse-painted, is the work of the artist Jean Dupard (1882–1964).

In the "Nicolle" cabinet, ca. 1926, Emile-Jacques Ruhlmann combined the ivory inlay and trim used in many of his pieces with veneered squares of red tortoise shell. Zebrawood.

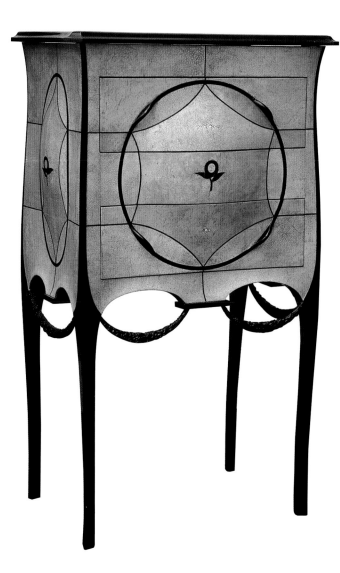

A shapely two-drawer chest, ca. 1914, by Paul Iribe (1883–1935), a couturier as well as a designer of interiors and furniture. Covered entirely in pink shagreen and accented with ebony.

The shape recalls the eighteenth century, but the pale-green shagreen surface is undeniably *Style Moderne*. By Andre Groult (1884–1967), ca. 1925.

notes on the defining characteristics

MOOD
soigné sophistication

SCALE
grand

COLORS
deep, saturated

ORNAMENT
stylized, with classical overtones

FURNITURE
sleek shapes, highly polished exotic veneers,
lacquers, shagreen, and parchment

TEXTILES
as rich as possible

KEY MOTIFS
waterfall, stylized flowers

LOOK FOR
rooms that scream "expensive"

sample color palette and fabric swatch

Designed by Emile-Jacques
Ruhlmann and made by
Stephany, this textile
covered the walls in the
designers "Hôtel d'un
riche collectionneur" at
the 1925 Paris exposition.

While established French designers continued to produce luxury goods for an exclusive clientele, the iconoclasts of the Union des Artistes Modernes, and others who shared their commitment to a modern aesthetic, embraced technology and the use of new materials. They designed furnishings that took into account the realities of modern materials and production techniques, balancing traditional elegance and stark functionalism, and often crossing over into avant-garde innovation.

The furniture and interiors they designed stands with the best of early Modernism, and has drawn increased recognition during the past decade. The most familiar of these are Jean-Michel Frank (1895–1941), who designed projects in America; Charlotte Perriand (1903–1999), and Jean Prouvé (1901–1984). After the decline of Art Deco, they were major contributors to the revival of French design.

Jean-Michel Frank (1895–1941) designed furniture with clean-lined contemporary forms, like this sycamore side chair, ca. 1930.

Robert Mallet-Stevens (1886–1945) used a steel frame for this adjustable armchair, ca. 1929–30. Armrests are ebonized wood, and upholstery is suede.

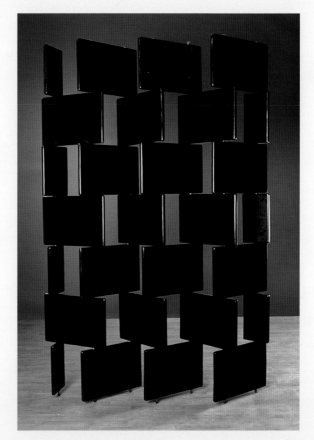

ABOVE: The furniture of Jean Prouvé reflects his early training as a black-smith. the angular "afrique" table, ca. 1952, is African wood and steel with burgundy lacquer.

RIGHT: An iconic symbol of early French modernism, this black lacquer screen, made ca. 1922–25 and composed of individual pivoting elements, was designed by Scottish-born Eileen Gray.

America's enthusiastic expression of Art Deco absorbed the country's infatuation with speed, transportation, and the machine age into what was variously called "Modernistic," "Streamline," "Jazz Age," and "Skyscraper Style." It offered welcome relief from the gloom of the Depression, with positive imagery and an optimistic attitude. In objects whose come-hither packaging was calculated to stimulate consumer purchasing, the period also saw the birth of the new profession of industrial design.

The United States had been conspicuous at the 1925 Paris exhibition by its absence, declining to exhibit on the grounds of having insufficient good modern design. Secretary of Commerce Herbert Hoover's judgment was accurate, though a blow to national pride. The exhibition, and its glorification of Le Style Moderne, became a catalyst for change, awakening the incipient Modern movement in America and leading to exhibitions in major museums and department stores to showcase the new style.

American translations of Le Style Moderne were less luxurious, more subdued, and more democratic than the original. Furniture was produced in pared-down, populist versions of the formal French designs. Most successfully, the new fashion stimulated an explosion of affordable, mass-produced objects like tableware, cocktail sets, small appliances, and decorative accessories that were at best witty reflections of popular culture, and at worst discardable kitsch.

America's most ambitious, and most successful, innovations of this era were in architecture, where motifs from machinery, ocean liners and aircraft, and Jazz-Age geometrics created a new design vocabulary—one that was then replicated in textiles, graphics, and decorative accessories. At its most fully realized, American Art Deco produced iconic structures such as the Chrysler Building, the Empire State Building, and Rockefeller Center, the colorful hotels of Miami's South Beach, and the elegant interiors of theaters and train stations in many major cities.

Early modernists like Austrian émigré Paul Frankl (1887–1958) introduced a new look in furniture. At Cranbrook Academy in Bloomfield Hills, Michigan, Finnish-born Eliel Saarinen (1873–1950) brought his Scandinavian sensibility to the new style, teaching modernist principles to a future generation of young American-born designers. And encouraged by manufacturers seeking to repackage their products with more consumer appeal, early industrial designers like Donald Deskey (1894–1989), Raymond Loewy (1893–1986), and Norman Bel Geddes (1893–1958) created designs in the modern vernacular that could be identified as uniquely American. Their accomplishments were considerable in helping to stimulate sales of consumer products during the Depression years and, more important, introducing new forms and new industrial materials like plastic laminate and tubular metal in mass-produced decorative objects and furniture. The New York World's Fair in 1939 was the last real showcase for Art Deco, as an excess of poorly conceived and tasteless objects brought it into decline. The same event, however, saw the first stirrings of a fresh new direction—one that would develop fully after the interruption of World War II.

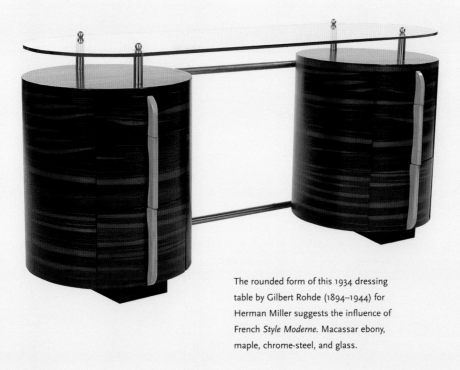

The rounded form of this 1934 dressing table by Gilbert Rohde (1894–1944) for Herman Miller suggests the influence of French *Style Moderne*. Macassar ebony, maple, chrome-steel, and glass.

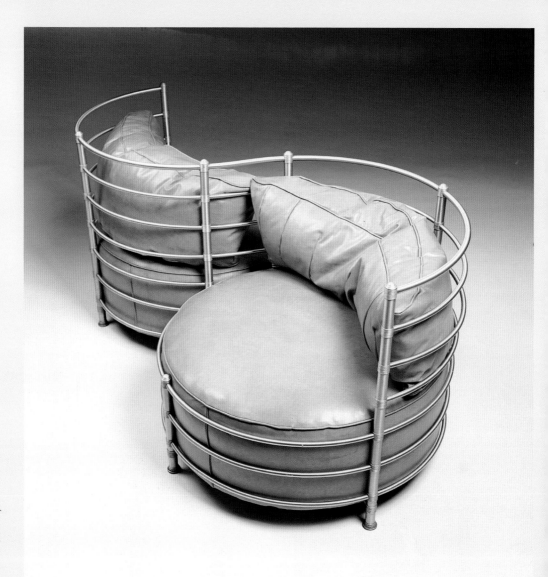

Brushed tubular aluminum forms a modern
"tête-à-tête" by designer Warren McArthur
(1885–1961), designed in 1932.

Sharp angles and an assertive color scheme mark this custom screen by early industrial designer Donald Deskey, who also designed interiors and furniture.

Among the first American-made designs in a new modern style were a series of ziggurat-shaped desks and storage pieces by Austrian-born Paul Frankl, which he called "Skyscraper" furniture. This mahogany bookcase is from 1928.

ABOUT THE PERIOD

America was the last of the major Western countries to embrace modernism, although American designers had long been aware of the developments in Europe, largely through translations of German design publications. When it first emerged in the 1930s, modernism in America formed a battleground between opposing camps: on the one hand the Bauhaus expatriates and those with architectural leanings, who favored spare, functional design; on the other, a tradition-minded public and followers of the French approach, for whom aesthetics were the priority and functionalism too austere and dehumanized. The conflict for dominance of the new market came to an abrupt conclusion with the outbreak of World War II.

As the war ended, a second wave of Modern design swept across America. Now known as Midcentury Modern, it was a homegrown style, enabled by new petroleum-based plastics, foam and fiberglass, and technologies developed for wartime. Spearheaded by the innovations of Charles (1907–1978) and Ray (1912–1988) Eames, Eero Saarinen (1873–1950), and George Nelson (1908–1986), and supported by the Museum of Modern Art and the media, it was embraced by a victory-proud public open to new ideas. It offered the right products, at the right time, at the right price. It was also the first original American style.

The period also brought new kinds of living space: high-rise urban apartment houses in the cities and Ranch House-style residences in the suburban developments that sprang up to fill the need for housing in an exploding postwar economy. In these homes, a new generation of young families lived a casual lifestyle that precipitated changes in both the look and layout of interiors.

Parallel to the evolving design climate was a sharper definition between the roles of furniture and product designers, and those who created interiors. Interior design matured from its origins with Elsie de Wolfe (1865–1950) at the turn of the twentieth century into a serious and financially significant profession that mirrored the explosive growth of the American furniture industry.

Midcentury Modern coexisted with more historicist-based styles, and is contemporaneous with the International Style in interiors. Despite its originality, it did not become dominant in America; though, a half-century later, it has enjoyed a major revival in the early years of the twenty-first century.

ABOUT THE STYLE

Midcentury Modern interiors are bright, inviting, and refreshingly unpretentious. Reflecting the happy optimism of the postwar era in America, they are casual, comfortable, and generally reflect the easy-to-live-with air that suits a space designed for family living and informal entertaining.

The flowing, open plan, first conceived by Frank Lloyd Wright and brought to its full flowering by Marcel Breuer and Ludwig Mies van der Rohe, is a hallmark of a Midcentury Modern interior, as in those of the International Style. The basic enclosure is a simple, rectilinear shell, easy to erect and generally painted white, though possibly accented with warm-tone wood paneling. Decorative moldings have been eliminated as a relic of the pre-modern era. Wall screens or wall sections define living areas without entirely separating them, retaining a feeling of continuity from one room to another and adding a feeling of spaciousness, even in homes of modest size. In these easy-living, casual homes, privacy, save for bedroom and bath, is not as critical as "togetherness," and the boundaries between inside and out are erased by sliding glass doors, floor-to-ceiling windows, and the use of natural colors and materials that link interior spaces with those beyond. (A similar type of indoor-outdoor residence had been pioneered by Schindler and Neutra in California two decades earlier.)

The kitchen seen via a pass-through into the dining and living areas, is now the highly visible center of home life. It is outfitted with the newest labor-saving modern appliances, products of the postwar boom in consumer-product manufacturing.

Wall-to-wall carpeting is almost ubiquitous, though in warmer climates natural wood, stone, or linoleum might provide a similar effect of continuity. Furniture is removed from the perimeter of a room and set in free-floating, asymmetrical arrangements. It might also be grouped around colorful "area rugs" that offer a versatile alternative to carpeting, or may be placed over it.

Window treatments follow the clean-lined look of the space, with hanging, floor-to-ceiling draperies pulling back to reveal simple sheer curtains or shades. Colors are lively and clear, and patterns are relatively simple, with abstract geometrics or other stylized motifs rather than representational ones. Textured woven blinds, printed velvets and linens, and nubby natural-fiber upholstery provides contrast to avoid the monotony of surfaces without architectural accents.

Concealed lighting, or light-scaled fixtures that might include skinny floor-to-ceiling pole lamps or textured ceramic ones, provide illumination. Decorative accents include colorful pottery, wall hangings, or lively abstract paintings or graphics.

The spare modern furniture in these interiors has abandoned all traces of traditionalism in favor of new forms and modern materials. "Good Design" is the mantra proposed by the Museum of Modern Art: it must utilize new materials and technology, serve a practical need, avoid unnecessary ornament, and be affordable to the average consumer. The scale of the furniture is relatively modest, in keeping with the size of most contemporary rooms.

Armless sofas and sectional upholstered pieces are the centerpieces of the furniture arrangement in the living area, offering many options for rearrangeable seating. Modularity is a new idea in case pieces as well, making it possible to create different arrangements from a limited number of individual units. Cabinetry emphasizes function over decorative effect—silhouettes are linear, laminates fashionable, metal an acceptable alternative to wood, and carving or decorative hardware studiously avoided. Flexible built-ins, open shelving, and pieces like folding tables, serving carts, and others that fill multiple functions are increasingly popular. During this period, a parallel strain of biomorphic design offers organic shapes in seating and accent furniture to relieve the sameness of too many straight-lined objects.

Midcentury Modern chairs are refreshingly varied and designed in accordance with anthropomorphic research on human proportions and comfort. Dozens of imaginative and now-iconic furniture designs have been conceived in this period by America's first generation of homegrown talent and produced by forward-thinking companies—most notably the venerable Herman Miller and the brand-new Knoll, both committed to producing furniture in the Modern style.

OPPOSITE: The airy interiors of this 1958 Beverly Hills residence, by Smith and Williams Architects, bears the hallmarks of Midcentury Modern, with slim-lined furniture, a neutral color scheme, and an open-plan design that merges inside and out.

RIGHT: This slim-legged 1958 design by Norman Cherner (1920–) reworks the earlier "Pretzel" chair by John Pile of the George Nelson office. Laminated plywood in varying thicknesses.

BELOW: At home in the Midcentury Modern living room or office—a "thin edge" cabinet of rosewood with metal legs by George Nelson for Herman Miller, 1955.

The ESU (Eames Storage Unit) 400, a versatile
design for flexible room-divider storage elements in
varying colors and configurations, designed ca. 1950
by Charles and Ray Eames for Knoll. Laminated
plywood or masonite, zinc, and aluminum.

Molded rosewood forms the shell of this lounge chair, with leather upholstery and a brushed aluminum swivel base. By Charles and Ray Eames for Knoll, 1957.

The LCM (Lounge Chair, Metal) by Charles and Ray Eames, whose innovative "potato chip" form for Knoll dates to 1946. Black aniline-dyed laminated plywood, tubular steel, and "slunkskin" upholstery.

The pedestal-base chair followed the cantilever in pro-
viding an alternative to four-legged seating pieces.
Eero Saarinen's "Tulip" was designed for Knoll in 1957.
Molded plastic with cast aluminum and painted base.

Using plastic-coated welded steel rods, sculptor
Harry (Arieto) Bertoia (1915–1978) designed a
collection of furniture for Knoll in 1952 based on
a wire grid. the "bird" chair and ottoman.

One of the organic designs that counter-
pointed straight-lined modernism, the
118-inch-long "cloud form" sofa by
Isamu Noguchi (1904–1988), designed
in 1948 for Herman Miller.

notes on the defining characteristics

MOOD easy living	**FURNITURE** light-scaled, machine-made forms
SCALE low and lean	**TEXTILES** perky prints, casual textures
COLORS lively	**KEY MOTIFS** small geometrics, atom and amoebic forms
ORNAMENT as little as possible	**LOOK FOR** Eames and Saarinen chairs, rooms that look easy to live in

sample color palette and fabric swatch

This small-scale geometric print by Ray Eames has a lively look that suits Midcentury Modern interiors.

Notwithstanding the enthusiastic reception awarded Midcentury Modernism, a concurrent strain of design refused to abandon its traditional heritage. In the heyday of America's first modern design, historicists like Edward Wormley (1907–1995) and T. H. Robsjohn-Gibbings (1905–1976) designed furniture that, while unquestionably of the twentieth century, drew on traditional forms, generally avoided plastics, and emphasized elegant materials and polished finishes over a more industrialized look. Catering to more exotic tastes, other designers produced furniture in lustrous lacquers, with applied ornament, or parchment and other surfaces recalling the luxurious extravagance of French Art Deco design, or movie-star glamour.

The interiors containing this type of furniture did not reprise traditional architectural details, utilizing a straight-lined modern surround and evoking a less severe aesthetic with more intense colors and textured surfaces. Walls might be painted, paneled, upholstered, or papered to create a rich background for the furnishings, and fabrics were likely to be lustrous velvets or silks. These and other "moderate Modernist" interiors were generally described as Contemporary, a word with fewer off-putting connotations than the more extreme-sounding Modern.

The strain of historicism has been constant, informing the work of interior designers from Dorothy Draper (1889–1969), and Billy Baldwin (1903–1984), to Angelo Donghia (1935–85), Mark Hampton (1940–1998), and many others, and seems likely to persist well into the twenty-first.

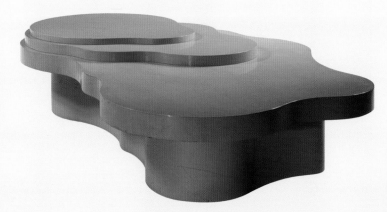

The "Mesa" coffee table, with an amoeba-like silhouette, was designed ca. 1950 by T. H. Robsjohn-Gibbings (1905–1976) for Widdicomb Furniture. Laminated birch with maple finish.

Swept-back legs and a boldly
curved back in an armchair
by Edward Wormley, 1954.
Mahogany and cane.

Shapely ca. 1950s lounge chair by
Vladimir Kagan (1927–). Walnut
and wool upholstery.

Harvey Probber (1922–2003)
combined clean modern lines
with luxurious finish in this
mahogany and walnut sideboard
from the 1950s.

The Studio Craft movement, although tracing its origins as far back as the 1930s, began to develop in America after the end of World War II. Paralleling the growth of midcentury modernism, it was a reaction to the impersonality of production furnishings, initiated by individual artisans creating one-off works in small studios, and developing into the sophisticated and highly professional practice that exists today. Incorporating a wide variety of skills and combining elements of crafts and vernacular design, handmade furniture and decorative objects have become an important subset of contemporary design, though remaining independent of any classification by style.

Some practitioners have adopted the philosophy of Arts and Crafts, and many draw inspiration from historic designs. Most often, however, they have pursued a gentler aesthetic than Bauhaus-inspired formalism and linearity—in works that emphasize hand-finishing, sculptural forms, and touchable materials similar to that seen in Scandinavian furniture.

After pioneers like Wharton Esherick (1887–1970) and George Nakashima (1905–1990) broke the first ground, an increasing number of young artists found creative expression in making furniture by hand. Centers for training woodworkers, like those begun by Danish-born Tage Frid (1915–2004) at Alfred University, and the Rhode Island School of Design, helped to encourage greater professionalism in the field. Specialized schools and departments in various parts of the country have brought master craftsmen to teach traditional skills that had been largely forgotten in the pursuit of industrialization. Through associations, craft shows, and galleries, the work of artisans in wood, fabric, metal, ceramics, and glass has gained prestige, often commensurate with that given to painting and sculpture.

By the latter part of the twentieth century, studio crafts were no longer a movement, but an established sector of design, and entered a new phase that began to blur the line between craft and art. Contemporary craft artists feel free to experiment with new forms, creating objects for which function is not only secondary, but often irrelevant.

Although there are many collectors of handcrafted furniture, or Art Furniture, as it is frequently called, these objects appear most often in contemporary interiors, where they coexist with machine-produced objects, and provide the contrast of emotion-generating design to counterbalance the impersonality of functionalism.

An interior designed around Art Furniture has the characteristics of any modern one, save for treating its objects with the reverence awarded fine art. The furniture itself might take varied forms; rectilinear, abstract, biomorphic, or occasionally anthropomorphic. It may be alternatingly practical, sculptural, or humorous, and its production may rely entirely on handicraftsmanship, or take advantage of modern technology in laminating or finishing details. Traditionally wood is the material of choice, though artisans have explored new ways of using metal, and even plastics, in their search for new forms of expression. Both timely and timeless, handmade furnishings can bridge the past to the future in design.

Sam Maloof (1916–) is one of the best-known contemporary furniture craftsmen. This armchair was designed in the 1960s, though he continues to make them. Black walnut with sculpted seat and back.

 modern made by hand

The pioneering work of Wharton
Esherick (1887–1970) helped spark
the revival of interest in handcrafted
furniture. He made this walnut and
cherry music stand in 1952.

A "conoid" bench, ca. 1960, one variation
of the classic seating for which George
Nakashima (1905–1990) became celebrated.
Walnut and hickory.

The "Minguren II" coffee table whose
form retains elements of the log from
which it was formed—typifying designs
by Nakashima.

ABOUT THE PERIOD

In the years just after World War II, when the steel-and-glass design vocabulary of the International Style was making its mark, an alternative, humanistic approach to Modernism was emanating from the group of countries just north of the European continent. The style they created came to be known as Scandinavian, after the peninsula that incorporates Norway, Sweden, and the islands of Denmark—something of a misnomer, since the Nordic nations also include Finland and Iceland.

Until early in the twentieth century, Scandinavian styles reflected those of its European neighbors, but as the last of these countries achieved independence (Norway in 1905, Finland in 1918, Iceland in 1944), they developed individual approaches to design but with shared ideals and a common aesthetic. Beginning as early as the 1930s, Alvar Aalto (1898–1976) in Finland and Bruno Mathsson (1907–1988) in Sweden, and later others like Hans Wegner (1914–) and Finn Juhl (1912–1989) in Denmark, were basing their designs for interiors and furniture on a love of natural materials, a respect for handicraft, and a long tradition of cabinetmaking skills.

In the Nordic countries, good design was considered a democratic right rather than an elitist privilege, following the much-quoted manifesto of Swedish critic Gregor Pahlsson: "More beautiful things for everyday use." They pursued the goal of socially responsible design, focusing on human needs as much as, and often more than, aesthetics. The resulting objects, and the interiors that surrounded them, offered a less radical and more accessible option for those put off by severe, European-born Modernism.

Through exhibitions at international fairs including those in Paris in 1925, New York in 1939, and the *Triennale* events in Milan in the 1950s, Scandinavian design— first Swedish glass, then Swedish Modern, and later Danish Modern furnishings— became an international success, and built an important export industry for the countries that developed it. Scaled to the modest proportions of most Nordic homes, Scandinavian furniture was well suited to the apartments and suburban ranch homes of post-World War II America, which became one of its most enthusiastic markets.

After almost a century of uneasy coexistence between handmade and machine production, the Nordic designers had achieved a happy compromise, making some pieces in small craft workshops and others in medium-size factories, but even the latter retained the not-too-slick look of handcrafted objects.

In the 1960s Nordic designers like Eero Aarnio (1932–) and Verner Panton (1926–1998) broke with tradition, introducing modern materials in molded forms and vivid colors, but their forward-thinking concepts ran counter to the conservative approach of most Nordic design. Two decades after Scandinavian style's explosive success, the focus on timelessness rather than fashion contributed to its decline and it was eclipsed by a wave of design innovation from Italy.

In the final decades of the twentieth century, Swedish home-furnishings giant IKEA's translations of Scandinavian style into inexpensive, cash-and-carry products for the mass market helped to initiate a revival of interest in the genre.

ABOUT THE STYLE

The Scandinavian-style interior does not seem to be designed but to have evolved naturally over the course of time and comfortable use. In these countries with a dislike of ostentation, even the most impressive space is rarely grand in scale but has a feeling of airy openness that makes it seem larger. Reflecting the Nordic love of nature and the strains of living in a harsh climate with relatively short summers, Scandinavian interiors are characteristically planned to bring the outdoors in, using mostly natural materials and maximizing access to natural light.

The interior architecture is simple, as in all Modernist interiors, without the cornices, moldings, or ornamental details of traditional styles. Walls, if not white, might be paneled in light wood, punctuated by expanses of windows that admit both light and the landscape.

Floors are generally of light wood, laid in vertical strips rather than decorative parquet. Over them wool rugs, hand-woven (or seeming so) are either folk-patterned flat weaves or shaggy ryas—originating in Finland, the rya rug, now made by machine, has become ubiquitous in the Scandinavian design vocabulary.

In place of heavy draperies, window treatments are airy curtains, shades, or wood blinds. Upholstery fabrics, more often plain than patterned, tend to be simple basket-weaves, tweedy textures, or natural leather.

A wood-burning fireplace is a likely feature of the Scandinavian interior—built into the wall, a traditional freestanding version in ceramic tile, or a modern shape of bright, enameled metal.

Nordic color schemes favor clear, natural hues—the blues of sky and water, the greens of foliage, the yellows of sunshine, combined with a variety of warm beiges and earth tones.

Supplementing the natural light are ceramic lamps and clean-lined lighting fixtures, adding decorative but unpretentious accents in keeping with the spare simplicity of the style. Beyond these, accessories may include ceramic bowls and vases, sculptural modern silver, and hand-blown glass—just enough to make the room look comfortable but uncluttered. Plants and flowers are reminders of nature.

In the design of Scandinavian furniture, comfort and function are more critical concerns than current fashion, and designers tend to focus on perfecting classics rather than on innovations. A number of these classics, however, have become familiar, and iconic, objects. Scandinavian-style chairs are generally straight-lined and designed to accommodate the body, often with woven rather than upholstered seats and shapely sculptural backs that add decorative interest as well as support. Sofas are linear rather than overstuffed, with squared-off or tight cushions.

Storage chests and cabinets are rectangular forms, on straight legs that maximize the look of slenderness rather than bulk. In their simplicity of line, details like the dovetail joints and tambour doors become subtle decorative accents. The wall system, a clever new concept of wall-mounted shelves and cabinetry, is flexible, functional, and space-efficient. Light woods such as native ash, beech and birch, or richly grained imported rosewood and teak, all with natural matte or oiled finishes, are decorated only by simple knobs or recessed pulls. Carving or other ornament is not so much rejected as it is deemed unnecessary.

PREVIOUS PAGE: This light-filled interior in the Villa Mairea in Finland, by Alvar Aalto, uses natural materials to create an airy, open space with the unpretentious look that characterizes Scandinavian style. The neutral palette is brought to life with contrasts of tone and texture, and the color complement of greenery.

BELOW: A simple sideboard of rosewood, birch, and painted wood, made ca. 1956 by Arne Vodder (1924–).

Bruno Mathsson of Sweden designed this practical folding dining table, a modern adaptation of the traditional gate-leg, ca. 1960.

This 1947 armchair by Danish designer Hans Wegner is known simply as "The Chair" and has become one of the iconic images of Nordic furniture. Teak and cane.

The "chieftain" armchair, based on ancient Egyptian forms, is a sculptured shape of teak and leather by Danish designer Finn Juhl, and made by master cabinetmaker Niels Vodder (1892–1982) in 1949.

The "egg" chair and ottoman was a
bold departure from understated Scandinavian style, when Danish architect
Arne Jacobsen (1902–1971) designed it
in 1957. Upholstery and foam over fiberglass shell, with aluminum swivel base.

RIGHT: The "artichoke" lamp by Danish designer Poul Henningsen (1894–1967) has been in continuous production since its introduction in 1957 by Louis Poulsen & Co. Copper and steel.

BELOW: This tea trolley, ca. 1936, is one of a series of designs in molded, laminated birch plywood designed by Finnish architect Alvar Aalto, the first internationally-known Nordic designer.

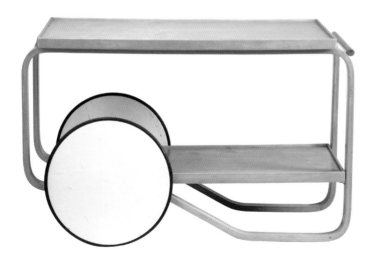

Austrian-born Josef Frank (1885–1967)
designed elegant furniture and textiles
for Swedish firm Svenskt Tenn. This
walnut and glass vitrine-on-stand was
designed in 1946.

notes on the defining characteristics

MOOD calm	**FURNITURE** clean-lined forms, oil-finished teak, rosewood, birch, or ash
SCALE modest	**TEXTILES** hand-woven fabrics, shaggy *rya* rugs
COLORS mostly natural	**KEY MOTIFS** plants, anything natural
ORNAMENT simple	**LOOK FOR** modern with a soft edge

sample color palette and fabric swatch

A lively blue-and-white floral in a classic Swedish cotton print by designer Josef Frank for Svensk Tenn.

sixties

ABOUT THE PERIOD

Spearheaded by a revolution in popular culture, the "Swinging Sixties" gave birth to a style that, while perhaps not on a par with the great design periods, paints a striking picture of the provocative decade in which it thrived. It was a breakaway look, or series of looks, that rebelled against the constraints of serious-minded Modernism, lacking any specific design aesthetic but with more than its share of visual impact.

The "youthquake" marked the decade dominated by a generation of young consumers who sought to change the world, repudiating the overdone or too-conventional contemporary. They recycled history in their search for the new and unusual, adapting classic geometric forms in bold shapes and patterns that alternated between psychedelic and Op art. These eye-popping colors and swirling shapes, the jarring rhythms of Beatles-generation music, and the extroverted clothing styles of Carnaby Street fashion were all reflected in assertive interiors that sometimes seemed to be laughing at themselves—and at design.

The blurring of class lines through postwar prosperity had also created a new bourgeoisie that rejected the elitist elements of traditional design and embraced the aggressively modern. Led by avant-gardists in London and New York, design of the decade emphasized bold silhouettes and unconventional shapes. Designers experimented with new types of plastic, molding technology, and flexible fabrics. Projects like the 1956 "House of the Future" in London, and one of the same name in America the following year, proposed biomorphic shapes and space-age inspiration for forward-thinking design, most of which proved more eye-catching than livable.

The diversity of Sixties style is seen in its other directions: the formal interiors of Englishman David Hicks (1928–1998), who created opulent effects with bold geometric patterns, and the unabashed ostentation of Hollywood-style rooms by California designers like William Haines (1900–1973).

The Sixties was an erratic but intriguing time, though one doomed to rapid obsolescence. As the decade waned, design took another turn, pursuing a more rational and less disjointed but in many ways far less entertaining, direction.

ABOUT THE STYLE

The Sixties interior is lively, bold, colorful, and, perhaps, in today's eyes, excessive in its extroverted lack of inhibitions. As overdone in its way as the periods of the eighteenth-century French kings, its object is to create an impression, not with costliness, but with sheer flamboyance.

The basic framework of the twentieth-century interior—rectilinear, flat-ceilinged, free of architectural details—provides a background for furnishings in brilliant, intense, and often clashing colors. The walls might be painted white, but are likelier to show off more intense, undiluted hues. Wall-covering made with silvery (or gold-tone) Mylar might be patterned in Op-art geometrics, and curtains or upholstery fabrics may use similar designs, though not generally mixing the two in a single room. Occasionally, three-dimensional wall treatments are assembled by large, tile-like sections of molded plastic, stamped out or injection-molded in brilliant-colored, shiny modules.

Silver or gold-tone threads might be woven into tweedy textured fabric upholstery on modular seating. Or psychedelic colors printed in surreal swirls and coils on new stretch fabrics are wrapped around freeform chairs and loveseats to emphasize their sinuous forms.

As in the preceding period, floors are covered with wall-to-wall carpet or smooth-surface vinyl, generally without pattern, but often accented with colorful area rugs.

The earth tones predominating throughout the previous decade have been abandoned in favor of undiluted bright shades—bubble-gum pink, zingy turquoise, and teal, paintbox hues that are likely to be the dominant element in the interiors.

Lighting is likely to emanate from decorative table lamps or standing fixtures. In a decade defined by the Space Age, atomic and rocket motifs are frequent inspiration for designs on wall-coverings, fabrics, and laminate surfaces, and these themes often inspire accessories as well. Often witty, but sometimes crossing over into kitsch such as the mesmerizing multicolored lava lamp or multicolored plastic-bead curtains used as room dividers, they are congenial accents for the Sixties interior.

sixties

Sixties furniture can look like anything ever seen, or never seen, at any other time. The geometric forms of Aarnio or Panton, or the sensual, ribbonlike silhouettes designed by Pierre Paulin (1927–) and Olivier Morgue (1939–) revolutionize the concept of how a chair may look and the materials of which it should be made. The Lucite chairs introduced a decade earlier by Estelle (1915–1998) and Erwine (1909–) Laverne have inspired many variations in see-through seating. This furniture that suggests biomorphic forms like eggs, tree-trunks, clouds, or amoeba shapes are comfortable, but may exist in uneasy combination with more conventional silhouettes.

Seating "landscapes"—vari-shaped and -sized elements of fabric-wrapped molded foam that could be installed on several levels—expanded the concept of sectional seating, and provided many new ways to arrange and rearrange the living room. It is a practical solution to the need for flexible furnishings in an increasingly mobile, transient society. The often-impractical "conversation pit" is a variant of this idea.

Chests and tables, though limited to a more conventional range of geometric silhouettes, continue to explore the possibilities of plastic surfacing.

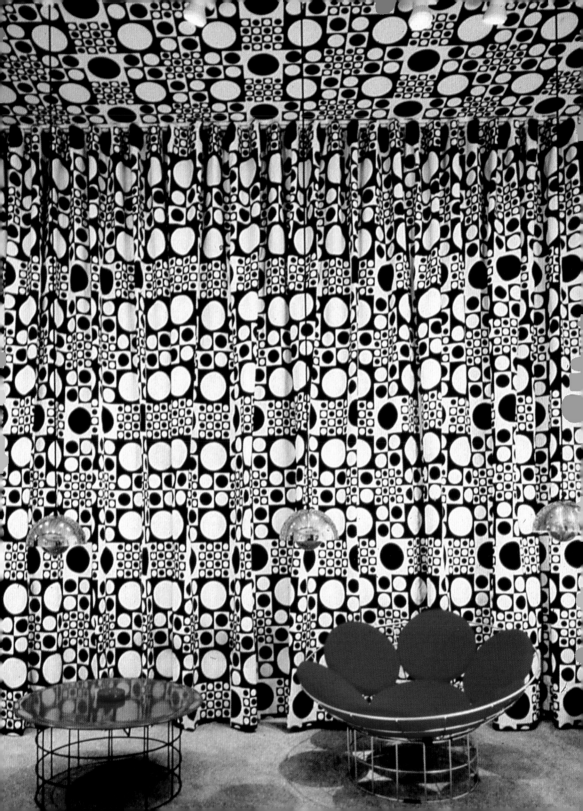

PREVIOUS PAGE: Enclosed in Op-art fabric and furnished with his whimsical wire-base seating, this
recreation of an interior by Verner Panton has the exuberance that recalls the best of 1960s style.

BELOW: Space-age seating form known as the "ball"
chair, ca. 1968, by Finnish designer Eero Aarnio.
Molded fiberglass with enameled aluminum base
and upholstered foam interior.

RIGHT: One of the "fun" series of lighting fixtures by Danish designer Verner Panton, this rare version was made in 1964 of aluminum disks.

BELOW: The 1968 "Djinn" chaise by French designer Olivier Morgue (1939–) for Airborne is a wiggle of stretch fabric over a serpentine steel frame.

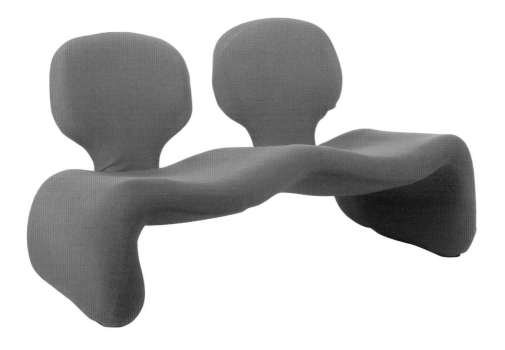

The "invisible chairs" by Estelle (1915–1997)
and Erwine (1909–2003) Laverne from 1957
were an experiment in molding see-through
Perspex plastic into a series of seating pieces.

notes on the defining characteristics

MOOD upbeat	**FURNITURE** biomorphic forms, Lucite and molded plastics
SCALE irrelevant	**TEXTILES** clashing colors, zingy patterns
COLORS bright, saturated	**KEY MOTIFS** Op, Pop, Space-Age symbols
ORNAMENT surreal and punchy	**LOOK FOR** rooms that scream for attention

sample color palette and fabric swatch

Andy Warhol flower paintings inspired the design of this extroverted area rug made by Edward Fields in the 1960s.

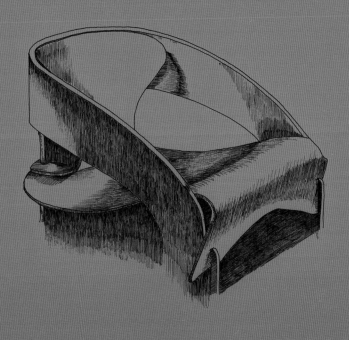

ABOUT THE PERIOD

Almost simultaneous with, and continuing after, the popularity of Scandinavian modern design, Italian Style was born in the years after World War II and became an international phenomenon in the 1970s. Its seeds were cultivated by the forward-thinking ideas of Gio Ponti (1891–1979), architect and designer whose influence was most widespread in his role as founder (1928) and longtime editor of the design magazine *Domus*, and a leading force in the establishment of the *Triennale* exhibitions in Milan. Begun in 1923 to help encourage the relationship between industry and the applied arts, the *Triennales* became the world's premier venue for innovative design and decorative arts.

The war had devastated much of Italy's industry. Seeking to rebuild both its shattered economy and the country's international image, Italian designers were brilliantly creative, making the most of minimal resources to explore new horizons in design. The results—witty and ingenious applications of plastics, metal, and experimental production methods, occasionally mixing in bits of social commentary—were a wake-up call to Modernism. They dramatically shifted the balance of power and influenced the course of twentieth-century design, particularly in furniture and lighting.

In the 1960s, Italian groups like Archizoom and Superstudio developed an approach to design that focused on the use of technology. Others followed their lead, formulating a new vocabulary that could be categorized only in terms of its diversity. Abandoning the idea that function must determine form, Italian design made form primary, teasing history with rational and irrational applications that challenged the meaning and concept of furniture. Such wide-ranging talents as Joe Colombo (1930–1971), Gae Aulenti (1927–), Marco Zanuso (1916–2001), Gaetano Pesce (1939–), and many others, have designed furniture that might stack or fold, expand or collapse; be molded of plastic or blown up like balloons; be straight-lined, overstuffed, or of indescribable shape.

Along with their contributions to interior and industrial design, Italian designers' innovative lighting virtually revolutionized a dormant field and represents perhaps their most groundbreaking achievement. Employing new technology that minimized bulb size and maximized illumination, designers like Achille Castiglione (1918–2002) devised lighting fixtures that not only were the first real complements to modern furniture, but also treated lighting as decorative objects rather than functional afterthoughts in interior decoration, pointing a new course for the future of lighting design.

Exhibited at the *Triennale* events and widely celebrated in the press, the work of Italian designers catapulted the country to a position of leadership and style innovation, rapidly eclipsing the dominance of Scandinavian Style and elbowing aside the avant-garde credentials of the Bauhaus aesthetic. In a now-historic 1972 exhibition, *Italy: The New Domestic Landscape*, New York's Museum of Modern Art placed its imprimatur on Italian design as the newest fashion and the wave of the future.

Starting even before the flourishing of Italian style in interiors and furnishings, the makers of Italian glass initiated their own renaissance, devising proprietary techniques for glassblowing and decoration that made their pieces as unique as the furniture and lighting designed by their compatriots.

In its disregard of tradition and concern with visual effect, Italian Modern design laid the groundwork for the movement that would be called Post-Modernism.

ABOUT THE STYLE

One of the most appealing qualities of an interior, or indeed, any object, designed in Italian Style is its refusal to take itself too seriously. Italian design is infused with wit and humor. As extroverted as its citizens, it is informal despite its elegance, colorful despite its understatement, and as likely to generate instant love as immediate dislike. The Italian Modern interior can be uncomfortable to inhabit, since its intent is to strike the eye more than to ease it.

The interior itself is not so much a designed space as it is a setting for the presentation of the objects that are the critical components of Italian Style. White walls are the most likely background, and the floors are bare, natural-tone wood. What matters most are the furnishings, set around the room with a casualness that belies the care that has been given to their selection.

What its objects lack in hand-crafted detail—and they rarely have any—they more than make up in panache. Stack-up seats and tables of bright molded plastic, a leather lounge shaped like a baseball glove, a compressed-foam chair that expands when unpacked, and other forms like nothing ever previously attempted, provide a repertoire of ideas to furnish an interior with style that clearly relates to its particular time and place.

Colors are vivid and applied with abandon to any surface. Patterns, if any, are equally aggressive, and are more likely to be drawn from Pop art or the designer's imagination than from any definable source.

Furniture by the Italian modernists is more likely to be made of plastic than any other material, though much of the upholstery is leather. Tables and storage pieces are crisply outlined with geometric precision, or shaped with injection-molding techniques from primary-hued plastic. Considering the space limitations of postwar housing, the majority of pieces are relatively modest in scale; the primary exception being sofas, which plumb the possibilities of modularity and flexibility with oversize elements, sometimes sinuous and sometimes square, that combine into an inviting everyone-sit-together seating group set in the center of the room.

Lighting, rather than accessories, is probably the most distinctive finishing touch—standing lamps or torchères in pencil-slim shapes, organic of handblown glass, snakelike coils of plastic, tiny bulbs strung on wires—contribute to the drama, and the personality, of the space.

PREVIOUS PAGE: In this 1970 interior by Joe (Cesare) Colombo (1930–1971), extroverted colors and whimsical furniture show the wit and originality that brought Italian design to international fame.

RIGHT: Monumental 79-inch-long cabinet by Gio Ponti, 1951. Italian walnut, with open upper display unit above a solid plinth base on tapered legs.

Brothers Achille Castiglioni (1918–2002) and Pier Giacomo Castiglioni (1913–1966) transformed an ordinary tractor seat into a provocative modern stool in 1957. In 1971, it was produced by Zanotta. Steel and beech.

The "Bocca" sofa (in America it's called "Marilyn,"
for Marilyn Monroe) by Studio 65 for Gufram, 1971.
Stretch upholstery over polyurethane foam.

Adjustability is a major attraction of this
articulated chaise longue designed by
Osvaldo Borsani (1911–1985) for Tecno, 1955.
Enameled steel, foam, and upholstery.

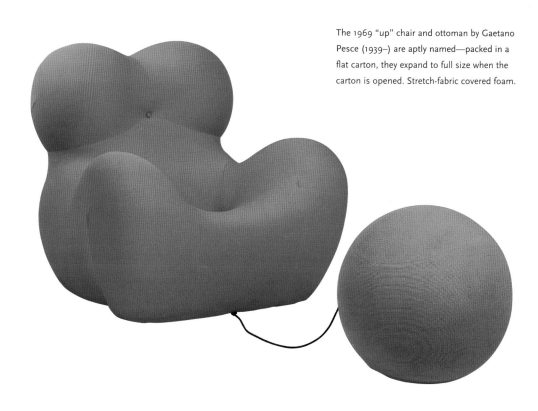

The 1969 "up" chair and ottoman by Gaetano Pesce (1939–) are aptly named—packed in a flat carton, they expand to full size when the carton is opened. Stretch-fabric covered foam.

The "Malitte" seating system designed in
1966 by artist Roberto Matta (1911–2002)
stacks several shapely units into a 64-inch
square. Polyurethane foam and stretch wool
upholstery with internal wood supports.

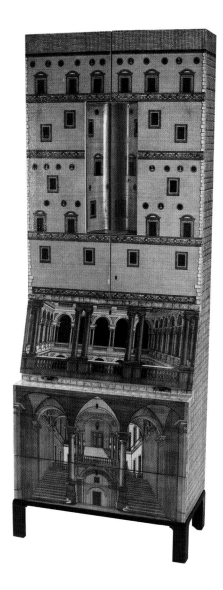

In the "Architettura" secretary, Piero Fornasetti (1913–1988) applied a witty mix of architectural motifs to a Gio Ponti form, 1951. Handpainted and lithographed wood.

One of the new generation of modern Italian designs in lighting, the three-arm Arredoluce "Triennale" floor lamp was introduced in the 1950s and became a classic.

notes on the defining characteristics

MOOD serious fun	**FURNITURE** adventurous shapes, adventurous materials
SCALE not relevant	**TEXTILES** bold
COLORS lively, intense	**KEY MOTIFS** linear forms, sleek abstracts
ORNAMENT minimal	**LOOK FOR** furniture with flair, lighting as art form

sample color palette and fabric swatch

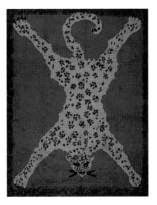

The vivid colors of the ca. 1970 "Tapipardo" wool rug, and its witty leopard-skin graphic, are congenial complements to an Italian modern interior.

post-modernism

ABOUT THE PERIOD

The term Post-Modern, like Modern, is a confusing one. It refers to a series of late-twentieth-century philosophical concepts reflected in many disciplines, including literature, poetry, and sociology as well as the visual arts. In design, however, it labels a specific movement that erupted as a response to International Style modernism. The fragmented movement evolved from ideas articulated by Robert Venturi in the 1966 book *Complexity and Contradiction in Architecture*, which found the designs of the International Style to be sterile and austere: in response to Mies van der Rohe's often-quoted "Less is more," he countered "Less is a bore."

Post-Modernism challenged the single-minded Bauhaus rejection of historicism, suggesting that modern architecture would regain emotional content by using classical elements that linked past and present. In his 1972 book *Learning from Las Vegas,* Venturi proposed that vernacular materials and forms give meaning to architecture, and that design could sometimes have no deeper purpose than simply to attract or amuse. The Post-Modernists rethought and restyled columns, pilasters, and pediments, applying them with wit, whimsy, and sometimes no reason whatever to both interiors and exteriors, though Post-Modernism made its strongest statements in architecture.

Foreshadowed by the antiestablishment thinking of earlier Italian radicals, Post-Modernism was influenced by Pop art, Dada, and hippie culture as well as classical design. In resisting accepted ways of thinking about and practicing design, it produced provocative and sometimes bizarre results: in seeking to join high art with popular culture, it is often translated into mass-market kitsch. But its challenge to the wholesale rejection of the past in the search for a meaningful design for the present was a valuable wake-up call, and its use of humor and exaggeration was a valuable reminder not to take design too seriously.

In its wake, interiors toward the end of the twentieth century took on a new eclecticism. Minimalism is the most direct response to postmodern excess, but along with the move to stripped-down modernism are a counterbalancing revival of traditional design, and a shift to greater eclecticism that favors combining classic and avant-garde furnishings in the same interior.

ABOUT THE STYLE

The Post-Modern interior is a striking environment and a clearly contemporary one. Its use of familiar classical motifs may seem almost a caricature, since it makes no pretense of authenticity, but it is intended as homage to the timeless meaning of the past. A large-scale space, it employs a wealth of architectural detail, stripped down and stylized for a strictly nontraditional look. Walls may be defined with columns, arches, alcoves, and exaggerated moldings, used to sculpt the space or simply to avoid the linearity of steel-frame construction. Palladian elements such as arches and pediments enhance windows and doorways. Its lively colors and provocative furnishings are a bold and arresting decorative statement, but more conservative tastes may be drawn for occasional visits rather than long-term occupancy.

So much architectural detail makes additional pattern unnecessary, but the absence of need is beside the point. Though walls are most often painted in solid colors, upholstery and floor coverings are frequently patterned in stylish abstract classical, geometric, or floral motifs.

The colors of Post-Modernism are drawn from color-field paintings and ice-cream vendors: vanilla, apricot, pistachio, black raspberry. Primary hues are discarded in favor of pastels and unexpected contrasts. This distinctive palette, applied to wall surfaces, carpet, and upholstery, adds liveliness that underscores the humor and irony of Post-Modern style, setting it apart from anything that preceded or followed.

Post-Modern furniture is innovative, provocative, and often tongue-in-cheek. Designed more for eye appeal than function, many of the pieces draw on architectural forms, but even more emerged entirely from their designers' imaginations. Italians are the unquestionable stars of the style, from 1976 and Studio Alchimia's experiments with new iconography, to the memorable 1981 debut by the group called Memphis, in which Ettore Sottsass (1917–) and a group of compatriots introduced designs that flew in the face of all established standards of practicality and taste. Their colorful pieces, though obviously modern in their use of metal and plastic, their unconventional shapes and lack of applied ornament, are the antithesis of austere. Zingy laminated surface patterns and bold combinations of colors rather than the more traditional types of furniture ornament, enliven these extroverted pieces.

Though often extreme and, as noted, not always utilitarian, Post-Modern designs have a winning silliness that evokes either of two emotional responses—immediate infatuation or intense dislike. Designers like Michael Graves (1934–), Frank Gehry (1929–), Philippe Starck (1949–), and many others have contributed to the reservoir of Post-Modernism with a cornucopia of design objects that, while uncomfortably competitive en masse, can shine as individual and provocative accents in a contemporary setting.

Postmodern accessories also rely on architecture for both form and decoration, but their smaller size allows for tweaking, reassembling, and improvisation of classical motifs. Colorful glass bowls and vases, striking silver and metal objects, and others in ceramic or lacquered wood, reflect the skewed historicism that informs Post-Modern design. They avoid the criticism of impracticality to which the furniture is subject, and are almost invariably charming.

PREVIOUS PAGE: The ideal Post-Modern interior—an erratic mix of color and pattern furnished a living room for the 1986 comedy film *Ruthless People*.

RIGHT: American architect Robert Venturi (1925–) designed the "Sheraton" side chair in silk-screened, laminated plywood, one of a series of tongue-in-cheek takes on period chairs. For Knoll, 1983.

A provocative form accented with lively color, the "first" chair by Michele De Lucchi (1951–) for Memphis group, 1983. Varnished tubular steel and wood.

RIGHT: "Proust's Armchair," ca. 1978, by Alessandro Mendini (1931–) for Studio Alchimia makes a provocative design statement in handpainted upholstered-and-carved wood.

BELOW: Beginning with "Easy Edges" in 1971, architect Frank Gehry (1930–) experimented with furniture made from layers of laminated corrugated fiberboard. the "little beaver" armchair is from the "Experimental Edges" series, ca. 1980.

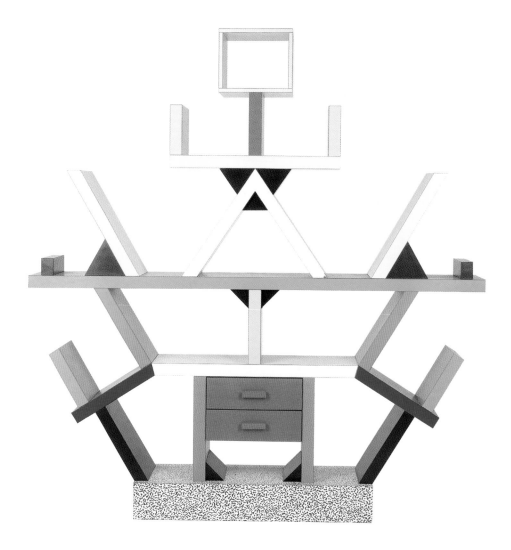

A paradigm of Post-Modern design, this angular "Carlton" bookcase-room divider was designed by Ettore Sottsass for Memphis, 1981. Multicolored plastic laminate.

post-modernism

field notes on defining characteristics

MOOD fun	**FURNITURE** whimsical takes on familiar forms
SCALE relatively large	**TEXTILES** quirky patterns
COLORS lively, clashing pastels	**KEY MOTIFS** columns and pediments
ORNAMENT stripped-down, stylized classical	**LOOK FOR** classical ornament, quirky colors

color palette and fabric

Alessandro Mendini's fragmented pattern of high-density color makes a hand-tufted rug with a Post-Modern air. For Studio Alchimia, ca. 1980.

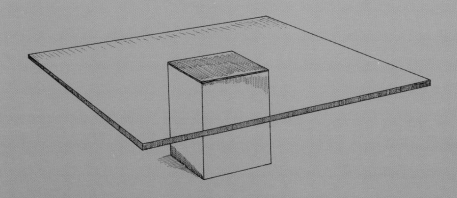

ABOUT THE PERIOD

More elusive to pinpoint than most twentieth century styles, Minimalism grew out of the 1960s art movement exemplified by such practitioners as Donald Judd, Robert Ryman, Dan Flavin, and others whose ascetic, academic approach treated artworks as objects rather than artistic expressions. The experience of art became physical and spatial, rather than emotional.

The theories spawned by Minimalist art crystallized into a design aesthetic that took Mies van der Rohe's "Less is more" to its most literal extreme. Interiors were stripped of nonessentials, creating Spartan spaces furnished with the fewest possible objects. Critics of the style, as well as its supporters, attested to its effectiveness in translating the anomie of modern life.

In the 1970s, the strikingly simple designs of American Ward Bennett (1917–2003), and the industrial-chic of High Tech (from the 1978 book of the same name) were precursors of the style, which became prominent decades later in the work of American Joe D'Urso (1943–) and London architect John Pawson (1949–). Their striking, astringent interiors presented a refreshing, though radical, alternative to the highly decorative interiors popularized by shelter magazines and showhouse presentations.

Minimalism was embraced by the media, but only the most adventurous felt comfortable in its unforgiving starkness. A related approach was taken by Deconstructivist architecture, which assembled structures in irregular and unpredictable configurations that were equally arresting, though often impractical to build.

More intellectual than aesthetic, Minimalism had a limited audience and a relatively short life. It became one of many options in a decade of inclusive design, overshadowed by styles that offered greater creature comforts but retaining a committed constituency of purists.

ABOUT THE STYLE

The Minimalist interior is undeniably striking, though sometimes intimidatingly severe. It evokes a feeling of enveloping space, in surroundings sculpted with geometric precision. It seems, in its utter lack of decoration, to be unplanned, or even unfinished, but the illusion is deceptive. Every element of the composition has been meticulously designed and placed. Minimalism can be viewed as an extension of the International Style, pared down to its barest essentials. More artwork than interior design, it is also more welcoming than it appears, offering a background that invites the occupants as decoration.

Walls are ruler-straight, or sharply angled, and might be simply painted white or finished in high-gloss lacquer, polished steel, or concrete. Though texture may be acceptable, specific pattern is avoided. Ceilings, whether high or low, are without decoration and appear to recede into space.

Expanses of windows are desirable, but only if the landscape is equally pristine. Floors may be smooth concrete, or covered with flat industrial carpeting, sisal, or jute. Other surfaces add subtle contrast—with polished or patinated steel, clear or frosted glass, textured slate, translucent plastic, or lacquered wood.

Lighting is most often concealed, becoming part of the background rather than the furnishings. Except for an object or two designed into the composition, decorative accents are banished, as is anything that might soften the linearity of the composition—no clutter or pattern is permitted to break the mood of the astringent but seductive surround.

Color is studiously avoided: white, black, and grey are the chosen palette, which can be varied with textures, tonalities, and applications of light.

Minimalist furniture fuses into its surroundings, punctuating the space like sculpture. Rectilinear or sharply angular, it is likely to include sectional seating that seems rooted to the floor, glass- or slate-top tables, and low, preferably built-in cabinetry. Horizontal lines are generally emphasized rather than verticals to enhance the feeling of openness.

OPPOSITE: In a New York apartment, a pristine interior of minimalist bent, but maximum finesse, by architect Michael Gabellini (1958–).

RIGHT: An overscaled armchair made of steel mesh, 1986, by Japanese designer Shiro Kuramata (1934–1991) seems to disappear into space.

BELOW: Mirror-polished stainless steel, a hard-edged material, is sculpted into soft-edged form in Israeli designer Ron Arad's (1951–) "big easy" limited-edition chair, 1989, for two.

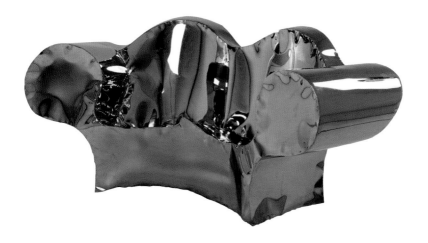

The "Non" chair, 2000, by Komplot Design for Kallemo is almost indestructible and can be used indoors or out. Molded PUR rubber on a steel frame.

Wood furniture at its Minimalist best, this table is by Kevin Walz (1950–) for Ralph Pucci, ca. 2002.

notes on the defining characteristics

MOOD unemotional	**FURNITURE** strictly linear
SCALE can vary	**TEXTILES** flat-pile upholstery, high-tech sheers
COLORS white, black, and grey	**KEY MOTIFS** none
ORNAMENT banished	**LOOK FOR** industrial finishes, Zen like space

sample color palette and fabric swatch

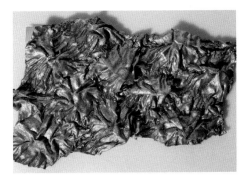

Metal textile by Maya Romanoff (1941–), intriguingly pleated, makes more of the Minimalist interior.

twenty-first century: an overview

MODERNISM STEERED THE STYLE DIRECTION OF THE TWENTIETH CENTURY, but it is too soon to speculate

on what the twenty-first will bring. The landscape of design has been reinvented, once again, by technologi-

cal advances that make the cataclysmic changes wrought by the Industrial Revolution seem tame. ■ Archi-

tecture has brought us organically shaped buildings with wrappings of metal, singular silhouettes that soar

like wings, glass walls with light-emitting diodes, and surfaces of materials harvested from scrap. The work

of Rem Koolhaas (1944–), Frank Gehry (1929–), Santiago Calatrava (1951–), Zaha Hadid (1950–), Jean Nou-

vel (1945–), and others has changed our expectations of how a building may look. ■ There are other con-

siderations: today's most advanced structures embrace issues like ecologically-sensitive sustainable materi-

als and universal design, and deal with solar power, recyclables, and energy-efficiency, considerations some-

times even more important than style. In such projects, the design of interiors is integrated into the broader

picture. ■ The design of furniture is taking directions too diverse to follow, let alone to classify or predict.

Designers are developing new forms from materials that make them possible, or finding new possibilities in

existing materials. New designs experiment with injected polypropylene, laser-cut polystyrene, flexible poly-

carbonate, and injection-molded foam, or alternatively with string, rope, or cutout aluminum. Familiar

objects are transformed, distorted, or reconfigured in abstract forms that cross the line between furniture

and art, sometimes even eschewing function in expressing ideas. Their designs are not always easy to like,

but their energy and vitality provoke interest, and often emotional responses not usually associated with

objects of design. Names of the moment include Ron Arad (1951–), Mark Newson (1963–), the brothers Rowan

(1971–) and Erwan (1976–) Bouroullec, Humberto (1953–) and Fernando (1961–) Campana, and Konstantin Grcic (1965–). ■ New textiles are made with plastics and thermoplastics, metallics, carbon fiber and resin, and fiberoptics that allow them to emit light. And lighting, in a new flourish of creativity, is exploiting the possibilities of miniaturization in sophisticated applications with no resemblance to lamps or chandeliers of a generation past. ■ The other side of the coin is a counter-trend, a return to natural materials: lighting fixtures and fabrics of paper, unfinished wood, or veneers woven into braids or interlocking forms that refer back to those in nature. Recyclable materials are being used for furnishings—such likely ones as bamboo and concrete, and such unlikely ones as seeds, spider webs, and garbage bags. ■ In dealing with a changing environment, the home itself will change. So-called smart houses, with preprogrammed lighting and appliances, are only the beginning: the next steps are furniture that can change size and shape, walls that are transformed with the season or the mood, and other innovations that provide more flexible living spaces. Such changes are not literal elements of style, but will invariably affect the look of future interiors, as information becomes a tool for design. ■ With today's instant communications, design has become increasingly international—cultural barriers have disappeared as designers from countries far removed in geographic space explore similar aesthetics. It is no longer possible, or even desirable, to place national labels on styles of design. The Netherlands, Germany, Japan, England, France, Sweden, and several others are contributing as vitally to the cutting edge of modern design as America and Italy. ■ The landscape of twenty-first century design is as intriguing as in any period in history, though its styles will be possible to define only some decades in the future, with an objectivity gained from the perspective of distance.

styles of the twenty-first century

ABOVE, LEFT: Using an unexpected material, the "knotted chair," more comfortable than it appears, is of twisted carbon fibers, coated with epoxy. By Dutch designer Marcel Wanders (1963–), designed 1995.

ABOVE, RIGHT: Experimenting with surrealist-colored molded urethane, Gaetano Pesce designed the "Pratt" chair series in 1991. Each of the nine models was firmer than the preceding one (No. 3, shown, can support the weight of a child).

RIGHT: Australian designer Mark Newson (1962–) shaped the "embryo" chair in 1988, anticipating the move of modernism in a direction towards biomorphic shapes. Neoprene and tubular steel.

Blurring the barriers between furniture, craft,
and art, "you can't lay down your memories,"
a limited-edition cabinet by Tejo Remy (1960–)
for Dutch collaborative Droog Design (1991),
is assembled from recycled drawers bound
with canvas belting.

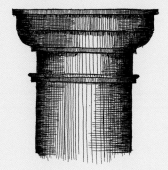

Tuscan

Doric

Ionic

Corinthian

Composite

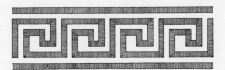

Fretwork/Greek Key

Guilloche

Acanthus

Rosette

Cartouche

Trophy

Gargoyle

Renaissance Panel

Bun foot

Scroll foot

Pad foot

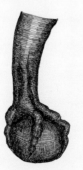

Ball and claw foot

Hairy paw foot

Bracket foot

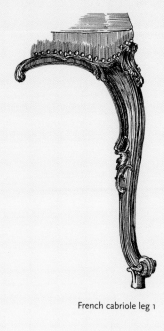

French cabriole leg 1

French cabriole leg 2

French sabot foot

English cabriole leg

Tapered neoclassical leg

Bonnet top

Double-dome top with finials

Broken pediment with center finial

Swan's neck scrolled pediment with pierced carving

glossary

ACAJOU / French term for mahogany.

ACANTHUS / Decorative representation of the leaves of the acanthus plant in classical ornament, especially on the lower part of **Corinthian** and **Composite** capitals.

ANILINE DYE / Chemical dyes made from coal tar derivatives, enabling more varied colorations possible than with only natural dyes.

APRON / The panel, often shaped or carved, running horizontally below the seat of a chair. Also, below the top of a table (connecting with the legs), or beneath the underframing of case pieces.

APPLIQUÉ / An ornament applied to a surface of a different material. Usually associated with textiles, where the design is cut out and sewn or pasted onto another material.

ARABESQUE / A decorative scroll pattern derived from vegetation and arranged into a symmetrical design. Similar to a **grotesque**, but without human or animal motifs.

ARCHITRAVE / The lowest horizontal member of the **entablature**.

ARCUATED / Architectural system based on arches, as differentiated from a columnar or **trabeated** system.

ARM / Elbow and forearm support in seating furniture.

ARMOIRE / A large cupboard or wardrobe, with one or two doors, designed for holding clothes. Originally intended for the storage of armor.

AUBUSSON / Tapestrylike handwoven rugs, without pile, of the type first produced in the workshops founded at Aubusson, France in the fifteenth century.

AXMINSTER / Tightly woven cut-pile carpets first produced in Axminster, England in the eighteenth century, made on special looms to imitate Turkish carpets.

BALL-AND-CLAW FOOT / Believed to be of Chinese origin, a furniture foot imitating a claw grasping a sphere. Most seen in English Georgian and Late American Colonial furniture.

BALLOON BACK / Chair back with the top **rail** and uprights rounded to give an overall balloon shape.

BALUSTER / The upright support in a balustrade; a short, often **turned**, square or circular post or column. Also used for furniture legs or to form part of a chair back. Also called banister.

BANISTER-BACK / Chair back with of a series of vertical **banisters** between the seat and top **rail**.

BANJO CLOCK / American pendulum wall clock with a circular case for the dial, a narrow tapering body, and a boxlike base that resembles a banjo.

BANQUETTE / French term for a small bench, usually upholstered.

BARGELLO / A needlework stitch producing a distinctive zigzag pattern.

BARREL CHAIR / English in origin, an easy chair whose back is completely rounded.

BASE / The moldings at the lowest part if a column, or the lowest supporting element of a piece of furniture.

BASEBOARD / A board or molding placed at the base of the wall and resting on the floor.

BAY / A unit of space designated by architectural elements such as columns, piers, and walls.

BEAUVAIS / A tapestry factory in Beauvais, France established in the seventeenth century.

BENTWOOD / Steam treated wood which is bent into curved shapes. First developed by Michael Thonet in Germany in the mid-nineteenth century.

BERGÈRE / French in origin, an upholstered armchair with enclosed sides and exposed frame, generally with lowered arms and loose-cushion seat.

BEVEL / A cut made at any angle other than a right one. Associated with the edges of mirrors or furniture.

BISQUE OR BISCUIT / **Pottery** fired once, without glazing or with a very thin glaze. Also refers to white, unglazed porcelain figurines.

BLIND FRETWORK / Applied fretwork as opposed to pierced or open fretwork, often for decoration based on **Chinoiserie** and Gothic designs.

BLOCK-FRONT / Case piece in which the front recedes in a flattened curve between convex sections. Thought to be Cuban in origin, the form is associated with colonial New England furniture.

BOBÊCHE / A socket for a candle with a wide rim to catch the wax.

BOISERIE / French term for wood lining, generally used to describe the elaborate carved woodwork and paneling, often gilded, in seventeenth- and eighteenth-century French interiors.

BOMBÉ / French term for the exaggerated swelling or flowing curve typical of commodes and chests in Rococo style.

BONE CHINA / Developed in England in the eighteenth century to compete with imported **porcelain**. Made with bone ash added to the clay and feldspathic rock to create a clear white color.

BONNET TOP / The arched topmost section of a case piece, typically eighteenth-century English or American, formed by a broken pediment, shaped into opposing curves. Also called a hooded top.

BOSS / Medieval in origin, the term for a project-ing knob or sphere at the intersection of vault rib or ceiling. Also, knoblike projections in decorations or metalwork on cabinetry.

BOULLE WORK / Brass and tortoiseshell **marquetry** technique perfected by André-Charles Boulle in seventeenth century France, as decoration for furniture.

BRACKET FOOT / A simple foot for case furniture formed from two pieces of wood joined at the corner.

BREAKFRONT / A three-section bookcase whose central section projects forward.

BRIGHT-CUT / Sharply **engraved** designs on silver that create a glittering effect.

BROADLOOM / Seamless carpets manufactured in broad strips, installed wall-to-wall in interiors.

BROCADE / Fabric, woven on a jacquard loom in intricate patterns with raised ornaments to resemble **embroidery**. Originally silk, satin, or velvet, often with gold and silver. Threads are carried across the width of the fabric, and on the reverse side.

BROKEN PEDIMENT / A **pediment** with a break in its crown. Refers to architecture or furniture.

BRONZE DORÉ / French term for **gilded** bronze. See **ormolu**.

BUFFET / A cupboard or sideboard. Refers to furniture for the dining room.

BUN FOOT / Flemish in origin, a furniture foot resembling a flattened sphere.

BUREAU / French term for a desk or writing table, originally covered with fabric for use as a writing surface.

BUREAU À CYLINDRE / French term for a **rolltop** desk which covers both the pigeon holes and writing surface when closed.

BUREAU PLAT / French term for a flat writing table or desk, usually with a flat leather covered surface. May have small drawers.

BUREAU MAZARIN / French term for a **bureau** popular in the seventeenth century with eight legs, curved stretchers, and usually two tiers of drawers flanking a kneehole recess.

BUTTERFLY TABLE / A small drop-leaf table whose leaves, resembling butterfly wings, are supported by a swinging bracket.

CABRIOLE LEG / A furniture leg or support formed in a S-shaped double curve, derived from an animal's leg, its parts designated as thigh, knee, ankle, and foot. Associated with Rococo and Queen Anne furniture.

CAMELBACK / A serpentine chair or sofa back, whose double curve resembles a camel hump.

CAMEO GLASS / Two layers of glass, each of a different color, with the top layer carved away to reveal a pattern, which then projects from the surface in relief.

CANAPÉ / French term, originally for a seventeenth century two-seater couch covered with a canopy, but generally applied to small sofas without canopies.

CANDELABRUM / Ornamental candlestick with multiple branches. Plural is candelabra.

CAPITAL / The sculpted top of a column forming a transition between the **shaft** and **entablature** or lintel.

CARTOUCHE / Ornament in the form of a motif enclosed in an ornate frame or shield; in architecture, generally an unrolled scroll or oval table with curled edges, often embellished with heraldry.

CARYATID / A sculpted female figure used in classical architecture or furniture, instead of a column, for support or decoration. Male figures are called atlantes.

CASEMENT / A window sash that opens on hinges at the side, swinging open its entire length.

CASSONE / A hinged-top Italian Renaissance marriage chest often richly adorned with paint, carvings, or inlaid decoration.

CASTING / Process of metalworking that involves melting the raw materials and pouring it into a mold to achieve a specific shape. The finished object is a casting.

CERAMICS / Generic term, derived from the Greek word for potter's clay, describing any objects made from baked clay, hardened by firing in a kiln. The finished objects may be earthenware, stoneware or porcelain, depending on the composition of the clay, the firing temperature, and the glazing. See **pottery**.

CHAISE / French term for a side chair.

CHAISE LONGUE / French term for a long chair for reclining, which is upholstered and supported by additional legs.

CHAMFER / The slanted surface made when an angle is trimmed or **beveled**, common in buildings and metalwork, also used to describe sides of case furniture.

CHANDELIER / Hanging light fixture suspended from the ceiling. Derived from the French term for candlestick.

CHASING / The finishing of a **casting** or other metal object to correct surface defects.

CHEST OF DRAWERS / A case piece completely fitted with drawers.

CHEST ON CHEST / A **chest of drawers** in two sections, one placed on top of the other.

CHESTERFIELD / An overstuffed couch with no exposed woodwork.

CHEVRON / A decorative or heraldic motif comprised of repeated V's.

CHINOISERIE / European interpretations of Chinese decorative motifs on lacquerwork, carvings, plaster, or textiles.

CHINTZ / A printed cotton that is either **glazed** or calenderized. Originally Indian, adopted by England beginning in the eighteenth century.

CHIP CARVING / Carving in low relief, using chisels and gouges to create simple, mostly geometric motifs. Associated with Early American Colonial furniture, also seventeenth century English.

CLUB FOOT / A furniture foot in the shape of the head of a foot; flaring into a flat, round pad.

COFFER / An ornamental panel sunk into a ceiling or soffit, usually square but sometimes polygonal.

COIFFEUSE / French term for a hairdressing or makeup table.

COLONNADE / A row of columns, supporting a horizontal lintel.

COMB BACK / A **Windsor** chair back whose spindles extend above the main back in imitation of old-fashioned high combs.

COMMODE / French term for a **chest of drawers** or cabinet, typically low and squat.

COMPOSITE / The Classical **Order**, a Roman variant of the Corinthian, distinguished by its **capital,** which combines **Corinthian acanthus** leaves with prominent **Ionic volutes**.

CONNECTICUT CHEST / Developed in colonial New England, a chest decorated with three carved panels over two or three drawers, decorated with chip-carving and split **spindles**. Used throughout the northern colonies as a dowery chest and for storage. See **Hadley chest.**

CONSOLE TABLE / A side table affixed to a wall and supported by one or two receding scroll-shaped legs, or a bracket.

CORINTHIAN / The most slender and elaborate of the Greek Classical **Orders,** consisting of **base** on a **plinth**, fluted **shaft**, and **capital** distinguished by two rows of **acanthus** leaves, and four small **volutes**. The height of the column is ten times the diameter of the shaft.

CORNICE / Uppermost projecting horizontal element of an **entablature**. Also the crowning horizontal molding on buildings, interior walls, drapery treatments, or case furniture.

COROMANDEL / A variety of black ebony wood from the East Indies, often used in Chinese screens.

COURT CUPBOARD / A low cupboard or double cupboard, usually on legs, used for display and service. From the French word for short, it is related to the credenza.

CREDENZA / Italian term for a serving table with a cupboard below the surface.

CREST RAIL / The top **rail** of a piece of furniture, generally referring to a chair back. Often shaped and elaborately decorated.

CREWEL / **Embroidery** executed with loosely twisted worsted yarn and a large eye needle to create floral and scroll patterns on unbleached cotton or linen.

CURULE LEG / An X-shaped leg derived from a classic Roman chair design.

DADO / The lower part of a wall, differentiated by a molding, color, or paneling from the upper section of the wall.

DAMASK / Glossy, patterned, **jacquard**-weave fabric, similar to brocade, but flatter and generally reversible, in which contrasting weaves are used for pattern and background. The pattern is highlighted as light strikes the different weaves.

DELFT / Tin-glazed ceramics first produced in Delft, Holland, made to emulate Chinese porcelain. Generally blue and white, but also in other colors. Similar to faience and majolica.

DEMILUNE / Top of a table or cabinet, half-circular in form.

DORÉ / French term for **gilded**. See **ormolu**.

DORIC / The oldest and simplest Classical **Order** distinguished by its lack of **base**, thick and broadly fluted **shaft**, and undecorated **capital**. The height of the column is eight times the diameter of the shaft.

DRESSER / A low **chest of drawers** with a mirror above for the storage of clothing. Also a **sideboard** or **buffet** for the storage and display of eating utensils.

DRESSING TABLE / Kneehole table with open center section and drawers on either side. Often with mirror attached.

DROP LEAF / Hinged flap or leaf on a table that raises to extend the table.

DROP LID / A desktop or cabinet front that is hinged at the bottom, and arranged to fall forward to form a writing surface. Also called fall front.

EARS / The frame of the wing on a wing chair, or the projecting ends on the crest rail of Chippendale-style chairs.

EARTHENWARE / Porous **pottery**, of coarse clay, fired at a low temperature. Heavy and opaque, it is often waterproofed with glazes.

ÉBENISTE / French term, originally for cabinet workers of the French Renaissance who specialized in furniture of ebony glued onto blackened pearwood. Later used to refer to those cabinetmakers who specialized in working with fine veneers.

EGG-AND-DART / A decorative molding composed of an alternating pattern of round and downward-pointing elements.

EMBOSSING / Technique of working metal by hammering from the reverse side to produce a relief pattern.

EMBROIDERY / Fabric decorated with a raised design or pattern made with a needle and thread.

ENAMEL / Glaze bonded to a metal or ceramic surface by heat. After firing, the glaze forms an opaque or translucent substance that is fixed to the ground. Also refers to paint with a similarly glossy finish.

ENFILADE / French term for the alignment of a series of doorways that provide an uninterrupted vista through a sequence of rooms.

ENGRAVING / Designs that are carved into the surface of a material such as glass or metal.

ENTABLATURE / The entire horizontal section of material carried on columns consisting of the **architrave**, **frieze**, and **cornice**.

ESCUTCHEON / A shield with a heraldic device. In furniture, the decorative metal plate around a keyhole, pull, or door knob.

ÉTAGÈRE / French term for an open shelf unit, which may be hanging or standing.

ETCHING / On glass, an acid **engraving** that produces a frosted appearance. In graphics, printing from copper plates coated with acid.

FAIENCE / Tin-glazed **earthenware** with colorful decoration, first produced in Faience in Northern Italy.

FALL FRONT / See **drop lid**.

FAUTEUIL / French term for an upholstered armchair with open sides.

FAUX-BOIS / An illusionistic wood grain effect for interiors, where inexpensive softwood paneling may be painted to imitate expensive woods. Also refers to outdoor furniture made to resemble tree branches.

FENESTRATION / The arrangement of windows on a building.

FESTOON / A design imitating a loop of drapery, usually depicting fruit and flowers. See **garland** and **swag**.

FIDDLE-BACK CHAIR / A chair back with a splat resembling a violin (variant on the urn-shape splat of Queen Anne style).

FILIGREE / Delicate, lacelike ornamental work, usually in metal.

FLAT TABLE / English term for a **drop leaf**.

FLAT-WEAVE / A basic textile weave without pile, generally referring to floor coverings.

FLOCKED / Wallpaper with a velvety or suedelike surface.

FLUTING / Shallow concave vertical grooves set in parallel strips, usually on the **shaft** of a column or on furniture supports. See **reeding**.

FRENCH WINDOWS / Pair of multi-paned windows extending, like doors, to the floor, and often opening onto an outdoor space.

FRET / Geometric band in a motif of interlacing lines resembling a series of rectilinear hook shapes. Derived from Greek ornamentation, and also known as Greek key or meander.

FRETWORK / Decorative woodwork in a pierced geometric design of interlocking horizontal and vertical lines resembling trellis work. Of Greek origin, also associated with Chinese and Gothic styles.

FRIEZE / The central horizontal member of an **entablature**. Also the decorative band or strip beneath the **cornice** of an interior wall. It may be carved, painted, fabric, or wallpaper.

FRINGE / A continuous band or ribbon of decorative edging, with hanging threads or tassels, used to trim drapery and upholstery.

FUMED OAK / Oak artificially treated to achieve a darker, weathered appearance by fumes of ammonia from uncorked cans placed in an airtight compartment. Widely used in furniture of the Arts and Crafts movement.

GABLE / The triangular wall space formed on the end of a building by two sides of a pitched roof.

GADROONING / A decorative pattern formed with a series of convex ridges. Seen on silver hollowware and furniture.

GALLERY TRIM / A miniature **railing** placed along the edge of shelf or table top. Often in brass, on Late Neoclassical furniture.

GARLAND / A wreathlike ornament of flowers or foliage. See **festoon** and **swag**.

GATELEG TABLE / A **drop-leaf** table with oval or rounded ends. Of Jacobean origin, but generally associated with American Colonial furniture.

GAUZE / A thin, transparent, fabric made of a netlike or plain weave.

GESSO / Plaster mixture for molded relief decoration, often applied to wood or other surfaces, and for painting or gilding.

GILDING / The application of gold leaf or gold pigment to an object of a different medium.

GIMP / A binding material used on the outer edges of upholstered furniture as a cover, often decorative.

GIRANDOLE / A wall sconce with multi-branched candleholders and back-plate fixed to the wall.

GLAZE / A glassine layer fused by firing onto a pottery body to achieve a smooth, non-porous surface and fix the decoration.

GOBELINS / Tapestries, ceramics, *pietra dura*, and other decorative arts produced at the Gobelins factory in Paris, France between the late seventeenth and late eighteenth century. The Gobelins tradition was continued with the **Savonerie** workshop.

GÔUT GREC / The early phase of French Neoclassicism dating from the mid-1750s to the late 1760s, contrasting with the Rococo style. The term broadly applies to architecture and decorative arts with classical motifs.

GRANDFATHER CLOCK / See **tall case clock**.

GROTESQUES / Classical decorative elements, generally vertical and symmetrical panels, with intertwined animals, figures, fruits, and plants. Named after ancient Roman decorations rediscovered in the Italian Renaissance and popularized by the painter Raphael, they are most closely associated with eighteenth-century Neoclassical design. Similar in appearance to arabesques.

GUÉRIDON / A small ornamental stand or **pedestal**.

GUILLOCHE / A continuous decorative band composed of interlacing circles.

HADLEY CHEST / A rectangular chest originating in early colonial America with hinged top and short legs formed by a continuation of the **stiles**. The front has three recessed panels with one or more drawers below. See **Connecticut chest**.

HIGHBOY / A **chest of drawers** supported by a stand or tablelike base fitted with drawers. A variant of the English **tallboy**, popular in eighteenth century America until the Revolution.

HOOPBACK CHAIR / Vertical back elements and top **rail** forming a continuous curve.

HUTCH / French term for a chest used to store food or clothing.

INCISED / Decoration that is deeply cut or carved, as differentiated from relief decoration.

INGLENOOK / A recessed seating area by a fire or hearth, with benches on either side. Associated with Arts and Crafts interiors.

INLAY / A decorative process in which pieces of one material are set into similarly-shaped holes cut into the surface of an object of a different material.

INTARSIA / Elaborate decoration created with inlay using different types of wood set into wood, a process developed in the Renaissance.

IONIC / The Classical **Order** distinguished by tapering, **fluted** column and bold **volutes** on the **capital**. The height of the column is nine times the diameter of the shaft.

JACQUARD / Intricate, multicolored patterned fabrics, woven on a Jacquard loom, invented in the early nineteenth century and enabling the inexpensive production of highly figured textiles at relatively modest cost. Also used for carpeting.

JAPANNING / A finishing process imitating Japanese lacquer work, popular in the eighteenth century, particularly in England. Furniture and metalwork are **enameled** with colored shellac and decoration is in relief, colored with paint, and often **gilded**.

KAS / A tall upright cabinet, clothespress, or wardrobe of Dutch origin, which usually has **ball feet**, a heavy **cornice**, and two doors.

KILIM / A flat woven Middle Eastern rug that is reversible and typically has striking geometric patterns.

KLISMOS / An ancient Greek chair with a deep top **rail** curving forward from the back with curved, splayed-out legs. Often imitated in nineteenth century classical revivals, particularly Empire, Regency, and American Empire.

KNEE / The upper, convex, curve or bulge of a **cabriole** leg, often embellished with carved ornaments.

KNEEHOLE DESK / A desk with a central, open space for leg room located under the writing surface and flanked by drawers on either side.

LACQUER / Of Asian origin, a type of hard, glossy, varnish made from the sap indigenous to China and Japan. Lacquer can be layered or combined with other materials for various decorative effects.

LADDER-BACK / A tall-backed chair with several horizontal slats between the posts.

LAMBREQUIN / Stiff, flat **valances** with decoratively shaped lower edges often descending at either side. See also **pelmet**.

LAMINATING / Various layers of wood bonded together, for strength or flexibility.

LOOP PILE / The uncut loops or cut loop tufts of surface yarn that form the wearing surface of the carpet.

LOVESEAT / A double chair or small sofa.

LOWBOY / A low chest set on legs, or a table with drawers. Often a companion piece to a highboy.

LOZENGE / A diamond-shaped motif, often describing marquetry or applied brass ornament.

LUSTERWARE / **Pottery** with a thin metallic glaze which produces a rich, iridescent color.

MAJOLICA / Italian and Spanish **pottery** coated with tin enamel and polychrome. See **Delft** and **Faience**.

MANTELPIECE / The framework surrounding a fireplace, generally in wood or stone, often treated as a decorative statement in an interior.

MARCHAND-MERCIER / Both a merchant and design-director who commissioned and sold furniture within the Parisian guild system in the eighteenth century.

MARLBOROUGH LEG / A straight-grooved furniture leg with a block as a foot. Used in English and American furniture, but most associated with late Chippendale designs.

MARQUETRY / A decorative pattern formed from different pieces of thin wood veneer, or occasionally other materials, and applied as a single sheet

to the surface of furniture. The process replaced intarsia by the eighteenth century.

MARQUISE / French term for a small **canapé** or large chair for two people. A type of **settee**.

MENUSIER / French term for a craftsperson who made furniture, mostly chairs, sofas, benches, tables, or other furniture from solid pieces of wood. The menusier practiced joinery and carving, as differentiated from the veneer work of the **ébeniste**.

MOIRÉ / Fabric with a waved or watered effect created by pressing the fabric between engraved cylinders, which emboss grained designs onto the material.

MULLIONS / Slim vertical or horizontal strips, most often of wood, dividing glass panels of a window or door.

MURAL / Decorative painting applied directly to a wall, or onto wallpaper or canvas, then mounted onto the wall.

MYLAR / Clear coated polyester film, metallized with aluminum, used as decorative wallcovering and in threads for fabric and upholstery, particularly in the 1950s and 1960s.

ORDER / The basis of classical architecture. The orders are composed of a column, with or without **base** or **capital**, supporting an **entablature**. The Greek orders include the **Doric**, **Ionic**, and **Corinthian**. The Romans added the **Tuscan** and **Composite**.

ORMOLU / French term for **gilt bronze**. See also **bronze doré.**

OTTOMAN / An upholstered bench or seat without arms and back.

PAD FOOT / A **club foot** resting on a disc, often found on a cabriole leg.

PALISANDER / German term for rosewood.

PAPIER-MÂCHÉ / Pulverized paper made into a pulp with an adhesive binder, often used to make furniture in the Victorian period.

PARCEL GILT / A partially **gilded** portion of a surface, often done with stencils.

PARQUETRY / Small pieces of colored hardwood assembled into a geometric pattern for flooring.

PATINA / Incrustation formed on a material, such as bronze, by a chemical reaction.

PEDESTAL / Supporting element of a vase or statue, or the lowest portion of a classical order. In furniture, a single-support element for a chair or table.

PEDIMENT / The triangular space formed at the end of a Greek temple, conforming to the slope of the roof. The term is applied to similar decorative motifs applied above windows, doors, and on furniture. Variations on standard form include the **broken** and **scroll pediment**.

PELMET / See **lambrequin**.

PEMBROKE / A small **drop-leaf** table with a drawer set in the **apron**.

PIECRUST TABLE / A round **pedestal** table with the raised edge of the top surface carved in scallops resembling the crimped edge of a pie. Seen in English and American furniture.

PIER GLASS / Tall mirror originally designed to hang on a pier between two windows. Now a common term for any wall mirror used over a console table.

PIER TABLE / Side table designed to stand against a pier, a columnlike section of masonry, in the space between two windows. Now refers to a console-type table used beneath a pier glass.

PIETRA DURE / An Italian Renaissance mosaic inlay of marbles and assorted semi-precious stones.

PILASTER / Vertical cross-section of a column, flat-faced and projecting from a wall, or carved as

ornament on furniture, usually depicting the characteristics and elements of a classic column.

PLINTH / Square portion at the **base** of a column. Also the platformlike, solid base section used in place of legs on case furniture.

POLYCHROME / Multicolored painted decoration applied to a building, object, or piece of furniture.

PORCELAIN / Vitrified, white, translucent **ceramic** made with kaolin clay, fired at extremely high temperature. Desirable for its lustrous glaze and imperviousness to moisture. Made in China from the ninth century; first European version developed in Germany in the early eighteenth century.

POTTERY / General term for objects made of clay hardened by firing in a kiln. See **ceramics**.

POUFFE / A round, heavily stuffed, cushion that serves as a seat popular in the nineteenth century.

PRESS / A cupboard or **armoire** for the storage of linens or clothing.

PRESSED-GLASS / Glass ornamented with a pattern in **relief,** made by pressing it into a mold.

QUATREFOIL / Gothic motif composed of four equal lobes separated by cusps. Suggesting the form of a four-leaf clover.

RAIL / Any structural horizontal member of a piece of furniture, such as a crest rail, or seat rail.

REEDING / Semi-cylindrical, convex vertical moldings set in close parallel strips. Opposite of **fluting**. The term also refers to a single, continuous ornament of stemlike form, on molding.

REPOUSSÉ / Technique of hammering metal from the back to create a protruding or relief image.

RIBBAND BACK / A chair back composed of a pattern of interlacing ribbons.

RINCEAU / Decorative scroll and leaf ornament,

usually horizontal and symmetrical, used on walls or paneling. Similar to **arabesque**.

ROSETTE / An ornamental rose shaped disk.

SABOT / French term for the decorative metal covering used for the feet of wood furniture.

SATIN / A flat woven fabric with rich, glossy surface and dull back. Made in many variations of texture and surface finish.

SAVONAROLA CHAIR / An Italian Renaissance X-shaped chair, derived from the Roman curule form, and named after the martyred monk Savonarola. It has a series of interlacing slats forming the base, and a wooden back and arms, often richly carved. A variant is the Dante chair, with only two sets of slats forming the base and continuing upward to shape the arms.

SAVONNERIE / High-pile hand-woven rugs produced in the French rug and tapestry works, founded by Louis XIII in the early seventeenth century on the site of a soap factory.

SCAGOLIA / Material composed of plaster and marble chips, used since antiquity to imitate marble.

SCONCE / The ornamental wall bracket for mounting a light source.

SCROLL ARM / Chair terminating at the hand in a scroll.

SCROLL FOOT / Foot in the shape of a flattened scroll, often appearing at the base of a **cabriole** leg.

SCROLL PEDIMENT / A **broken pediment** with each end shaped in the form of a reverse curve, and terminating in an ornamental scroll.

SECRÉTAIRE À ABATTANT / French term for a desk with a vertical fall front enclosing drawers and pigeonholes. It will generally have doors above the fall front, and drawers below.

SECRETARY / A desk with shelves or storage areas both above and below the writing surface.

SEMANIER / A tall bedroom chest with seven drawers, originally used for each day of the week.

SERPENTINE / The juxtaposition of concave and convex forms to create a sinuous line.

SETTEE / Derived from the **settle**, it is composed of two or more engaged armchairs.

SETTLE / Of American colonial origin, a timber bench with arms and flat back, to accommodate two or more people.

SGABELLO CHAIR / A small wooden armless chair, of Italian Renaissance origin, usually with a carved **splat** back, octagonal seat, and carved trestle supports.

SHAFT / The body or trunk of a column extending from the top of the **base** to the bottom of the **capital.**

SHIELD BACK CHAIR / An open chair back resembling the shape of a shield.

SIDEBOARD / Dining room case furniture for serving and storage, a composite of center serving table with drawers, and flanking pedestals with drawers or cupboards. Developed by Shearer and Hepplewhite in eighteenth century England.

SLEIGH BED / A bed with a high headboard and slightly lower footboard, suggesting the shape of a horse-drawn sleigh. Developed in America in the early nineteenth century, it was derived from Empire scrolled-end bed designs.

SLIPPER CHAIR / A high-backed, upholstered chair with short legs and low seat, intended for bedroom use.

SPINDLE / Long, slim length of **turned** wood, varied with swellings or turned moldings.

SPLAT / The central, vertical panel of a chair back, stretching from the seat to the top **rail**.

STAMPING / Designs pressed into metal with a tool.

STILE / The structural, vertical member in the framework of a piece of furniture.

STONEWARE / A heavy, opaque, non-porous pottery, fired at medium temperature, in which the body and glaze fuse to form an integrated, vitrified layer.

STRETCHER / The horizontal crosspiece between furniture legs, used initially for support and strengthening, but sometimes serving as elements in the design.

STRINGCOURSE / A continuous horizontal member, such as a molding, decorating the face of a wall.

STRINGING / A decorative border on furniture, composed of a narrow band or contrasting veneer.

SWAG / Length of fabric looped or draped between two **supports** or carved decoration in a similar form. See **festoon** and **garland**.

TABOURET / A low upholstered stool for sitting.

TAFFETA / A smooth, crisp, tight-weave fabric with a lustrous surface, often woven to create an effect of iridescence.

TALLBOY / Tall case piece, generally with seven or more drawers, divided by a cornice into two sections with the lower section supported on raised legs. Composite of a chest set on a larger chest on legs. See **highboy**.

TALL CASE CLOCK / A pendulum floor clock with a tall case developed in England in the mid-seventeenth century. Also called **grandfather clock**, popular in colonial America.

TAMBOUR / French term for a flexible rollover top, roll-top desk, or table. Also thin strips of wood adhered to canvas backing to form a flexible sheet to conceal storage areas.

TAPERED LEG / A straight rectangular furniture leg that narrows down evenly toward the foot.

TERRA COTTA / Baked or fired clay, usually brownish red in tone, used as **pottery**, small sculptures, and roof tiles, as well as facing material on buildings.

TESTER / The canopy that joins the post of a four-poster bed. From the eighteenth century, originally flat, it became draped and valanced, with a wood cornice.

TILT-TOP / A table top attached to the base with a hinge allowing the top to swing into a vertical position for storage. Popular in eighteenth-century English and American furniture.

TOILE / Linen or cotton canvaslike fabric, usually printed with allover scenic designs. Toile de Jouy, the best known of this type, have been produced in Jouy-en-Josas, France, since the eighteenth century.

TORCHÈERE / Originally a stand or table for a candle or lamp, is usually embellished with carving and **gilded**. Also any standing floor lamp casting light upward toward the ceiling.

TRABEATED / Architectural composition based on a post-and-lintel system, rather than an **arcuated** system.

TRACERY / Ornamental openwork of masonry found in the upper parts of Gothic style windows; also, similar decorative motifs on walls, furniture, and other objects.

TRIFID FOOT / Three-toed foot on furniture, seen in eighteenth century England and America.

TRIPOD / A three-legged **pedestal** table.

TRUMEAU / From the French word for pier, originally referring to the wall area between windows, now indicating the decorative treatment of the space over a mantel, door, or window, generally consisting of mirroring or painting.

TURNING / A decorative or structural furniture part produced by rotating wood on a lathe and shaping it into rounded forms with cutting tools. See **spindle**.

TUSCAN / The Classical **Order**, a Roman adaptation of the Greek **Doric**, distinguished by the unfluted shaft and a simple **capital** closely related to the **Doric**.

TYMPANUM / The triangular or segmental spaces enclosed by a **pediment** or an arch on a building; on furniture, the area beneath the pedimented top of a tall chest.

UNDERGLAZE / The decoration applied to pottery before the final application of glazing.

VALANCE / A horizontal element of fabric or other materials, hung across the top of windows, doors, or bed hangings, generally to conceal the top of curtains or draperies. See **lambrequin** or **pelmet.**

VELVET / Fabric of silk or other fibers, woven with a thick, short pile and plain back. Plain or sometimes patterned.

VENEER / A very thin layer of decorative wood, or occasionally other materials, applied to the surface of a lesser material. Wood veneers are obtained by slicing the vertical section of a log to produce a series of sheets with identical, figured grain, which may then be used to create ornamental patterns on case furniture or table tops.

VERDIGRIS / The greenish **patina** found on aged brass, bronze, or copper.

VITRINE / A display cabinet with a glass front or door.

VOLUTE / A scroll or spiral, shaped like a ram's horn, as found on an **Ionic** column, or used as decorative motif on furniture.

WAINSCOT CHAIR / Named for its similarity to **wainscoting**, usually with a carved or **inlaid** panel **splat**, and a high seat. A footstool is a typical accompaniment.

WAINSCOTING / Wood paneling covering the **dado** level of the wall.

WARP / The threads that run lengthwise on a loom; the vertical threads of a fabric.

WEFT / The threads that run crosswise from selvage to selvage, and are woven in and out of the **warp** threads by a shuttle or bobbin. Also called filler threads.

WHEEL-BACK CHAIR / A chair back composed of spokes radiating from the center imitating a wheel.

WILTON / Carpet with a velvety appearance created by cut loops of the pile, developed in Wiltshire, England, during the first half of the eighteenth century, using a jacquard pattern device.

WINDSOR CHAIR / A domestic chair developed in eighteenth century England with **spindle** back, and sloped seat. Popular in eighteenth and nineteenth century America, where distinctive variations include fan-back, bow-back, comb-back, and hoop-back designs, all with turned legs and shaped seats.

WING CHAIR / A high-backed upholstered easy chair with projecting wings or **ears** on either side of the chair back, originally implemented to deter drafts. In colonial America, called an easy chair.

YOKE BACK / A cross-bar in the form of two S-curves, resembling an oxen yoke, used for the top rail of a chair back.

for further reading

GENERAL

Abercrombie, Stanley and Sherrill Whiton. *Interior Design and Decoration*. 5th Edition. New York: Prentice Hall, 2001.

Axelrod, Alex, ed. *The Colonial Revival in America*. New York: W.W. Norton, 1985.

Banham, Joanna, et al. *Victorian Interior Design*. London: Cassell, 1991.

Beard, Geoffrey. *Craftsmen and Interior Decoration in England, 1660–1820*. London: Bloomsbury Books, 1981.

Beard, Geoffrey. *Upholsterers and Interior Furnishings in England, 1530–1840*. New Haven, CT.: Yale University Press, 1997.

Blakemore, Robbie. *A History of Interior Design and Furniture from Ancient Egypt to Nineteenth-Century Europe*. New York: Van Nostrand Reinhold, 1997.

Bowett, Adam. *English Furniture 1680–1714: From Charles II to Queen Anne*. London: Antique Collectors' Club, 2002.

Brunhammer, Yvonne. *L' Art De Vivre: Decorative Arts and Design in France 1789–1989*. New York: Thames and Hudson, 1989.

Calloway, Stephen. *The Elements of Style*. Revised Edition. New York: Simon & Schuster, 1996.

Cook, Clarence. *The House Beautiful: An Unabridged Reprint of the Classic Victorian Stylebook*. Reprint. New York: Dover Publications, 1995.

Cooper, Jeremy. *Victorian and Edwardian Décor: From Gothic Revival to Art Nouveau*. New York: Abbeville Press, 1987.

Denenberg, Thomas Andrew. *Wallace Nutting and the Invention of Old America*. New Haven, CT.: Yale University Press, 2003.

Eastlake, Charles L. *Hints on Household Taste: The Classic Handbook of Victorian Interior Decoration*. New York: Dover Publications, 1986.

Edwards, Clive D. *Victorian Furniture: Technology and Design*. New York: St. Martin's Press, 1993.

Eidelberg, Martin, ed. *Design 1935–1965: What Modern Was: Selections from the Lilian and David M. Stewart Collection*. New York: Harry N. Abrams, 2001.

Fairbanks, Jonathan, and Elizabeth Bates. *American Furniture 1620 to the Present*. New York: Marek, 1981.

Fitzgerald, Oscar P. *Four Centuries of American Furniture*. Revised Edition. Iola, WI.: Krause Publications, 1995.

Fleming, John and Hugh Honour. *Penguin Dictionary of Decorative Arts*. Revised Edition. London: Penguin, 1990.

Frank, Isabelle, ed. *The Theory of Decorative Art: An Anthology of European and American Writings*. New Haven, CT.: Yale University Press, 2000.

Friedman, Joe. *Inside Paris: Discovering the Period Interiors of Paris*. New York: Rizzoli, 1990.

Gere, Charlotte, et al. *Nineteenth-Century Design: From Pugin to Mackintosh*. New York: Harry N. Abrams, 2000.

Gilbert, Christopher. *English Vernacular Furniture, 1750–1900*. New Haven, CT.: Yale University Press, 1991.

Glancey, Jonathan. *Modern: Masters of the Twentieth-Century Interior*. New York: Rizzoli, 1999.

Gloag, John. *A Social History of Furniture Design from 1300 B.C. to A.D. 1960.* New York: Crown Publishers, 1968.

Gore, Allan. *The History of English Interiors.* Reprint. London: Phaidon Press, 1995.

Greene, Jeffrey. *American Furniture of the Eighteenth Century: History, Technique, Structure.* Newton, CT.: Taunton Press, 1996.

Harwood, Buie, et al. *Architecture and Interior Design through the Eighteenth Century: An Integrated History.* New York: Prentice Hall, 2001.

Heisinger, Kathryn and George Marcus. *Landmarks of Twentieth-Century Design: An Illustrated Handbook.* New York: Abbeville, 1993.

Jones, Owen. *The Grammar of Ornament: Illustrated by Examples from Various Styles of Ornament.* Reprint. New York: DK Publishing, 2001.

Lucie-Smith, Edward. *Furniture: A Concise History.* London: Thames and Hudson, 1978.

de Noailles Mahey, Edgar. *A Documentary History of American Interiors: From the Colonial Era to 1915.* Reprint. New York: Simon & Schuster, 1986.

Mang, Karl. *History of Modern Furniture.* New York: Harry N. Abrams, 1979.

Massey, Anne. *Interior Design of the Twentieth Century.* Revised Edition. London: Thames and Hudson, 2001.

Morley, John. *The History of Furniture: Twenty-Five Centuries of Style and Design in the Western Tradition.* Boston: Little, Brown and Co., 1999.

Pallot, Bill B. G. *The Art of the Chair in Eighteenth-Century France.* Paris: A.C.R. Gismondi Editeurs, 1989.

Peck, Amelia, ed. *Period Rooms in The Metropolitan Museum of Art.* New York: Metropolitan Museum of Art, 1996.

Pegler, Martin. *The Dictionary of Interior Design.* New York: Crown, 1966; Reprint. New York: Fairchild, 1988.

Peirce, Donald C. and Hope Alswang. *American Interiors, New England and the South: Period Rooms at the Brooklyn Museum.* Brooklyn, N.Y.: Brooklyn Museum, 1983.

Pevsner, Nikolaus. *Pioneers of Twentieth-Century Design: From William Morris to Le Corbusier.* London: Penguin, 1960.

Pradere, Alexandre. *French Furniture Makers: The Art of the Ebeniste from Louis XIV to the Revolution.* Translated by Perran Wood. Los Angeles: J. Paul Getty Museum, 1991.

Praz, Mario. *An Illustrated History of Interior Decoration from Pompeii to Art Nouveau.* London: Thames and Hudson, 1987.

Raymond, Pierre. *Masterpieces of Marquetry.* Translated by Brian Considine. Los Angeles: J. Paul Getty Museum, 2001.

Riley, Noel and Patricia Bayer. *The Elements of Design: A Practical Encyclopedia of the Decorative Arts from the Renaissance to the Present.* New York: Free Press, 2003.

Rogers, Meyric R. *American Interior Design: The Traditions and Development of Domestic Design from Colonial Times to the Present.* New York: Bonanza Books, 1947.

Sossons, Adrianna Boidi. *Furniture: From Rococo to Art Deco.* Köln: Evergreen, 2000.

Sparke, Penny. *A Century of Design: Design Pioneers of the Twentieth Century.* Woodbury, N.Y.: Barrons, 1998.

Strange, Thomas Arthur. *English Interiors, Furniture, Decoration, Woodwork, and Allied Arts During the Last Half of the Seventeenth Century, the Whole of the Eighteenth Century, and the Early Part of the Nineteenth*. Reprint. London: Studio Editions, 1986.

Tate, Allen and C. Ray Smith. *Interior Design in the Twentieth Century*. New York: Harper & Row, 1986.

Thornton, Peter. *Authentic Decor: The Domestic Interior 1620–1920*. Revised Edition. London: Seven Dials, 2001.

Verlet, Pierre. *French Furniture of the Eighteenth Century*. Virginia: University of Virginia Press, 1991.

Whitehead, John. *The French Interior in the Eighteenth Century*. New York: Dutton Studio Books, 1992.

Wilk, Christopher, ed. *Western Furniture: 1350 to the Present Day: In the Victoria and Albert Museum London*. London: Cross River Press, 1996.

Wilson, Richard Guy. *The Colonial Revival House*. New York: Harry N. Abrams, 2004.

Winkler, Gail Caskey and Roger Moss. *Victorian Interior Decoration: American Interiors, 1830–1900*. New York: H. Holt, 1986.

de Wolfe, Elsie. *The House in Good Taste*. Reprint. New York: Rizzoli, 2004.

Woodham, Jonathan M. *Twentieth-Century Design*. Oxford: Oxford University Press, 1997.

LOUIS XIV

Apra, Nietta. *The Louis Styles: Louis XIV, Louis XV, and Louis XVI*. London: Orbis, 1972.

WILLIAM AND MARY

Baarsen, Reiner, et al. *Courts and Colonies: The William and Mary Style in Holland, England, and America*. Washington: University of Washington Press, 1989.

Cooper, Nicholas. *Houses of the Gentry, 1480–1680*. New Haven, CT: Yale University Press, 2000.

Mowl, Timothy. *Elizabethan and Jacobean Style*. London: Phaidon Press, 1993.

EARLY AMERICAN COLONIAL

Garrett, Wendell. *American Colonial: Puritan Simplicity to Georgian Grace*. New York: Monacelli Press, 1998.

LOUIS XV

Scott, Katie. *The Rococo Interior: Decoration and Social Spaces in Early Eighteenth-Century Paris*. New Haven, CT.: Yale University Press, 1995.

ENGLISH QUEEN ANNE

Vandal, Norman L. *Queen Anne Furniture: History, Design, and Construction*. Newton, CT.: Taunton Press, 1990.

EARLY GEORGIAN

Coleridge, Anthony. *Chippendale Furniture: The Work of Thomas Chippendale and His Contemporaries in the Rococo Taste: Vile, Cobb, Langlois, Channon, Hallett, Ince and Mayhew, Lock, Johnson, and Others, Circa 1745–1765*. London: Faber and Faber, 1968.

Chippendale, Thomas. *The Gentleman and Cabinet Maker's Director*. Reprint. New York: Dover Publications, 1966.

LATE AMERICAN COLONIAL

Downs, Joseph. *American Furniture: Queen Anne and Chippendale Periods in the Henry Francis Du Pont Winterthur Museum*. Atglen, PA.: Schiffer Publishing, 2001.

Heckscher, Morrison H. *American Furniture in the Metropolitan Museum of Art, Late Colonial Period: The Queen Anne and Chippendale Styles*. New York: Metropolitan Museum of Art, 1986.

LOUIS XVI

Geck, Fracis. *French Interiors and Furniture Vol. 9: The Period of Louis XVI*. Roseville, MI.: Stureck Educational Services, 1996.

LATE GEORGIAN

Harris, Eileen. *The Genius of Robert Adam: His Interiors*. New Haven, CT.: Yale University Press, 2001.

Hepplewhite, George. *The Cabinet-Maker and Upholsterer's Guide*. Reprint. New York: Dover Publications, 1969.

Musgrave, Clifford. *Adam and Hepplewhite and Other Furniture*. New York: Taplinger, 1966.

Roberts, Hugh. *For the King's Pleasure: The Furnishings and Decoration of George IV's Apartments at Windsor Castle*. London: Thames and Hudson, 2002.

Sheraton, Thomas. *The Cabinet-Maker and Upholsterer's Drawing Book*. Reprint. New York: Dover Publications, 1972.

FEDERAL

Evans, Nancy Goyne. *American Windsor Chairs*. New York: Hudson Hills Press, 1996.

Garett, Wendell. *Classic America: The Federal Style and Beyond*. New York: Rizzoli, 1992.

Montgomery, Charles F. and Ask, Gilbert. *American Furniture, the Federal Period in the Henry Francis Du Pont Winterthur Museum*. Atglen, PA.: Schiffer Publishing, Ltd., 2001.

FRENCH EMPIRE

Chenevière, Antoine. *Russian Furniture: The Golden Age 1780–1840*. London: Weidenfeld & Nicholson, 1988.

Deschamps, Madeleine. *Empire*. New York: Abbeville Press, 1994.

Gere, Charlotte. *Nineteenth-Century Decoration: The Art of the Interior*. New York: Harry N. Abrams, 1989.

Fontaine, Pierre-Françoise-Léonard and Charles Percier. *Receuil de décorations interieurs*. Reprint. New York: Dover Publications, 1981.

REGENCY

Morley, John. *Regency Design, 1790–1840*. New York: Harry N. Abrams, 1993.

Musgrave, Clifford. *Regency Furniture: 1800–1830*. London: Faber and Faber, 1961.

Parisssien, Steven. *Regency Style*. London: Phaidon Press, 1992.

_____. *Palladian Style*. London: Phaidon Press, 1999.

Vincent, Nancy. *Duncan Phyfe and the English Regency, 1795–1830*. New York: Dover Publications, 1980.

Watkin, David. *Thomas Hope and the Neo-Classical Idea*. London: Murray, 1968.

BIEDERMEIER

Chase, Linda and Karl Kemp. *The World of Biedermeier*. London: Thames and Hudson, 2001.

Wilkie, Angus. *Biedermeier*. New York: Abbeville Press, 1987.

AMERICAN EMPIRE

Voorsanger, Catherine Hoover, ed. *Art and the Empire City: New York, 1825–1861*. New Haven: Yale University Press, 2000.

GOTHIC REVIVAL

Aldrich, Megan. *Gothic Revival*. London: Phaidon, 1997.

Howe, Katherine S. *The Gothic Revival Style in America, 1830–1870*. Houston: Museum of Fine Arts, 1976.

Mahoney, Kathleen. *Gothic Style: Architecture and Interiors from the Eighteenth Century to the Present*. New York: Harry N. Abrams, 1995.

Pugin, Augustus Welby Northmore, et al., eds. *A. W. N. Pugin: Master of Gothic Revival*. New Haven, CT.: Yale University Press, 1996.

ROCOCO REVIVAL

Heckscher, Morinson H. *American Rococo, 1750–1775: Elegance in Ornament*. New York: Harry N. Abrams, 1992.

Schwarz, Marvin D. *The Furniture of John Henry Belter and the Rococo Revival: An Inquiry into Nineteenth-Century Furniture Design Through a Study of the Gloria and Richard Manney Collection*. New York: E. P. Dutton, 1981.

RENAISSANCE REVIVAL

Wilson, Richard Guy, et al. *The American Renaissance, 1876–1917*. Brooklyn, N.Y.: Brooklyn Museum, 1979.

AESTHETIC

Aslin, Elizabeth. *The Aesthetic Movement: Prelude to Art Nouveau*. New York: Frederick A. Praeger, 1969.

Burke, Doreen Bolger, et. al., eds. *In Pursuit of Beauty: Americans and the Aesthetic Movement*. New York: Rizzoli, 1986.

Frankel, Lory. *Herter Brothers: Furniture and Interiors for a Gilded Age*. New York: Harry N. Abrams, 1994.

Lambourne, Lionel. *The Aesthetic Movement*. London: Phaidon Press, 1996.

Lynn, Catherine. *In Pursuit of Beauty: Americans and the Aesthetic Movement*. New York: Rizzoli, 1986.

Spencer, Robin. *The Aesthetic Movement*. London: Dutton/Studio Vista, 1972.

ENGLISH ARTS AND CRAFTS

Anscombe, Isabelle. *Arts and Crafts Style*. London: Phaidon Press, 1996.

Parray, Linda. *William Morris*. New York: Harry N. Abrams, 1996.

AMERICAN ARTS AND CRAFTS

Cathers, David. *Gustav Stickley*. London: Phaidon Press, 2003.

Heinz, Thomas A. *Frank Lloyd Wright Interiors and Furniture*. London: Academy Editions, 1994.

Kaplan, Wendy, et al. *The Art That is Life: The Arts and Crafts Movement in America, 1875–1920*. Boston: Bulfinch, 1987.

Makinson, Randell L. *Greene and Greene: Architecture as a Fine Art, Furniture, and Related Designs*. Layton, UT.: Gibbs Smith, 2001.

Volpe, Tod M., et al. *Treasures of the American Arts and Crafts Movement, 1890–1920.* New York: Harry N. Abrams, 1991.

ART NOUVEAU

Arwas, Victor. *Art Nouveau: The French Aesthetic.* London: Andreas Papadakis, 2000.

Duncan, Alastair. *Art Nouveau.* London: Thames and Hudson, 1994.

_____. *Masterworks of Louis Comfort Tiffany.* New York: Abradale Press, 1998.

Greenhalgh, Paul, ed. *Art Nouveau, 1890–1914.* New York: Harry N. Abrams, 2000.

GLASGOW STYLE

Kaplan, Wendy, ed. *Charles Rennie Mackintosh.* New York: Abbeville Press, 1996.

McKean, John. *Charles Rennie Mackintosh: Architect, Artist, Icon.* Stillwater, MN.: Voyageur Press, 2000.

AVANT-GARDE AND THE WEINER WERKSTATTE

Brandstätter, Christian. *Wiener Werkstatte: Design in Vienna 1903–1932.* New York: Harry N. Abrams, 2004.

Sweiger, Werner J. *Weiner Werstatte, Design in Vienna: 1903–1932.* London: Thames and Hudson, 1982.

Troy, Nancy. *The De Stijl Environment.* Cambridge, MA.: MIT Press, 1983.

INTERNATIONAL STYLE

Blaser, Werner. *Mies van der Rohe: Furniture and Interiors.* Woodbury, NY.: Barrons, 1982.

Droste, Magdalena. *Bauhaus, 1919–1933.* Köln: Taschen, 1990.

_____. *Marcel Breuer, Design.* Köln: Taschen, 1994.

Le Corbusier. *The Decorative Art of Today.* Translated by James I. Dunnell. Cambridge, MA.: MIT Press, 1987. First published as *L'Art décoratif d'aujourd'hui.* Paris: Editions G. Crès, 1925.

Marcus, George H. *Le Corbusier: Inside the Machine for Living.* New York: The Monacelli Press, 2000.

McLeod, Mary, ed. *Charlotte Perriand: An Art of Living.* New York: Harry N. Abrams, 2003.

Weltge-Wortmann, Sigrid. *Bauhaus Textiles: Women Artists and the Weaving Workshop.* London: Thames and Hudson, 1993.

Wingler, Hans M. *The Bauhaus.* Translated by Wolfgang Jabs. Cambridge, MA.: MIT Press, 1969.

FRENCH ART DECO

Arwas, Victor. *Art Deco.* Revised Edition. New York: Abradale Books, 2000.

Battersby, Martin. *The Decorative Twenties.* Revised Edition. New York: Whitney Library of Design, 1988.

_____. *The Decorative Thirties.* Revised Edition. New York: Whitney Library of Design, 1988.

Bayer, Patricia. *Art Deco Interiors: Decoration and Design Classics of the 1920s and 1930s.* London: Thames and Hudson, 1998.

Benton, Charlotte and Tim, eds. *Art Deco 1910–1939.* London: Victoria and Albert Publications, 2003.

Breeze, Carla. *American Art Deco: Modernistic Architecture and Regionalism.* New York: W. W. Norton, 2003.

Clark, Robert J. *Design in America: The Cranbrook Vision, 1925–1950*. New York: Harry N. Abrams, 1984.

Duncan, Alastair. *American Art Deco*. London: Thames and Hudson, 1986.

Hillier, Bevis and Stephen Escritt. *Art Deco Style*. London: Phaidon Press, 1997.

Robinson, Cervin and Rosemarie Haag Bletter. *Skyscraper Style: Art Deco New York*. Oxford: Oxford University Press, 1975.

Wood, Ghislaine, ed. *Essential Art Deco*. Boston: Bulfinch, 2003.

STYLE MODERNE AND FRENCH MODERN

Bony, Anne. *Furniture and Interiors of the 1940's*. Paris: Flammarion, 2003.

Bréon, Emmanuel and Rosalind Pepall, eds. *Ruhlmann: Genius of Art Deco*. New York: Metropolitan Museum of Art, 2004.

Brunhammer, Yvonne and Tise, Suzanne. *The Decorative Arts in France: Le Societé des Artistes Décorateurs, 1900-1942*. New York: Rizzoli, 1990.

Camard, Florence. *Ruhlmann*. New York: Harry N. Abrams, 1999.

Constant, Caroline. *Eileen Gray*. London: Phaidon Press, 2000.

Pinchon, Jean-François. *Robert Mallet-Stevens: Architecture, Furniture, Interior Design*. Cambridge, MA.: MIT Press, 1990.

Sulzer, Peter. *Jean Prouve Complete Works, Volume 1: 1917–1933*. Basel: Birkhauser, 2000.

_____. *Jean Prouve Complete Works, Volume 2: 1934–1944*. Basel: Birkhauser, 2000.

Taylor, Brian B. *Pierre Chareau: Designer and Architect*. Köln: Taschen, 1998.

Troy, Nancy J. *Modernism and the Decorative Arts in France: Art Nouveau to Le Corbusier*. New Haven, CT.: Yale University Press, 1991.

Vellay, Marc and Kenneth Frampton. *Chareau: Architect and Craftsman, 1883–1950*. New York: Rizzoli, 1986.

MIDCENTURY MODERN

Albrecht, Donald, et al. *The Work of Charles and Ray Eames: A Legacy of Invention*. New York: Harry N. Abrams, 1997.

Hanks, David E. *High Styles: Twentieth-Century American Design*. New York: Whitney Museum, 1985.

Heisinger, Kathryn B. and George H. Marcus. *Design Since 1945*. Philadelphia: Philadelphia Museum of Art, 1983.

Jackson, Lesley. *Contemporary: Architecture and Interiors of the 1950s*. London: Phaidon Press, 1994.

Larrabee, Eric. *Knoll Design*. New York: Harry N. Abrams, 1981.

Noyes, Eliot F. *Organic Design in Home Furnishings*. New York: The Museum of Modern Art, 1941.

Wilson, Richard Guy, et al. *The Machine Age in America, 1918–1941*. New York: Harry N. Abrams, 1987.

MODERN MADE BY HAND

Adamson, Jeremy. *The Furniture of Sam Maloof*. New York: W. W. Norton, 2001.

Nakashima, Mira. *Nature, Form, and Spirit: The Life and Legacy of George Nakashima*: New York: Harry N. Abrams, 2003.

Smith, Paul. *Objects for Use: Handmade by Design*. New York: Harry N. Abrams, 2001.

SCANDINAVIAN MODERN

Aav, Marianne and Nina Stritzler-Levine. *Finnish Modern Design*. New Haven, CT.: Yale University Press, 1998.

Fiell, Charlotte and Peter. *Scandinavian Design*. Köln: Taschen, 2003.

McFadden, David, ed. *Scandinavian Modern Design, 1880–1980*. New York: Harry N. Abrams, 1982.

SIXTIES

Bony, Anne. *Furniture and Interiors of the 1960s*. Paris: Flammarion, 2004.

Jackson, Lesley. *The Sixties*. London: Phaidon Press, 2000.

ITALIAN MODERN

Branzi, Andrea. *The Hot House: Italian New Wave*. Cambridge, MA.: MIT Press, 1984.

Polano, Sergio. *Achille Castiglioni: Complete Works, 1938–2000*. Milan: Electa, 2001.

Radice, Barbara. *Memphis: Research, Experience, Results, Failure, and Successes of New Design*. New York: Rizzoli, 1984.

Sparke, Penny. *Design in Italy: 1870 to the Present*. New York: Abbeville Press, 1990.

POST-MODERNISM

Bangert, Albrecht, et al. *Eighties Style: Design of the Decade*. New York: Abbeville Press, 1990.

Collins, Michael and Andreas Papadakis. *Post-Modern Design*. London: Academy Editions, 1989.

Jencks, Charles. *The New Paradigm in Architecture: The Language of Postmodernism*. Seventh Edition. New Haven, CT.: Yale University Press, 2002.

Miller, R. Craig, et. al. *U.S. Design: 1975–2000*. New York: Prestel, 2002.

Philippe, Simone, ed. *Stark*. Köln: Taschen, 2000.

Sparke, Penny. *Modern Japanese Design*. New York: E. P. Dutton, 1987.

Tasma-Anargyros, Sophie. *Andrée Putman*. Woodstock, NY.: The Overlook Press, 1997.

MINIMALISM

Pawson, John. *Minimum*. London: Phaidon Press, 1998.

Rawsthorn, Alice. *Marc Newson*. London: Booth-Clibborn Editions, 2000.

Riley, Terence, et. al. *The Un-Private House*. New York: Museum of Modern Art, 2002.

Sudjic, Deyan. *Ron Arad*. London: Lawrence King, 1999.

THE TWENTY-FIRST CENTURY

Marcus, George. *What is Design Today?* New York: Harry N. Abrams, 2003.

index

A

Aalto, Alvar, 338, 345
Aarnio, Eero, 338, 352, 354
Adam, Robert, 9, 122, 124, 125, 126, 132–33, 134, 136, 140
Aesthetic style: color palette of, 209, 215, 215; defining characteristics of, 215; description of, 208–10; Eastern influence in, 218–19, 219; furniture of, 210, 212–14, 215–16, 217, 218, 219; Herter Brothers' style in, 208, 216; lighting of, 210; origins of, 208; ornamentation of, 209–10, 214, 215; textiles of, 209, 215, 215
American Arts and Crafts style. See also Art Nouveau style; English Arts and Crafts style: defining characteristics of, 243; description of, 234–36; dining room in, 237, 238; furniture of, 236, 238–42, 243, 245, 246–47; lighting of, 236, 241; Mission Style in, 234–35; origins of, 234–35; ornamentation of, 235, 243; textiles of, 235, 243, 243
American Empire style:

color palette of, 173, 179, 179; description of, 172–74; furniture of, 173–74, 176–78, 179; origins of, 172–73; ornamentation of, 173–74, 179; parlor in, 175, 176; textiles of, 173, 179, 179
Arad, Ron, 385, 388
armchairs, 20, 32, 76, 80–81, 81–82, 116, 129, 135–36, 155, 164, 219, 227, 236, 239–40, 246, 247, 252, 255–56, 278, 280–82, 290, 292–93, 302, 305, 310, 331, 333, 340, 343–44, 377, 385
armoires, 43, 58
Art Deco. See French Art Deco style
Art Furniture. See studio crafts
Art Nouveau style: color palette of, 251, 259, 259; defining characteristics of, 259; description of, 250–52; furniture of, 252, 254–58, 259; lighting of, 252, 260–61, 261; living room in, 253, 254; origins of, 250–51; ornamentation of, 252, 259; textiles of, 251, 259, 259
Arts and Crafts style. See American Arts and

Crafts style; English Arts and Crafts style
avant-garde style: color palette of, 278, 285, 285; defining characteristics of, 285; description of, 276–78; dining room in, 279, 280; furniture of, 278, 280–84, 285; origins of, 276–77; ornamentation of, 277–78, 285; textiles of, 277–78, 285, 285; Wiener Werkstatte and, 277–78, 280–84, 285

B

Barcelona tables, 295
The Baroque. See Louis XIV style; William and Mary style
Bauhaus school, 290, 292, 372
beds, 155, 164, 213, 217. See also daybeds; liten-bateau beds
Belter, John Henry, 194–95
benches, 197, 224, 226, 335
bentwood furniture, 278, 282–84
Biedermeier style, 150, 168, 169
bookcases, 127, 130, 137, 144, 189, 230, 236, 239,

296, 315, 377
Bouroullec brothers, 388–89
breakfast tables, 146
buffets, 58
bureaus, 22, 54, 64, 68, 101, 117
butterfly tables, 43

C

cabinets, 28, 30–31, 43, 68, 74, 89, 124, 199, 203, 219, 236, 242, 252, 256, 257–58, 283, 302, 306, 320, 323, 346, 364, 391
Campana brothers, 389
cantilever chairs, 293
card tables, 174, 177
case furniture, 11, 28, 30–31, 38–39, 42–43, 52, 55, 59, 67, 68, 74, 78, 80–81, 83, 89, 98, 98, 100–102, 102, 106–7, 112, 117, 124, 126, 126–28, 130, 137, 142, 144, 146, 150, 154, 156, 168, 169, 173, 178, 187, 189–90, 199, 202–4, 219, 224, 228, 230, 236, 238–39, 242, 252, 256, 257–58, 290, 296, 302, 304, 306–8, 320, 323–24, 331, 346, 364, 368, 391. See also armoires; bookcases;

buffets; cabinets; chests; commodes; highboys; linen presses; lowboys; secretaries; tallboys
Castiglione brothers, 361, 366
center tables, 20, 189
chairs, 11, 18, 20–21, 28, 32, 38–39, 44, 52, 56, 58, 63–64, 66–67, 74, 76–77, 80–81, 81–82, 99, 103, 106, 112, 116, 124, 129, 134, 135, 135–36, 142, 145, 145, 150, 155, 162, 164, 168, 169, 174, 176, 187, 191, 217, 219, 224, 227, 230, 236, 239–40, 246, 247, 252, 254–56, 266, 268–69, 278, 280–82, 290, 292–93, 302, 304–5, 320–21, 323, 325–27, 331, 333, 340, 343–44, 352, 354, 356, 364–66, 376–77, 385–86, 390. See also armchairs; cantilever chairs; chaise longues; dining chairs; egg chairs; fauteuil chairs; hall chairs; ladder-back chairs; lounge chairs; Malitte seating system; Morris chairs; parlor chairs; pedestal-base

chairs; stack chairs; stools; turned chairs; wainscot chairs; Windsor chairs; wing chairs; specific types
chaise longues, 252, 254, 290, 294, 364
chandeliers, 156
chests, 28, 30, 38–39, 42–43, 78, 190, 302, 307–8
Chippendale, 9–10, 72–74, 80–81, 81–83, 94, 97, 98, 102–4, 106–7, 122, 124, 127, 129
clocks, 100, 142
coffee tables, 330, 335
Colombo, Joe, 360, 364–65
commodes, 52, 55, 83, 112, 117, 128
console tables, 54, 64, 87, 90, 118, 118
crafts guilds, 230, 230–31

D
Davis, Andrew Jackson, 186–87, 189
daybeds, 164
Deskey, Donald, 313, 315
desks, 101, 106–7, 134, 136, 156, 166, 202, 236, 238, 246, 302, 304. See also bureaus
dining chairs, 32, 246

dining tables, 342
Dresser, Christopher, 208, 214
dressers, 199, 204
dressing tables, 313
drum tables, 166

E
Eames, Charles and Ray, 318, 324–25, 329
Early American Colonial style: color palette of, 36, 45, 45; defining characteristics of, 45; description of, 36–39; furniture of, 38–39, 41–44, 45; lighting of, 37; origins of, 36; ornamentation of, 36, 37–39, 45; parish room in, 40–41; textiles of, 37, 45, 45; William and Mary style in, 38, 42
Early Georgian style: Chippendale style in, 72–74; color palette of, 73, 79, 79; defining characteristics of, 79; description of, 72–74; dining room in, 75, 76; furniture of, 72, 73–74, 76–78, 79; lighting of, 73–74; origins of, 72; ornamentation of, 73–74, 79; textiles of, 73, 79, 79

egg chairs, 344
English Arts and Crafts style. See also American Arts and Crafts style; Art Nouveau style: color palette of, 223, 229, 229; crafts guilds in, 230, 231; defining characteristics of, 229; description of, 222–24; furniture of, 224, 226–28, 229, 230; grand parlor in, 225, 226; origins of, 222; ornamentation of, 223–24, 229; textiles of, 223, 229, 229
English Baroque. See William and Mary style

F
Far Eastern influence, 218–19, 219
fauteuil chairs, 21, 56, 116
Federal style: Adam style in, 140; color palette of, 141, 147, 147; defining characteristics of, 147; description of, 140–42; furniture of, 142, 144–46, 147; Hepplewhite style in, 140, 142, 145; lighting of, 141; origins of, 140; ornamentation of, 141–42, 147; parlor in, 143, 144;

Sheraton style in, 140, 142, 146; textiles of, 141, 147, 147

Frankl, Paul, 312, 315

French Antique style. See Rococo Revival style

French Art Deco style: color palette of, 301, 309, 309; defining characteristics of, 309; description of, 300–302; French modernists in, 300, 310–11; furniture of, 302, 304–8, 309, 310–11, 310–13, 312–13, 313–15, 314–15; lighting of, 302; Modernistic Style in, 312–13, 313–15; origins of, 300–301; ornamentation of, 301–2, 309; salon in, 303, 304; textiles of, 301, 309, 309

French Country style. See French Provincial style

French Empire style: Biedermeier style in, 150, 168, 169; color palette of, 151–52, 157, 157; defining characteristics of, 157; description of, 150–52; furniture of, 152, 154–56, 157; lighting of, 156; music room in, 153, 154; ornamentation of, 151–52, 157; tex-

tiles of, 151, 157, 157

French modernists, 310–11, 310–11

French Provincial style, 58, 58–59

G

gateleg tables, 39

Gehry, Frank, 372, 377

Glasgow style: color palette of, 265–66, 271, 271; defining characteristics of, 271; description of, 264–66; furniture of, 265–66, 268–69, 271; interior in, 267, 268; lighting of, 265; Mackintosh-MacDonald partnership in, 264–66; origins of, 264–65; ornamentation of, 265–66, 271, 271; textiles of, 265–66, 271, 271

Godwin, E. W., 208, 210

Gothic Revival style. See also Victorian style: color palette of, 187; description of, 186–87; furniture of, 187, 189–91; lighting of, 187; origins of, 185–86; ornamentation of, 187; saloon in, 188, 189; textiles of, 187

Gray, Eileen, 300, 310

Greene brothers, 234, 237, 238

Greuby Art Pottery, 236, 241

Groult, Andre, 302, 308

gueridon tables, 154

Guimard, Hector, 250, 255

H

hall chairs, 191

hall trees, 212

Hepplewhite style, 9, 122, 124, 126, 134–35, 135, 135–36, 140, 142, 145

Herter Brothers, 200, 203–4, 208, 216, 217

highboys, 39, 98, 98, 102, 106–7, 142

Historicist Modern style, 330, 330–31

Hoffmann, Josef, 277–78, 280, 282, 284–85

Hope, Thomas, 160, 162, 164

Horta, Victor, 250, 254

I

illustrations, of furniture details, 392–97

International Style: color palette of, 289, 297, 297; defining characteristics of, 290, 297; description of, 288–90; Farnsworth House in, 291, 292; furniture of,

290, 292–96, 297; lighting of, 290; origins of, 288–89; ornamentation of, 290, 297; textiles of, 289, 297, 297

Italian Modern style: color palette of, 362, 369, 369; defining characteristics of, 369; description of, 360–62; furniture of, 362, 364–68, 369; interior in, 363, 364; lighting of, 362, 368; origins of, 360–61; ornamentation of, 361–62, 369; textiles of, 362, 369, 369

J

Juhl, Finn, 338, 343

K

Kent, William, 72, 86–87, 90, 90

L

ladder-back chairs, 38, 44, 268

lamps, 241, 246, 261, 345, 355, 368

Late American Colonial style: bedroom in, 97, 98; Chippendale style in, 94, 97, 98, 102–4, 106–7; color palette of, 96, 105, 105; defining characteristics of, 105; description of, 94–96; furniture of, 96, 98–104, 105, 106–7; lighting of, 95–96; origins of, 94–95; ornamentation of, 95–96, 105; Queen Anne style in, 94, 97, 98, 99, 106–7; textiles of, 95, 105, 105

Late Georgian style: Adam style in, 122, 124, 125, 126, 136; Chippendale style in, 122, 124, 127, 129; color palette of, 123–24, 131, 131; defining characteristics of, 131; description of, 122–24; furniture of, 124, 126–30, 131, 135–36; Hepplewhite style in, 122, 124, 126, 134–35, 135–36; lighting of, 124; origins of, 122–23; ornamentation of, 122–24, 131; saloon in, 125, 126; Sheraton style in, 122, 124, 134–35, 135–36; textiles of, 123, 131, 131

Laverne, Estelle and Erwin, 352, 356

Le Corbusier, 288, 294

Le Style Moderne. See French Art Deco style

library tables, 217, 246

linen presses, 230

lit-en-bateau beds, 155

Lock, Matthias, 87, 90, 90

Louis Sue, 302, 304

Louis XIV style: bedroom in, 19; color palette of, 17, 23, 23; defining characteristics of, 23; description of, 16–18; furniture of, 17, 19–22, 23; lighting of, 17–18; origins of, 16; ornamentation of, 17, 23; textiles of, 17, 23, 23

Louis XVI style: color palette of, 111–12, 119, 119; defining characteristics of, 119; description of, 110–13; furniture of, 112–13, 116–18, 118–19; origins of, 9, 110; ornamentation of, 111–13, 119; salon in, 114–15, 115; textiles of, 111, 119, 119

Louis XV style: color palette of, 51–52, 57, 57; defining characteristics of, 57; description of, 50–52; French Provincial Style of, 58, 58–59; furniture of, 52, 54–56, 57; lighting of, 51–52, 57; origins of, 9, 50; ornamentation of,

51–52, 57; salon in, 53; textiles of, 51, 57, 57

lounge chairs, 320, 325, 331, 365

lowboys, 67, 100, 106–7

M

MacDonald, Margaret, 264–66, 267–69

Mackintosh, Charles Rennie, 264–66, 267–69, 278

Majorelle, Louis, 250, 256–57

Malitte seating system, 367

Mallet-Stevens, Robert, 300, 310

Mare, Andre, 302, 304

Mendini, Alessandro, 377, 379

Midcentury Modern style: color palette of, 319–20, 329, 329; defining characteristics of, 329; description of, 318–21; furniture of, 319–21, 323–28, 329, 330–31, 333, 335; Historicist Modern style in, 330, 330–31; interiors in, 322, 323; lighting of, 320; origins of, 318–19; ornamentation of, 319–20, 329; studio crafts in, 332–33,

333–35; textiles of, 319–20, 329, 329

Mies van der Rohe, 288, 292, 295, 319, 372

Minimalist style: color palette of, 383, 387, 387; defining characteristics of, 387; description of, 382–83; furniture of, 383, 385–86, 387; interior in, 384, 385; origins of, 382; ornamentation of, 383, 387; textiles of, 383, 387, 387

mirrors, 76, 145

Mission Style. See American Arts and Crafts style

Modernistic Style, 312–13, 313–15

modern made by hand. See studio crafts

Morgue, Olivier, 352, 355

Morris Chairs, 224, 240

Morris, William, 222–24, 225, 226–28, 234, 240

Moser, Kolomon, 277–78, 283

music stands, 334

N

Nakashima, George, 332, 335

Nash, John, 160

Nelson, George, 318

Neo-Palladian style: col-

ors of, 87, 91, 91; defining characteristics of,
91; description of,
86–87; furniture of, 87,
89–90, 91; hall in, 88,
89; lighting of, 87; ori-
gins of, 86; ornamenta-
tion of, 86–87, 91; tex-
tiles of, 86–87, 91, 91
Neutra, Richard, 288, 319

O

ottomans, 325, 327, 344,
366

P

Panton, Verner, 338, 352,
354–55
parlor chairs, 76
pattern, as style element,
11
pedestal-base chairs, 321,
326
Pembroke tables, 146
period styles: dates of, 7;
definition of, 6–8; ele-
ments of, 10–11
Phyfe, Duncan, 140, 172,
178
pier tables, 174, 177
Ponti, Gio, 360, 364, 368
Post-Modernist style:
color palette of, 373,
379, 379; defining char-
acteristics of, 379;
description of, 372–74;

furniture of, 373–73,
376–78, 379; interior in,
375, 376; origins of,
372–73; ornamentation
of, 373–74, 379; textiles
of, 373, 379, 379
Pugin, Augustus W. N.,
185–86, 191

Q

Queen Anne style: color
palette of, 63, 69, 69;
defining characteristics
of, 69; description of,
62–64; dining room in,
65, 66; furniture of,
63–64, 66–68, 69, 99,
101, 106–7; in Late
American Colonial
style, 94, 97, 98, 99,
106–7; lighting of, 63;
origins of, 9, 62; orna-
mentation of, 62–64,
69; textiles of, 63, 69,
69

R

Régence style. See Louis
XV style
Regency style: Bieder-
meier style in, 168, 169;
color palette of, 161–62,
167, 167; defining char-
acteristics of, 167;
description of, 160–62;
dining room in, 163,

164; furniture of, 162,
164–66, 167; lighting of,
162; origins of, 160–61;
ornamentation of,
161–62, 167; textiles of,
161, 167, 167
Reitveld, Gerrit, 276, 280
Renaissance Revival style.
See also Victorian style:
color palette of, 199;
description of,
198–200; furniture of,
199–200, 202–4; light-
ing of, 199; origins of,
198; ornamentation of,
199–200; salon in, 201,
202; textiles of, 199
Rococo Revival style. See
also Victorian style:
color palette of, 193;
description of, 192–94;
furniture of, 193–94,
196–97; grand parlor in,
195, 196; lighting of,
193; origins of, 192;
ornamentation of,
192–94; textiles of, 193
Rococo style. See Early
Georgian style; Louis
XV style; Queen Anne
style

S

Scandinavian style: color
palette of, 339–40, 347,
347; defining character-

istics of, 347; descrip-
tion of, 338–40; furni-
ture of, 340, 342–46,
347; interior in, 341,
342; lighting of, 340,
345; origins of, 338–39;
ornamentation of,
339–40, 347; textiles of,
339–40, 347, 347
screens, 214, 219, 311, 315
secretaries, 154, 169, 178,
368
serving tables, 165
settees, 226, 284
Sheraton style, 9, 122,
124, 134–35, 135, 135–36,
140, 142, 146
sideboards, 126, 126, 142,
146, 214, 224, 228, 331,
342
side chairs, 58, 76,
135–36, 145, 169, 176,
217, 236, 240, 252, 255,
310, 376–77
side tables, 20, 212
Sixties style: color palette
of, 351, 357, 357; defin-
ing characteristics of,
357; description of,
350–52; furniture of,
352, 354–56, 357; light-
ing of, 351–52, 355; ori-
gins of, 350–51; orna-
mentation of, 351–52,
357; Panton interior in,
353, 354; textiles of, 351,

357, 357

sofas, 52, 56, 103, 104, 112, 116, 162, 164, 168, 169, 174, 176, 196, 252, 254, 284, 314, 328, 364. See also benches; chaise longues; settees; tete a tete sofas

sofa tables, 165

stack chairs, 365

Starck, Philippe, 372

Stickley, Gustav, 234, 239–40, 242

stools, 66, 366

Streamline Style. See Modernistic Style

studio crafts, 332–33, 333–35

T

tables, 20, 22, 39, 42–43, 54, 63–64, 74, 82, 87, 90, 107, 112, 116–18, 117–18, 142, 146, 146, 154, 162, 165–66, 174, 177, 189, 212, 214, 217, 246, 290, 295, 302, 311, 313, 330, 335, 342, 345, 385. See also Barcelona tables; breakfast tables; butterfly tables; card tables; center tables; coffee tables; console tables; dining tables; dressing tables; drum tables; gateleg tables;

gueridon tables; library tables; Pembroke tables; pier tables; serving tables; side tables; sofa tables; tea tables

tallboys, 28, 39

tea tables, 42, 82

tea trolleys, 345

tete a tete sofas, 314

Thonet, Gebruder, 254

Thonet, Michael, 194, 278

Tiffany style, 250, 260–61, 261

Townsend, John, 94, 101, 101

turned chairs, 38, 44

21st-century styles: furniture of, 388; lighting of, 389; textiles of, 389

V

van de Velde, Henri, 250, 255

Venturi, Robert, 372, 376

Victorian style. See also Gothic Revival style; Renaissance Revival style; Rococo Revival style: color palette of, 184, 205, 205; defining characteristics of, 205; furniture of, 184–85, 189–91, 196–97, 202–4, 205; lighting of, 184; ornamentation of, 184–85, 205; overview

of, 184–85; textiles of, 184, 205, 205

vitrines, 258, 346

W

Webb, Philip, 222, 227–28

Wegner, Hans, 338, 343

William and Mary style: bedroom in, 29; color palette of, 27, 33, 33; defining characteristics of, 33; description of, 26–28; furniture of, 28, 29–32, 33, 38, 42; lighting of, 27, 28; origins of, 26; ornamentation of, 26, 28, 30–31, 33; textiles of, 27, 33, 33

Windsor chairs, 142, 145

wing chairs, 64, 67, 103

Wormley, Edward, 330–31

Wright, Frank Lloyd, 234, 244–45, 246–47, 319

p. 19 Réunion des Musées Nationaux/Art Resource, NY; p. 20 (top) © Christie's Images Incorporated 2005; p. 20 (bottom) Partridge Fine Arts, PLC, London; p. 21 (top) Ingrao Gallery, New York; p. 21 (bottom) © Christie's Images Incorporated 2005; p. 22 © Christie's Images Incorporated 2005; p. 23 PRELLE, Paris; p. 29 National Trust Photographic Library; p. 30 (top and bottom) © Christie's Images Incorporated 2005; p. 31 © Christie's Images Incorporated 2005; p. 32 (top and bottom) © Christie's Images Incorporated 2005; p. 33 © 2005 F. Schumacher & Co., New York City; pp. 40–41 HISTORIC NEW ENGLAND; p. 42 (top) © Christie's Images Incorporated 2005; p. 42 (bottom) PRATT ANTIQUES, Woodbury, Ct.; p. 43 (top, middle, and bottom) © Christie's Images Incorporated 2005; p. 44 (top and bottom) © Christie's Images Incorporated 2005; p. 45 BRUNSCHWIG & FILS, Inc.; p. 53 The J. Paul Getty Museum, Los Angeles. © The J. Paul Getty Museum; p. 54 (top and bottom) Partridge Fine Arts PLC, London; p. 55 (top and bottom) Partridge Fine Arts PLC, London; p. 56 (top) © Christie's Images Incorporated 2005; p. 56 (bottom) MALLETT Antiques PLC, London/MALLETT Inc., New York; p. 57 PRELLE, Paris; p. 58 French Country Living; p. 59 (top and bottom) © Christie's Images Incorporated 2005; p. 65 National Trust Photographic Library; p. 66 (top) MALLETT Antiques PLC, London/MALLET Inc., New York; p. 66 (bottom) © Christie's

Images Incorporated 2005; p. 67 (top) MALLETT Antiques PLC, London/MALLETT Inc., New York; p. 67 (bottom) Partridge Fine Arts PLC, London; p. 68 Galerie Ariane Dandois, Paris; p. 69 BRUNSCHWIG & FILS, Inc.; p. 75 Erich Lessing/Art Resource, NY; p. 76 (top) Partridge Fine Arts PLC, London; p. 76 (bottom) © Christie's Images Incorporated 2005; p. 77 (left) MALLETT Antiques PLC, London/MALLETT Inc., New York; p. 77 (right) © Christie's Images Incorporated 2005; p. 78 (top) © Christie's Images Incorporated 2005; p. 78 (bottom) Ingrao Gallery, New York; p. 79 BRUNSCHWIG & FILS, Inc.; p. 82 (top) MALLETT Antiques PLC, London/MALLETT Inc., New York; p. 82 (bottom) Ingrao Gallery, New York; p. 83 © Christie's Images Incorporated 2005; p. 88 National Trust Photographic Library; p. 89 © Christie's Images Incorporated 2005; p. 90 (top) Partridge Fine Arts PLC, London; p. 90 (bottom) Ingrao Gallery, New York; p. 91 © 2005 F. Schumacher & Co., New York City; p. 97 (top) HISTORIC NEW ENGLAND; p. 97 (bottom) HISTORIC NEW ENGLAND; p. 98 (left and right) © Christie's Images Incorporated 2005; p. 99 (left) © Christie's Images Incorporated 2005; p. 99 (right) Bernard & S. Dean Levy Inc., New York; p. 100 (left) Bernard & S. Dean Levy Inc., New York; p. 100 (right) © Christie's Images Incorporated 2005; p. 101 (top and bottom) © Christie's Images Incorporated 2005; p. 102 © Christie's Images Incorporated 2005; p. 103 (left) © Christie's

Images Incorporated 2005; p. 103 (right) Bernard & S. Dean Levy Inc., New York; p. 104 © Christie's Images Incorporated 2005; p. 105 © 2005 F. Schumacher & Co., New York City; pp. 114–115 Giraudon/Art Resource, NY; p. 116 (top and bottom left) © Christie's Images Incorporated 2005; p. 116 (bottom right) Partridge Fine Arts PLC, London; p. 117 (top) Partridge Fine Arts PLC, London; p. 117 (bottom) © Christie's Images Incorporated 2005; p. 118 (top and bottom) Partridge Fine Arts PLC, London; p. 119 PRELLE, Paris; p. 125 National Trust Photographic Library; p. 126 (top) © Christie's Images Incorporated 2005; p. 126 (bottom) Ingrao Gallery, New York; p. 127 Partridge Fine Arts PLC, London; p. 128 Partridge Fine Arts PLC, London; p. 129 (top) Partridge Fine Arts PLC, London; p. 129 (bottom) Ingrao Gallery, New York; p. 130 Jeremy, Ltd., London; p. 131 BRUNSCHWIG & FILS, Inc.; p. 133 Galerie Ariane Dandois, Paris; p. 136 (top left and bottom) MALLETT Antiques PLC, London/MALLETT Antiques Inc., New York; p. 136 (top right) © Christie's Images Incorporated 2005; p. 137 Hyde Park Antiques, Ltd., New York; p. 143 HISTORIC NEW ENGLAND; p. 144 © Christie's Images Incorporated 2005; p. 145 (top left) PRATT ANTIQUES, Woodbury, Ct.; p. 145 (top right) © Christie's Images Incorporated 2005; p. 145 (bottom) Bernard & S. Dean Levy Inc., New York; p. 146 (top) © Christie's Images Incorporated 2005; p. 146 (bottom left and right) Bernard & S.

Dean Levy Inc., New York; p. 147 © 2005 F. Schumacher & Co., New York City; p. 153 Erich Lessing/Art Resource, NY; p. 154 (top left and right) Galerie Ariane Dandois, Paris; p. 154 (bottom) © Christie's Images Incorporated 2005; p. 155 (top left) Partridge Fine Arts PLC, London; p. 155 (top right) Galerie Ariane Dandois, Paris; p. 155 (bottom) Galerie Ariane Dandois, Paris; p. 156 (top) © Christie's Images Incorporated 2005; p. 156 (bottom) Galerie Ariane Dandois, Paris; p. 157 PRELLE, Paris; p. 163 National Trust Photographic Library; p. 164 (top and bottom) © Christie's Images Incorporated 2005; p. 165 (top) Galerie Ariane Dandois, Paris; p. 165 (bottom) Hyde Park Antiques, Ltd., New York; p. 166 (top and bottom) Partridge Fine Arts PLC, London; p. 167 © 2005 F. Schumacher & Co., New York City; p. 169 (top, bottom left, and bottom right) RITTER ANTIK INC NY; p. 175 Courtesy Boscobel Restoration, Inc.; p. 176 (top) Hirschl & Adler Galleries, Inc., New York; p. 176 (bottom) © Christie's Images Incorporated 2005; p. 177 (top) © Christie's Images Incorporated 2005; p. 177 (bottom) Hirschl & Adler Galleries, Inc., New York; p. 178 Hirschl & Adler Galleries, Inc., New York; p. 179 © 2005 F. Schumacher & Co., New York City; p. 188 National Trust Photographic Library; p. 189 (left and right) © Christie's Images Incorporated 2005; p. 190 Associated Artists, LLC; p. 191 (top) Associated Artists, LLC; p. 191 (bottom) H. Blairman & Sons Ltd., London; p. 195 Courtesy of the Pilgrimage Garden

Club of Natchez, Mississippi; **p. 196** © Christie's Images Incorporated 2005; **p. 197** Galerie Ariane Dandois, Paris; **p. 200** Courtesy Victoria Mansion. Photography by J. David Bohl.; **p. 201** © Christie's Images Incorporated 2005; **p. 202** Associated Artists, LLC; **p. 203** © Christie's Images Incorporated 2005; **p. 204** © Christie's Images Incorporated 2005; **p. 205** PRELLE, Paris; **p. 211** V&A Picture Library; **p. 212 (left and right)** Associated Artists, LLC; **p. 213 (top left)** John Alexander; **p. 213 (top right)** Paul Reeves, London; **p. 213 (bottom)** Paul Reeves, London; **p. 214 (top)** Associated Artists, LLC; **p. 214 (bottom)** H. Blairman & Sons Ltd.; **p.** © 2005 Bradbury & Bradbury Art Wallpapers. All rights reserved.; **p. 217 (top left)** Associated Artists, LLC; **p. 217 (top right and bottom)** © Christie's Images Incorporated 2005; **p. 218** © Christie's Images Incorporated 2005; **p. 219 (top left, right, and bottom)** © Christie's Images Incorporated 2005; **p. 225** National Trust Photographic Library; **p. 226** John Alexander, Ltd.; **p. 227 (top)** John Alexander, Ltd.; **p. 227 (bottom)** Paul Reeves, London; **p. 228 (top and bottom)**; John Alexander, Ltd.; **p. 229** MORRIS & CO., New York/© Sanderson 2005; **p. 230** Paul Reeves, London; **p. 231 (top)** Paul Reeves, London; **p. 231 (bottom)** Cathers & Dembrosky, New York; **p. 237** Tim Street-Porter; **p. 238** Cathers & Dembrosky, New York; **p. 239** Cathers & Dembrosky, New York; **p. 240 (top and bottom)** Cathers & Dembrosky, New York; **p. 241 (top and bottom)** Cathers & Dembrosky, New

York; **p. 242** Cathers & Dembrosky, New York; **p. 243** © 2005 Bradbury & Bradbury Art Wallpapers. All rights reserved; **p. 246 (top)** Cathers & Dembrosky, New York; **p. 246 (bottom)** © Christie's Images Incorporated 2005; **p. 247 (top)** wright, Chicago; **p. 247 (bottom)** Cathers & Dembrosky, New York; **p. 253** Erich Lessing/Art Resource, NY; **p. 254** Phillips, de Pury & Company, New York; **p. 255 (left and right)** © Christie's Images Incorporated 2005; **p. 256** Maison Gerard Ltd.; **p. 257 (left and right)** © Christie's Images Incorporated 2005; **p. 258** © Christie's Images Incorporated 2005; **p. 259** PRELLE, Paris; **p. 261 (left)** Macklowe Gallery Ltd., New York; **p. 261 (right)** © Christie's Images Incorporated 2005; **p. 267** Photo © Hunterian Art Gallery, University of Glasgow, Mackintosh Collection; **p. 268 (top and bottom right)** Cassina USA; **p. 268 (bottom left)** Phillips, de Pury & Company, New York; **p. 269** © 2005 F. Schumacher & Co., New York City; **p. 277** © 2005 IMAGNO/Brandstaetter Images. All rights reserved; **p. 278** Phillips, de Pury & Company, New York; **p. 279** Phillips, de Pury & Company, New York; **p. 280** wright, Chicago; **p. 281** unika vaev/Hoffmann images; **p. 287** © Scott Frances/Esto. All rights reserved; **p. 288 (top and bottom)** Phillips, de Pury & Company, New York; **p. 289** wright, Chicago; **p. 290** Phillips, de Pury & Company, New York; **p. 291** wright, Chicago; **p. 292** Phillips, de Pury & Company, New York; **p. 293** Christopher Farr;

p. 299 Courtesy Philippe Garner; **p. 300 (top)** © Christie's Images Incorporated 2005; **p. 300 (bottom)** Galerie Vallois, Paris; **p. 301 (top)** Galerie Vallois, Paris; **p. 301 (bottom)** Maison Gerard Ltd.; **p. 302** Delorenzo Gallery, New York; **p. 303** Galerie Vallois, Paris; **p. 304** Galerie Vallois, Paris; **p. 305** PRELLE, Paris; **p. 306 (left and right)** Phillips, de Pury & Company, New York; **p. 307 (top)** Phillips, de Pury & Company, New York; **p. 307 (bottom)** Galerie Vallois, Paris; **p. 309** wright, Chicago; **p. 310** wright, Chicago; **p. 311 (left)** © Christie's Images Incorporated 2005; **p. 311 (right)** Virginia Museum of Fine Arts, Richmond; **p. 318** Julius Schulman; **p. 319 (top and bottom)** wright, Chicago; **p. 320** wright, Chicago; **p. 321 (top)** wright, Chicago; **p. 321 (bottom)** Phillips, de Pury & Company, New York; **p. 322** Wright, Chicago; **p. 323** wright, Chicago; **p. 324** Phillips, de Pury & Company, New York; **p. 325** © 2005 LUCIA EAMES dba EAMES OFFICE (www.eamesoffice.com); **p. 326** Phillips, de Pury & Company, New York; **p. 327 (top, middle and bottom)** wright, Chicago; **p. 329** © Moderne Gallery; **p. 330** © Moderne Gallery; **p. 331 (top)** wright, Chicago; **p. 331 (bottom)** © Moderne Gallery; **p. 337** Photo M. Kapanen/Alvar Aalto Museum; **p. 338 (top)** Phillips, de Pury & Company, New York; **p. 338 (bottom)** wright, Chicago; **p. 339 (top)** wright, Chicago; **p. 339 (bottom)** Phillips, de Pury & Company, New York; **p. 340** wright, Chicago; **p. 341 (top and bottom)** wright, Chicago; **p. 342** wright, Chicago;

p. 343 Svensk Tenn, Stockholm; **p. 349** R 20th Century; **p. 350** wright, Chicago; **p. 351 (top and bottom)** wright, Chicago; **p. 352** wright, Chicago; **p. 353** Edward Fields, Inc., New York; **p. 359** Courtesy Philippe Garner; **p. 360 (top)** wright, Chicago; **p. 360 (bottom)** wright, Chicago; **p. 361** wright, Chicago; **p. 362 (top)** Kartell, S.p.A. Italy ; **p. 362 (bottom)** wright, Chicago; **p. 363** wright, Chicago; **p. 364** wright, Chicago; **p. 365** Phillips, de Pury & Company, New York; **p. 366 (left and right)** wright, Chicago; **p. 367** Phillips, de Pury & Company, New York; **p. 373** Courtesy Touchstone Pictures; **p. 374 (top)** wright, Chicago; **p. 374 (bottom)** Phillips, de Pury & Company, New York; **p. 375 (top)** © Christie's Images Incorporated 2005; **p. 375 (bottom)** Phillips, de Pury & Company, New York; **p. 376** wright, Chicago; **p. 377** Phillips, de Pury & Company, New York; **p. 382** Courtesy Gabellini & Associates. Photo by Paul Warchol Photography, Inc.; **p. 383 (top)** wright, Chicago; **p. 383 (bottom)** Phillips, de Pury & Company, New York; **p. 384 (top)** KOMPLOT DESIGN. Boris Berlin & Poul Christiansen for KALLEMO AB; **p. 384 (bottom)** RALPH PUCCI International; **p. 385** © 2005 THE MAYA ROMANOFF CORPORATION. All rights reserved; **p. 388 (top left and right)** Phillips, de Pury & Company, New York; **p. 388 (bottom)** wright, Chicago; **p. 389** Phillips, de Pury & Company, New York